WISDEN AT THE OVAL

WISDEN AT THE OVAL

AN ANTHOLOGY

Edited by
Jon Surtees

With forewords by
Micky Stewart and Alec Stewart

B L O O M S B U R Y
LONDON · OXFORD · NEW YORK · NEW DELHI · SYDNEY

John Wisden & Co Ltd
An imprint of Bloomsbury Publishing Plc

50 Bedford Square   1385 Broadway
London   New York
WC1B 3DP   NY 10018
UK   USA

www.bloomsbury.com

WISDEN and the wood-engraving device are trademarks of John Wisden & Company Ltd,
a subsidiary of Bloomsbury Publishing Plc

First published 2017

www.wisden.com
www.wisdenrecords.com
Follow Wisden on Twitter @WisdenAlmanack
and on Facebook at Wisden Sports

British Library Cataloguing-in-Publication Data
A catalogue record for this book is available from the British Library.

Library of Congress Cataloguing-in-Publication data has been applied for.

ISBN: HB: 978-1-4729-4265-4
ePub: 978-1-4729-4264-7

2 4 6 8 10 9 7 5 3 1

Typeset in Minion by Deanta Global Publishing Services, Chennai, India
Printed and bound in Great Britain by CPI Group (UK) Ltd, Croydon CR0 4YY

To find out more about our authors and books visit www.wisden.com.
Here you will find extracts, author interviews, details of forthcoming events and
the option to sign up for our newsletters.

For Rachel

Contents

Contents

Forewords

My word, how The Oval has changed since I first saw it from the top deck of a tram travelling to Victoria. Those were the early years of the Second World War, when I was a boy of seven or eight and The Oval was covered in barbed wire, having been converted into a Prisoner of War camp. Rumour has it that it only accommodated one prisoner during the whole of the London Blitz! Nevertheless, this first sight of The Oval had a huge influence on me and my love for the game of cricket – and Surrey particularly – from that early age. I read every cricket book available at the local library and, once life had returned to normality after the war, my father made me a schoolboy member in 1947, in time to see Don Bradman's Australians the following year.

Before my membership, I had watched Surrey at every opportunity from the wooden benches on both the Archbishop Tenison's School and gasholder sides of the ground. There were no back rests on most of them! Sometimes I would watch from the very worn-down Vauxhall Stand, and it was from there, in 1946, that I saw my first day of Test cricket, when India took on Wally Hammond's England.

Though there had been no cricket at The Oval during the war years, MCC had compiled a programme of Saturday one-day matches at Lord's, featuring many of the leading county players. My father took me to some of these and eventually allowed me to go with some of my mates. Even then I was aware of Lord's having a very special atmosphere,

1

one which I continue to enjoy to this day. However, The Oval has always had a different atmosphere – welcoming and friendly – which is enjoyed by everyone. I greatly appreciated it as a player, never more so than during Surrey's seven consecutive County Championships in the 1950s (though I missed the first two because of National Service).

I have seen huge change in the game of cricket, both on and off the field, and The Oval has changed a lot as well. That old Vauxhall Stand has been replaced by the magnificent OCS Stand, with all modern facilities. Those old wooden benches on both sides of the ground have been replaced with comfortable terraced seating and, most recently, by the Peter May Stand with its upper garden terrace. The entrance to The Oval is unrecognisable from what it had been for decades. Importantly, however, despite all the change, The Oval has retained its special atmosphere. As a spectator, I relished it at the 1948 and 1953 Ashes Tests and it was just as apparent during the 2005 and 2015 Ashes (despite England losing the matches in 1948 and 2015). Great credit is due to the team of people who work so hard to ensure that it remains such a friendly environment.

In 2017, I will reach my 70th year as a member at The Oval, a span which includes 20 years as a player, ten as captain, eight as manager/ coach and two as president. Surrey County Cricket Club and The Oval has been the major player in the life of the Stewart family. My wife Sheila deserves a medal for making it all possible, not only for me, but also for our two sons, Neil and Alec, who have brought great pride to the family in their different ways.

Alec's career with Surrey and England is well documented (and nowhere better than in *Wisden*), but Neil has made a major contribution over many years in coaching and developing Surrey and England cricketers. They were both introduced to The Oval at a very young age and often played on the outfield before the day's play. They loved it. Now, dare I say it, our daughter Judy and her husband Kevin have an eight-year-old who made his debut for Surrey Under-9s this year – enough said!

MICKY STEWART, November 2016

The Oval is very much my second home – and has been since I was first brought to this great ground more than 50 years ago. I have been very lucky to have worked for so long at this iconic cricket venue. Flicking through the pages of this book reminds me of the amazing amount of cricketing history that has occurred here. I could never have imagined the central role it would play in my life, nor that the office I work from as Director of Cricket would be just one floor above the dressing rooms into which, as a young boy, I used to carry my dad's gear.

During those days, my brother and I used to wait for my dad at the end of play and we'd use the time to practise batting or bowling on the outfield. We never wanted it to end. Nowadays, when hundreds of families spill onto the ground at lunch or tea and do the same thing, I like to watch and imagine their excitement.

After becoming a professional cricketer, I began to learn what it was like to play in the middle of The Oval, rather than on the outfield. While the surroundings were not always the greatest, especially when the weather was bad, it was a unique feeling to play there. The famous gasometers were always an inspiration to me. As a young cricketer, I would look up and remember that those gasometers stood there when Bradman played his last Test at this ground in 1948, when Michael Holding and Viv Richards destroyed England when I was aged just 13, and when W. G. Grace played in this country's first-ever home Test match in 1880.

Reading some of the *Wisden* extracts in this book transports you back to those days and gives me more insight into the historic achievements of those great players. As a cricketer, I always respected *Wisden*, and looking through so many fascinating reports has reminded me of the high standards it has always kept.

Aside from my family links and loyalty to Surrey, The Oval played a huge part in my international career. I played 12 Test matches and ten one-day internationals there. The century I scored in a Texaco Trophy ODI in 1992 remains a very special memory.

In 2003, I was lucky enough to play my final Test – indeed my last professional match – at The Oval. Though I appreciated the significance of the occasion for myself personally, my focus was entirely on securing the win for England that would have seen us draw the series. The South African team formed a guard of honour as I walked out to bat in my final Test, just as England had done for Bradman 55 years earlier. It was a great honour and I felt enormously proud – until the moment I got to the end of the line of players and encountered my old friend Shaun Pollock. Offering his hand for me to shake and with a smile on his face, he said: "Remember how many runs Sir Don Bradman got in his last game here?" I did remember and was relieved to get off the mark! To win that match by nine wickets and leave the outfield for the last time as a player was an incredible feeling. The fact that I did so as a winner was very important and something for which I will always be grateful.

There's never been a time in my life when I haven't been a regular visitor at The Oval. Even though I did not immediately go into cricket management after retiring as a player, part of my working life was as an ambassador for Surrey. Now, as Director of Cricket at Surrey, part of my responsibility is to sign players for the club. The likelihood of a player deciding to join Surrey increases the moment they realise that I am offering them the chance to call The Oval their home ground. This is the case with all players, including all-time greats such as Ricky Ponting and Kumar Sangakkara, both of whom were very aware of what the ground meant to their fellow countrymen when they agreed to come and play their final stints of first-class cricket with Surrey.

Having travelled all round the cricketing world in my playing career and now being back at The Oval on a full-time basis, I can say in all honesty that there is nowhere in the world I would rather call my cricketing home.

ALEC STEWART, November 2016

Introduction

In 2010 Kyle Orton was earning around $8.9m a year as the starting quarterback for the Denver Broncos, holding an iconic position once occupied by the great John Elway. Orton played his football in the 76,000 capacity Invesco Field at Mile High and was considered one of the most high-profile sportsmen in a country of well over 300 million people. However, as he stood in a quiet corridor behind the Long Room at The Oval Cricket Ground – where his team were practising before their match at Wembley against the San Francisco 49ers – Orton was silent in reverence as the ground's heritage was explained to him.

A hushed "1845?" was the first sign that this titan of American sports was in awe of the weight of history represented by a series of black and white photographs on the wall in front of him. He may never know of the feats achieved by the Surrey greats that were pictured there – it was simply the fact that sport had been played in this place for 165 years. That was beyond his comprehension.

Prior to his NFL career, Orton had taken a history major at Purdue University in Indiana, so he may well have been able to make a few quick mental associations. He might have known that, in the year this ground was founded, Florida and Texas became the 27th and 28th states of the Union and that James K. Polk was inaugurated as the 11th President of the United States. He would surely have been aware that the ground predated the American Civil War, Abraham Lincoln's Emancipation Proclamation and the erection of the Statue of Liberty.

What he would not have known was the significance of the very corridor where he was standing, down which Donald Bradman had walked in 1948, the cheers of a grateful public ringing in his ears, to play what would be his last innings in a Test match. Orton would not have heard of Bradman but, as a fellow professional sportsman, would surely appreciate the dominance he was able to exert and the perfect tragedy that was about to unfold.

Another thing of which the great quarterback was unaware was sitting just behind him in the Sandham Room that forms part of the small museum at The Oval: a full collection of the *Wisden Cricketers' Almanack*, one of three in the possession of Surrey County Cricket Club. The historian inside Orton would have loved the fact that that the events at this ground had been painstakingly chronicled for the previous 146 years.

While The Oval is so much more than just a cricket ground, the almost symbiotic relationship it holds with the pages of *Wisden* has ensured that the *Almanack* represents a true record of its cricketing history. The two have so much in common that a collection like this was inevitable. As I write, The Oval has no fewer than 171 years of history to explore, 153 of which have been chronicled by *Wisden*.

Initially, *Wisden* covered more than just cricket, its first edition in 1864 including the rules of quoiting, the fact that carpets were first manufactured in Kidderminster in 1735, a brief history of China and the winners of various classic horse races. At that time, The Oval was not just a place for cricket; the ground served as the country's first real attempt at a national sporting stadium. It hosted the first FA Cup final in 1872 – plus a further 19 finals over the next two decades – and the first points by the England rugby team came at the ground the same year. The first goal by the national football team was scored at The Oval in 1873, and the venue was used for nine more England football matches as well as six more England rugby matches, including Ireland's inaugural game in 1875.

As cricket and publishing continued to evolve, both The Oval and *Wisden* have grown to become much-loved English institutions. Many of the great names of the Golden Age helped popularise *Wisden* among the late Victorians and also established The Oval as one of the pre-eminent places in the country to play cricket. Without The Oval, *Wisden* would have been a considerably poorer read; and without *Wisden*, perhaps The Oval would not have developed its reputation so early on.

What is clear as you read through one edition after another is that The Oval is one of the greatest cricket grounds in the world. Add in its wider Victorian heritage and there is a very strong argument to be made that this is the most historic sports stadium in the world.

Sport in England today is very different to what it was in the early decades of the 20th century, and very few of the Victorian sporting palaces are relevant in the modern world. Yet The Oval has become a world-class modern facility that carries its history into the present day. A ground that was once an icon of cricket's Golden Age is now a major venue of a game with the same name but an almost unrecognisable sensibility.

It is this realisation that provides the fundamental link between *Wisden* and The Oval. No other sport can boast a historical tome as comprehensive, admired and ancient, one that is still influencing, documenting and reporting the game today. Equally, no other sport has a venue so steeped in history and yet is still a place where you can watch the game throughout the summer.

Cricket is privileged to have a number of these cathedrals. The publication of this book marks The Oval's ascension to the tiny group of grounds that have staged 100 Test matches: it joins the Melbourne Cricket Ground, the Sydney Cricket Ground and, apparently, a small patch of turf on the edge of Regent's Park in London that others call the Home of Cricket. The Oval may have missed out on a podium spot in the race to 100 Tests, but it stands above all its rivals as a pantheon of history. Indeed, the entire story of cricket's evolution can be told through the events that have taken place at this ground.

We can begin by making the assertion that the modern game started with the advent of the Test match. The first of these took place in Melbourne, but Test cricket found a home in England at The Oval in 1880, where W. G. Grace hit 152 and Australian captain Billy Murdoch 153 not out as England won by five wickets.

Two years later, The Oval gave birth to the game's greatest contest – the Ashes – as England were shocked by the 'demon' Fred Spofforth and lost to Australia by seven runs. In an early sign of the British press tending toward the dramatic, the *Sporting Times* famously declared that English cricket was dead and the body would be cremated and taken to Australia. The story goes that the bails from that match were burned, placed into an urn, taken to Australia, and given to England captain Ivo Bligh by some Melburnian women after he led England to a 2–1 victory in the subsequent series.

As the game evolved and players went on to ever greater feats of personal brilliance, The Oval was the first to witness a Test double-century, courtesy of Murdoch in 1884. At the same ground 25 years later, Australian left-hander Warren Bardsley became the first player to score a century in both innings of a Test during the final match of the 1909 Ashes.

The Oval staged two landmark Test matches in the early years of the 20th century. In the Ashes Test of 1902, Gilbert Jessop scored a second-innings century in 75 minutes before Wilfred Rhodes and George Hirst saw England home to a one-wicket victory, having famously determined "to get them in singles". Ten years later, The Oval staged two Tests in the triangular series involving England, Australia and South Africa, the first of which featured England's Sydney Barnes taking match figures of 13 for 57 (including eight for 29 in the second innings) against South Africa.

While Test cricket gained momentum, the game's next great development was the formalisation of the domestic first-class game and the creation of the County Championship, which was first officially contested in 1890. The opening three competitions were won by Surrey, who have been residents at The Oval ever since the ground opened in 1845.

To truly develop and widen its popularity, a sport needs an icon. With W. G. Grace playing his final first-class match in 1908 – his last three games were all at The Oval – there was a vacancy for an international cricketing hero. Step forward John Berry Hobbs, known universally as Jack. As a young professional, Hobbs played in Grace's last game, and he would go on to bestride the sport until his own retirement in 1934, wearing the Brown Cap of Surrey and playing 369 first-class matches at The Oval. He averaged over 50 at the ground, hitting 90 centuries, and retired from Test cricket after the Oval Test of 1930 which concluded Don Bradman's first Ashes series in England.

Eight years later, with England searching for a figure to combat the brilliance of Bradman, a young Yorkshireman called Len Hutton walked out to bat on a Saturday morning in the final Ashes Test of the series at The Oval. He was still there on Tuesday morning – an extraordinary feat even allowing for the traditional Sunday rest day – and hit 364 of England's 903 for seven declared. Hutton's individual score, England's team total and the subsequent margin of victory (an innings and 579 runs) all remain national records.

After the Second World War, during which time the ground was requisitioned and turned into a Prisoner of War camp, The Oval played host to the end of an era when, in 1948, Don Bradman played his final Test innings. His failure to score the four runs he required to average 100 in Test cricket created an even greater historical legacy.

The spiritual predecessor of The Oval's 2005 Ashes Test was England's victory there in 1953, which returned the urn to these shores for the first time in 19 (war-interrupted) years. This was achieved with a headline-grabbing performance as England beat Lindsay Hassett's Australia by eight wickets, and the national outpouring which followed would be echoed when the heroes of 2005 achieved a similar feat 52 years later.

Asian cricket was beginning to make its mark on the game and in 1954 Pakistan became the first side to win a Test on their first tour of England with a 24-run victory at The Oval. The result was a forerunner to the great Asian teams that would visit the ground in the coming years.

In July 1956, Surrey and England spinner Jim Laker became the first man to take all ten wickets in a Test innings. This took place, of course, at Old Trafford in Manchester. However, Laker had warmed up for the feat by taking ten for 88 for Surrey against Australia at The Oval two months earlier.

Two years later, the defining achievement of English domestic cricket was completed at The Oval when Surrey took four points from a draw with Somerset, thereby collecting their seventh consecutive County Championship title. It remains the record against which all levels of domestic dominance are judged.

One of the crowning cricketing achievements of the 1960s was Freddie Trueman becoming the first bowler to take 300 Test wickets. It was touch and go throughout the summer of 1964 as to where the

Yorkshireman would reach the landmark. Ever the showman, Trueman waited until the final Ashes Test of the summer at The Oval, where he had Neil Hawke caught at slip by Colin Cowdrey to achieve the milestone.

Four years later, the ground saw another historical moment for English cricket. For one thing, it was one of the most extraordinary Ashes Tests. With England running out of time, the crowd took to the outfield on the final afternoon to help the groundsmen mop the playing area following an incendiary storm – allowing the home team to win with just six minutes to spare. But the match also laid the basis for one of the game's great political scandals, as Basil D'Oliveira hit 158 but was not selected for the scheduled winter tour of South Africa.

In 1971 India recorded their first Test victory in England, their four-wicket win at The Oval also securing the series. This may not have been seen as momentous outside of the subcontinent, but it marked the beginnings of the rise of India to a 21st-century cricketing superpower.

Earlier in 1971, limited-overs cricket made its bow on the world stage and, while the ground cannot lay a claim as the home of the first one-day international, it was a venue in the first Cricket World Cup, staging three games in 1975, including West Indies' defeat of New Zealand in the semi-final.

The West Indians returned the following year for a famous Oval Test which featured a double-century for Viv Richards and 14 wickets for Michael Holding. As well as being one of the all-time great Test matches, it attracted a passionate, packed and partisan crowd – largely supporting the tourists – as The Oval became an icon of a new golden age, that of Caribbean Cricket.

West Indian dominance lasted all the way through the 1980s and included the 1984 'Blackwash' of England, which reached its conclusion at The Oval. Seven years later, the ground played host to what many saw as the end of that era, when England managed to draw the series with a five-wicket victory. A traditionally generous Oval crowd rose to their feet and applauded Richards off the field for the final time in a Test match.

For English fans the ground would go on to play an important role in the 1990s, often providing a morale-boosting and charismatic victory at the end of a series that was already lost. Alas, the win would stoke optimism for the winter tour – optimism that was usually crushed long before Christmas.

In 1998 The Oval staged one of Sri Lanka's greatest moments when Muttiah Muralitharan baffled England while taking 16 wickets and introducing the world to an entirely new breed of spin bowler. England's misery was compounded by Sanath Jayasuriya's 213 as Sri Lanka romped to their first victory on English soil.

With the game transforming faster than ever, the ground has maintained and indeed increased its relevance as cricket seamlessly evolved into its third century.

It may not have seemed much at the time, but The Oval helped give birth to arguably the single biggest change in the history of the game when Surrey seamer Martin Bicknell lolloped in to bowl to Middlesex opener Paul Weekes on June 13, 2003. Bicknell produced an excellent example of his stock ball on a good length outside the off stump; Weekes let it go by. This was the first day on which Twenty20 cricket was played professionally anywhere in the world, and The Oval was staging one of the matches on the opening night (attracting a crowd of over 10,000). Surrey went on to win the inaugural trophy.

The Ashes reached its apogee in September 2005 – certainly in English hearts – when Michael Vaughan led England to victory for the first time since 1987. A newly modernised ground provided the arena for a contest screened live on free-to-air television at the end of the most dramatic series ever played. When the urn was lifted, the outpouring of English catharsis promoted the ground from merely a famous and popular sporting arena to the scene of one of the most iconic triumphs in English sporting history.

As if spurred by the 2005 Test, The Oval has continued to set the standard in many areas: corporate sponsorship (with a number of household brands paying large sums to insert their name into the ground's official title); the continued rise of Twenty20 cricket (in 2016, one in every seven tickets sold for an English domestic Twenty20 match was to a game at The Oval); and increasingly regular staging of major international events including the Champions Trophy, the World Twenty20 and, in 2019, the next Cricket World Cup. All this has reinforced The Oval's status as one of the world's leading cricket grounds, more than 170 years since cricket was first played in Kennington.

These events have been painstakingly documented in *Wisden* by some of the best journalists in sport. Indeed, many of them have done so while sitting in the Sydney Pardon Press Box, which was named after the *Almanack*'s longest-serving editor (35 editions between 1891 and 1925).

One of my aims in compiling this book was to provide readers with the opportunity to immerse themselves in some of the game's greatest matches, understand some of its great characters and follow the evolution of cricket from a Victorian pastime to a major international sport.

An unexpected pleasure that unfolded throughout the many hours I've spent with my head buried in *Wisden* was to observe the evolution of the book's language. The very first *Wisden* was a direct contemporary of Jules Verne's *Journey to the Centre of the Earth*. With a new edition having been published every year since then, the gradual change in *Wisden*'s language is a fascinating linguistic journey, from a time when the writers were publishing alongside George Eliot and Thomas Hardy to the relatively modern reportage used now. *Wisden* should always maintain its classic style, but for its canon to contain such a varied mix of prose is something of which it should be proud.

There is something gloriously evolutionary about The Oval as well. To look out over the outfield towards the gasholders, one can easily imagine the likes of Charles Dickens, William Gladstone and Prince Albert watching a game unfold, much as you can find Mick Jagger, John Major and Stephen Fry taking in a game today. A wonderful example of the different characters attracted to the game.

Beyond this, The Oval's location is a wonderful metaphor for its beauty. Tucked away in an under-appreciated working-class neighbourhood yet just ten minutes from the Houses of Parliament, she (the ground has always been a she) has been quietly going about her business since an age that would be unrecognisable to anyone living today.

As befits a resident of Kennington, The Oval has always been important and influential but never boastful or assumptive. It is these qualities that have ensured its endurance for over 170 years. Throughout this time, it has never had a better friend than *Wisden*.

JON SURTEES, April 2017

Chapter 1

The Greatest Match

It is a bold claim to isolate a specific game or moment as "the greatest" to have taken place at a ground. But such is the iconic status of England's 2005 Ashes triumph – a series that moved Wisden editor Matthew Engel to use that very term – that many are happy to label the final Ashes Test of 2005 as the greatest game to have been played at The Oval.

The tour had started with an England victory in their first-ever Twenty20 international, but Australia clinched the one-day series 2–1 with a win in the deciding match at The Oval.

The Test series entered the national conversation like no other in living memory. The last to be broadcast live on free-to-air television, the quality and drama of the cricket captivated sports fans across the world, with all parts of the UK grinding to a halt so the public could marvel at the feats of Michael Vaughan's Ashes heroes.

Naturally, the 2006 Wisden gorged itself on the feast of stories and statistics. A picture of Andrew Flintoff and Shane Warne, taken at The Oval, appeared on its cover.

ENGLAND V AUSTRALIA, FIFTH TEST

Hugh Chevallier, 2006

September 8, 9, 10, 11, 12, 2005. Match drawn.

The Test series had started with defeat at Lord's before England secured dramatic wins at Edgbaston and Trent Bridge either side of a thrilling draw at Old Trafford. They arrived at The Oval needing to avoid a loss to regain the Ashes for the first time since surrendering the urn in 1989.

The Ashes series ended in the sort of obscure anti-climax which baffled outsiders were inclined to associate with cricket before the summer of 2005. But this time it did not produce bewildered shakes of the head. It delivered one of the most exhilarating moments in the history of English sport, never mind cricket.

As England moved towards the draw that clinched the Ashes, the roads went quiet as the nation headed for the TV screens to concentrate on the moment. Next day, the noise was on the streets as England paraded the replica trophy from an open-top bus, and the game's new fans jumped into the Trafalgar Square fountains in delight as they awaited the team's arrival.

Could stuffy old cricket really have caused all this? The answer was yes. The euphoria released when England brought back the Ashes after an absence of 16 years 42 days confirmed that cricket's place in the country's soul had survived eight successive humiliating series against the Australians. But more than that, what was noticeable was how young those in Trafalgar Square were: many were unborn when Mike Gatting's team won in 1986-87. A new generation had been enticed to the game by this amazing summer. Cricket was unmissable; cricket was cool.

Perhaps it should have been no surprise. This was the climax of what was already being called the Greatest Series Ever. And despite that impossible billing, it matched expectations in all but its very end. It helped that the stage was perfectly set: with England 2–1 up, only defeat could prevent the triumphant restoration of the Ashes. It meant that tension suffused every move. And Ponting had two enemies to overcome: England were a known quantity, the September weather was not.

The buzz beforehand was so loud even the Arabic television channel Al Jazeera came to see what the fuss was about. Actually, it was about arms and legs. One of each was what it would cost to buy a ticket on the grey market. (Figures of £1,000 for a £66 seat were bandied around, though seldom substantiated.) The other limbs fascinating the media were Glenn McGrath's elbow and Simon Jones's ankle: each was suspect, each vital to the plot. Australia sighed with relief when the elbow passed a fitness test, England with dismay when the ankle failed. Forced into their only change of the series, the selectors overlooked poor Chris Tremlett, twelfth man since Lord's, and called up Paul Collingwood to deepen the batting: not a positive statement. McGrath gently elbowed aside Kasprowicz.

The crowd were so partisan that even the toss was greeted with a bellow of delight: Vaughan had won it, and naturally batted. This had become the pattern of England's success, and in no time the openers were singing along at around five an over. A true pitch, lightning outfield and hot sun – belying the latest-ever start for a Test in England – made scoring look easy. At least it did for an hour, until Warne made an early entrance. Suddenly, the game wore a different face. By his 11th over, despite scant turn and little more bounce, Warne had single-handedly rescued Australia, doing something new in his 128th Test: never before had he taken the first four wickets in a first innings. The score lurched from 82 for nought to 131 for four.

It looked as though England had squandered the advantage. But if one thing was certain this summer, it was that nothing was certain. Strauss and Flintoff knuckled down, initially defending against Warne and attacking the others. Soon after tea, Flintoff opened his shoulders and hit Warne for three successive fours. As Strauss reached a hundred dripping with quality cuts and drives, England were smiling again. The pair added 143, but with both going before the close the Australians still narrowly shaded the first day. Next morning, the tail lifted England to 373, almost par on this pitch.

After a wretched series, Australia's opening partnership had to come good. Langer was all fight, lofting Giles for two sixes in his first over, and heavily outscored a hesitant, scratchy Hayden, traditionally the more fluent, but now playing for his place as well as the Ashes. At least the runs were coming – until they weren't. To general disbelief, the batsmen took the light immediately after tea. The skies had filled in but, with the forecast iffy, it made no sense. Play eventually resumed 30 minutes late next morning, and it was a case of stop-start thereafter.

Australia were 185 when a wicket finally fell. In his 13th over, Harmison, largely anodyne till now, was riled by two bouncers being ruled wides and by two fours, the first bringing up Langer's century, the second his 7,000th Test run. Harmison instantly bit back, beating Langer for pace and fury. Rain interrupted again, though Hayden later found time to reach his first hundred for 14 months, more gritty than pretty. At 277 for two on the third evening, Australia looked impregnable. Impregnable, though, was no use; victory was Ponting's only currency, and the decision to go off for light again was unfathomable.

The murk on the fourth morning was similarly unfathomable, but now the batsmen did stay on, heralding a prodigious passage of play. Bowling unchanged from the Pavilion End from the start until six overs after lunch, Flintoff was awesome. Relentlessly hitting a length, he found seam, a hint of swing, four wickets and a place in Ashes legend. His figures of 14.2–3–30–4 (for an overall five for 78) could only hint at the intensity of the battle. Australia lost seven wickets for 44, their last five for 11. Hoggard, his late swing the perfect foil for Flintoff, contributed a sublime spell of four for four from 19 balls to finish things off.

Far from a commanding lead, Australia trailed by six, failing to make 400 in a series of four or more Tests for the first time since 1978-79. Ponting's only option was to blast England out double quick, but the light remained sepulchral. McGrath idiotically bowled a bouncer, and they were off – though not before Warne found extravagant, anxiety-inducing spin to remove Strauss. On their return, in marginally brighter conditions, all the Australian players sported sunglasses. The pantomime caught on: with Warne a constant threat, some spectators theatrically unfurled umbrellas against non-existent rain. Nearby Aussies promptly stripped off their shirts and basked in illusory sunshine. The umbrellas won. To applause that might have been thunder, everyone trooped off. It meant no more cricket; the paying public, for once, didn't care.

The final day dawned, brightly, with every result possible and tension upgraded from danger level to crisis point. England were 34 for one, but they had to get through a notional 98 overs without giving Australia a look-in. With the score on 67, McGrath struck twice with two exquisite deliveries. The hat-trick ball looped into the slips, sparking huge appeals and much queasiness. Somehow, umpire Bowden got it right. Not out: it had hit Pietersen's shoulder. Next over, he was dropped off Warne; had it stuck, England would have been 68 for four. They were nurturing the shoots of a recovery when Lee found Pietersen's edge. The ball flashed at head height to Warne, safest of first slips. He parried it. As his despairing lunge failed to grab the rebound, the stands erupted.

The release of tension was short-lived. Warne snaffled Trescothick and Flintoff to give Australia the edge: at lunch, they were 133 behind, just five wickets to filch and more than 70 overs left. Some found it all too much. David Graveney, the chairman of selectors, headed for the car park to calm himself down, missing an epic shoot-out between Pietersen, oozing conviction, confidence and courage, and Lee, touching 95mph. Supported by Collingwood, whose 72-minute ten justified his selection, and then Giles, Pietersen reeled off shots outrageous in any circumstances, unimaginable in these. By tea, he had pulled, punched, slashed and smashed his way to an extraordinary maiden Test hundred, applauded by Warne (his Hampshire captain), 23,000 in the stands and millions in their living-rooms.

Even then, Australia – 227 behind, three batsmen to dislodge, nearly 50 overs available – had a chance of victory. Not for long. No one could say precisely when the draw and England's Ashes became inescapable: certainly before Pietersen fell for an unforgettable 158, including seven sixes. Giles consolidated his reputation for reliability with 59, his highest Test score, and Warne wheeled away for a lion-hearted six wickets – 12 in the match, a staggering 40 in the series.

Yet the denouement of this Test, unlike the previous three, was pure bathos. Even though there was nothing to be gained from Australia starting their second innings, ICC regulations dragged the players back out. Four meaningless balls later, they came off for the umpteenth and last time, in fading light. The game theoretically remained live for another 16 minutes, and then, to a roar audible in Sydney, the umpires, adding their own piece of theatre, removed the bails: the Ashes were England's.

England

M. E. Trescothick c Hayden b Warne	43	– lbw b Warne		33
A. J. Strauss c Katich b Warne	129	– c Katich b Warne		1
*M. P. Vaughan c Clarke b Warne	11	– c Gilchrist b McGrath		45
I. R. Bell lbw b Warne	0	– c Warne b McGrath		0
K. P. Pietersen b Warne	14	– b McGrath		158
A. Flintoff c Warne b McGrath	72	– c and b Warne		8
P. D. Collingwood lbw b Tait	7	– c Ponting b Warne		10
†G. O. Jones b Lee	25	– b Tait		1
A. F. Giles lbw b Warne	32	– b Warne		59
M. J. Hoggard c Martyn b McGrath	2	– not out		4
S. J. Harmison not out	20	c Hayden b Warne		0
B 4, lb 6, w 1, nb 7	18	B 4, w 7, nb 5		16

1/82 (1) 2/102 (3) 3/104 (4)   (105.3 overs)   373   1/2 (2) 2/67 (3)   (91.3 overs) 335
4/131 (5) 5/274 (6) 6/289 (7)   3/67 (4) 4/109 (1)
7/297 (2) 8/325 (8) 9/345 (10) 10/373 (9)   5/126 (6) 6/186 (7) 7/199 (8)
                                             8/308 (5) 9/355 (9) 10/335 (11)

McGrath 27–5–72–2; Lee 23–3–94–1; Tait 15–1–61–1; Warne 37.3–5–122–6; Katich 3–0–14–0; *Second innings—* McGrath 26–3–85–3; Lee 20–4–88–0; Warne 38.3–3–124–6; Clarke 2–0–6–0; Tait 5–0–28–1;

Australia

J. L. Langer b Harmison	105	– not out	0
M. L. Hayden lbw b Flintoff	138	– not out	0
*R. T. Ponting c Strauss b Flintoff	35	–	
D. R. Martyn c Collingwood b Flintoff	10	–	
M. J. Clarke lbw b Hoggard	25	–	
S. M. Katich lbw b Flintoff	1	–	
†A. C. Gilchrist lbw b Hoggard	23		
S. K. Warne c Vaughan b Flintoff	0		
B. Lee c Giles b Hoggard	6		
G. D. McGrath c Strauss b Hoggard	0		
S. W. Tait not out	1		
B 4, lb 8, w 2, nb 9	23	Lb 4	4

1/185 (1) 2/264 (3) 3/281 (4)   (107.1 overs)   367   (no wkt, 0.4 overs)   4
4/323 (2) 5/329 (6) 6/356 (7)
7/359 (5) 8/363 (8) 9/363 (10) 10/367 (9)

Harmison 22–2–87–1; Hoggard 24.1–2–97–4; Flintoff 34–10–78–5; Giles 23–1–76–0; Collingwood 4–0–17–0. *Second innings*—Harmison 0.4–0–0–0;

Umpires: B. F. Bowden and R. E. Koertzen.   Third umpire: J. W. Lloyds.
Referee: R. S. Madugalle.

Close of play: first day, England 319-7 (Jones 21, Giles 5); second day, Australia 112-0 (Langer 75, Hayden 32); third day, Australia 277-2 (Hayden 110, Martyn 9): fourth day. England 34-1 (Trescothick 14, Vaughan 19).

THE ASHES 2005 – SERIES REVIEW Stephen Brenkley, 2006

If there has been a more compelling series, history forgot to record it. If there is a better one in the future, you would beg to be there. England regained the Ashes after a gap of 16 years and 42 days, when bad light brought a formal end to the Fifth Test: a series full of extraordinary climaxes and reversals, in the end just dwindling away in the more usual cricketing fashion to the point where an Australian victory became impossible, even in this summer.

Australia needed 338 runs to win from the 17.2 overs remaining to draw level at 2–2 and retain the Ashes. So 2–1 to England it was, though but for a run here, a wicket there or a catch almost anywhere it could conceivably have been either 4–1 or 0–4. It is somehow soothing to relate the bare facts and the strangely prosaic conclusion. The contest was gripping from the beginning. As it reached the end, not just regular English cricket-followers, but the whole country and the rest of the cricketing world were in its thrall. It was so intense and played with such purpose that it supplanted football on the back pages and much else on the front pages. Television viewing figures went through the roof.

The First Test was topsy-turvy, but eventually resulted in an easy Australian victory, leading most people – including, crucially, the Australians themselves – to assume their dominance would remain unchallenged. The Second ("The Greatest Test", many thought) produced the first sensational finish and a two-run England win. Australia just held out to save the Third. England clung on to edge the Fourth. And, though the Fifth reached a conclusion more bizarre than thrilling, everyone was so galvanised by the whole affair and, in England, by the impending return of the urn that no one minded.

By the halfway mark, a debate had begun about whether it was the best Ashes series of all; it moved swiftly on to whether it was the best Test series ever, with a substantial body of informed opinion thinking it was. At various times, the matches entered that peculiar realm where you could not look away but found it unbearable to keep watching.

But there was another dimension too. The image of England's monumental all-rounder Andrew Flintoff consoling a distraught Brett Lee immediately after England had won the Second Test flashed round

Planet Cricket. It seemed to show a world where forgotten virtues of honour, decency, respect and commiseration for your opponent still held sway. After years when every aspect of English cricket had been savaged or mocked, the game was now being reborn in the country where it had been conceived and nurtured, and looking like something with a great deal to teach rival sports and the rest of an often bad-tempered country.

When the series outcome was finally confirmed, after an audacious maiden Test century by Kevin Pietersen prevented Australia from having a decent tilt at the victory they required, there was an outpouring of relief and jubilation. The scenes at The Oval, splendidly refurbished and packed with 23,000 spectators on five successive days, were astonishing enough. There were countless renditions of "Jerusalem" which, like it or not, had become accepted as the team anthem, as well as "Land of Hope and Glory" and "There'll Always Be An England". The little scene when England's captain, Michael Vaughan, planted a kiss on the replica of the Ashes urn brought the house down, in the way that the hoisting of the FA Cup by the winning captain once did. And it was done with the judgment and delicacy of touch that had been apparent in his leadership throughout.

NOTES BY THE EDITOR   Matthew Engel, 2006

Around the country, kids who had never picked up cricket bats were suddenly pretending to be Freddie or Vaughany or Harmy or KP. And though autumn finally came, and jumper-goalposts inevitably replaced dustbin-wickets, there was evidence that the craze did not subside with the England team's sore heads, and that cricket had truly recaptured a slice of the nation's heart. For anyone who had lived through the dark years, it felt like a kind of liberation. Journalists still tended to write that we had witnessed Probably The Greatest Test (Edgbaston), Probably The Greatest Series, and Probably The Greatest Crowd To Greet A Victorious England Team. There is no need for the nervous adverb. This was The Greatest. The 2005 Ashes surpassed every previous series in cricket history on just about any indicator you choose. There had been close contests before, and turnarounds, and tension (1894-95, 1936-37, 1956, 1960-61 Australia v West Indies, 1981...), but never had cricket been so taut for so long...

England's years of failure and ultimate victory were crucial to this glorious story. Had they held the Ashes a series or two back, there wouldn't have been the pent-up emotion and resentment that made the release so wonderful. Had their victory been obvious, there wouldn't have been the build-up of tension that drew in so many of the uncommitted. Had England failed, it would have been melodrama rather than drama; anticlimax not climax; repression not catharsis. The patriotism was essential to the plot.

But in the final analysis, this was not primarily a victory for England. It was a victory for Australia too. It was – and this cliché is for once the simple truth – a victory for cricket. This was the old game routing its enemies, including those inside the walls. The 2005 Ashes constituted cricket in its purest form. There was no artificial colouring, no artificial flavouring, no added sugar. Nothing had to be sexed up or dumbed down. Everything was already there...

It was a triumph for the real thing: five five-day Test matches between two gifted, well-matched teams playing fantastic cricket at high velocity and high pressure with the perfect mix of chivalry and venom. Here was the best game in the world, at its best. And now millions more people know about it.

KEVIN PIETERSEN – CRICKETER OF THE YEAR   Paul Hayward, 2006

After capping a stellar debut Test series with an extraordinary performance at The Oval, Kevin Pietersen was named one of Wisden's *Five Cricketers of the Year. His 158 was the first of many great innings he would play at The Oval, a ground he lists as one of his favourites and one with which he will forever have a strong association as an England and Surrey player.*

When talent announces itself these days we rush to buy tickets for the burnout. This modern scepticism attached itself to Kevin Pietersen long before his bludgeoning and decisive innings of 158 on the final day of the Ashes. The genre for Pietersen's rise as cricketer and celebrity is one known to David Beckham, Jenson Button of Formula 1 and the self-basting Gavin Henson, Welsh rugby's icon for the iPod generation. With all these ubiquitous idols we observe the billboard competing with the scoreboard. It's a truism of modern sport that many young athletes have the party before they have fully done the work. In fact, there are those who worry that sport now exists as a fame academy – a factory for the making of deals – with the game itself an incidental part of the manufacturing process.

Pietersen certainly did the work at The Oval, and he sure as hell had the party afterwards. But when Pietersen stopped the victory bus to dive into Starbucks to relieve himself, cynics expected him to come out clutching a deal establishing him as the new face of the caramel macchiato.

He wasted no time affirming his status as cricket's first rock star. "Get your hair cut, Pietersen!" one MCC member barked as Michael Vaughan's men finally made it back to the Long Room after a long day of handshakes, hangovers and grins. The heckler was expressing the prejudices of those who regarded the lurching hero with suspicion.

The talent is the thing. Always the talent. If the gift is authentic it's easier to ignore the peripheral ringing of tills and vacuous celebrity chatter. On that front, Pietersen struck 473 runs in five Tests against Australia. This, after "KP" – as in the nuts – had recorded an average in 23 one-day internationals of 73.09. These are the figures of a resoundingly good cricketer. The ICC anointed him both Emerging Player and One-Day Player of the Year. His belligerent and fearless innings at The Oval lit the imagination's touch paper way beyond cricket. His team-mate Ashley Giles observed: "It was real grandchildren stuff. 'Gather round and I'll tell you about that innings I played with Pietersen, with the white stripes and the earrings.'" In the ensuing tide of English euphoria it was swiftly forgotten that KP had been dropped three times, most calamitously by Shane Warne, his Hampshire colleague and friend. That simple error turned Pietersen into a household name and millionaire. Sport's soundtrack is the music of chance.

The 158 may be a landmark Pietersen will never surpass. "Yes, I do think about that sometimes," he says. "But nothing I did that day was more important than us winning the Ashes. It was all about us winning the Ashes."…

Pietersen's six dropped catches in the series put gunpowder in the muskets of his critics, who detected a dilettante streak. Geoff Boycott received no thanks from Camp KP for reminding the new hero that greatness is achieved over years, not hours, and that frivolity has destroyed many promising careers.

Boycott, and others, will cite the skunk hairdo, the £50,000 earrings, the Three Lions tattoo, the dates with Caprice and a former Big Brother contestant, and the Los Angeles celebrity party to which Pietersen gained access with help from the dissolute actor Mickey Rourke. There he was romantically linked with Paris Hilton – an heiress, incidentally, not somewhere nice to stay in France. The game has never seen anything like this. Pietersen is surely the first man in flannels who chose to be famous – who set out to be world-renowned – just as Beckham and Henson have in their chosen fields. So now we stand back to find out whether he will be remembered as the cricketer who ate himself or a legend of the willow. Take your eyes off him if you can.

Chapter 2

The Birth of the Ashes

T est cricket was first played in England at The Oval in 1880, a fact which owed much to the efforts of Surrey secretary C. W. Alcock (who as secretary of the Football Association founded the FA Cup and arranged the first international football match). Wisden's report of the match ran to just 223 words, a brevity lamented by its compiler.

The Test between England and Australia was the only one that summer, with the two countries meeting at the ground on a biennial basis over the next decade, a period in which many of the great early names of English cricket produced some remarkable performances. These matches featured two centuries by W. G. Grace (his ton in 1880 was the first scored by an Englishman in Tests), the first Test double-century (1884) and, not least, the birth of the Ashes themselves (1882).

Thankfully, the extraordinary Test of 1882 was exhaustively recorded in Wisden, and it is reproduced here, including the statistics specifically requested by the compiler. The events of 2005 may have been 123 years in the future, but there are some fascinating parallels to explore.

ENGLAND V AUSTRALIA, ONLY TEST   1881

September 6, 7, 8, 1880. England won by five wickets.

Test cricket was born in Melbourne in 1877 and three years later it arrived in England with a one-off match at The Oval. Wisden provided a succinct report.

The compiler much regrets that the limited space allotted to the Australians' matches in this book precludes the possibility of giving a lengthened account of this famous contest.

He must therefore rest content to put on record the following facts anent the match: that in the history of the game no contest has created such world-wide interest; that the attendances on the first and second days were the largest ever seen at a cricket match; that 20,814 persons passed through the turnstiles on Monday, 19,863 on the Tuesday, and 3,751 on the Wednesday; that fine weather favoured the match from start to finish; that the wickets were faultless; that Mr Murdoch's magnificent innings of 153 not out was made without a chance, and contained one five, 18 fours, three threes, 13 twos and 41 singles; that Mr W. G. Grace's equally grand innings was made with only one hard chance, and comprised 12 fours, ten threes, 14 twos, and 46 singles; that superb batting was also shown by Mr Lucas, Lord Harris, Mr McDonnell, and Mr Steel; that the fielding and wicket-keeping on both sides was splendid; that a marvellous change in the aspect of the game was effected on the last day; that universal regret was felt at the unavoidable absence of Mr Spofforth; and that England won the match by five wickets.

England 420 (W. G. Grace 152, A. P. Lucas 55, Lord Harris 52) **and 57-5;**
Australia 149 (F. Morley 5-56) **and 327** (W. L. Murdoch 153*).

ENGLAND V AUSTRALIA, ONLY TEST   1883

August 28, 29, 1882. Australia won by seven runs.

The 1882 Test is arguably the most influential cricket match ever played, its result playing a huge part in ensuring the continued popularity of Test cricket. Australia's victory so surprised the Wisden *correspondent that the pre-match season averages of both teams were included as proof of a major upset. The* Sporting Times *proclaimed the death of English cricket, adding that the body would be cremated and the ashes taken to Australia. Legend has it that a group of women presented the urn to England captain Ivo Bligh in Australia the following winter.*

Before entering into any of the details of the play in this match, the compiler desires to place before the readers of *Wisden* the names of the rival teams and their batting and bowling averages in first-class matches from the commencement of the season to the time they engaged in this memorable struggle.

Batting averages:

AUSTRALIA		ENGLAND	
Mr W. L. Murdoch	36.22	Mr A. P. Lucas	38.3
Mr T. Horan	31.16	Hon. A. Lyttleton	35.1
Mr H. H. Massie	27.31	Mr C. T. Studd	34.12
Mr A. C. Bannerman	23.21	W. Barnes	30.36
Mr J. M. Blackham	21.19	G. Ulyett	30.22
Mr G. Giffen	21.6	R. G. Barlow	29.25
Mr G. J. Bonnor	19.21	Mr A. G. Steel	29.18
Mr S. P. Jones	15.12	Mr A. N. Hornby	29.9
Mr H. F. Boyle	11.7	Dr W. G. Grace	24.1
Mr T. W. Garrett	9.20	M. Read	24
Mr F. R. Spofforth	9.20	E. Peate	11.18

Bowling averages:

AUSTRALIA		ENGLAND	
Mr H. F. Boyle	12.77	R. G. Barlow	11.53
Mr F. R. Spofforth	13.87	E. Peate	11.118
Mr T. W. Garrett	27.2	G. Ulyett	14.23
		Mr C. T. Studd	16.9
		Mr A. G. Steel	20.4
		W. Barnes	35

It will be observed that in *every* instance the batting average of each member of the Australian team is lower than that of the English batsman placed opposite him, and that the bowling averages of the two men who had the largest share of the trundling for England are both better than either of those of the two bowlers who sent down the largest number of overs for Australia.

A perusal of these statistics must in the first place create a feeling of surprise that when the two elevens met there was the slightest probability of the English one being defeated. Secondly, no sensation but one of the highest admiration of the achievement of the Australian team can be felt when the result of the match is considered; and thirdly the figures prove, if figures prove anything, that the inevitable result of a series of encounters between the two elevens would be victory for the Englishmen in a very large proportion of the matches; and they further offer the strongest protest to the oft-raised cry of the decadence of English cricket.

With these few remarks the compiler proceeds to give a short account of the contest, leaving the reader to attribute the Australian victory to the fact that the Colonists won the toss and thereby had the best of the cricket; to the fact that the English had to play the last innings; to the brilliant batting of Massie; to the superb bowling of Spofforth; to the nervousness of some of the England side; to the glorious uncertainty of the noble game; or to whatever he or she thinks the true reason.

Monday. Murdoch beat Hornby in the toss and deputed Bannerman and Massie to commence the innings. Massie was clean bowled by a yorker on the leg stump at six. At 21 Murdoch played a ball from Peate on to his wicket, and, after adding a single, Bonnor was clean bowled middle stump. Horan came in, and then, at 26, Bannerman was splendidly caught by Grace at point, left hand, low down, having been in an hour and five minutes for nine runs. Horan was bowled, leg stump, at 30. Blackham joined Giffen, and, with the total unchanged, was bowled with the second ball he received. Garrett was the new batsman, and a double change of bowling was found necessary before the newcomer was well caught at long-off just after luncheon. At 50 a splendid ball from Barlow just took the top of Boyle's wicket. Jones came in and rain fell for a few minutes. At 59 Blackham skied a ball and was caught, and Spofforth, the last man, joined Jones. The Demon hit a four, and then Jones was caught at third man, the innings closing for 63. At 3.30 Grace and Barlow started the first innings of England. Spofforth bowled Grace at 13, and Barlow was caught at forward point at 18. With Lucas and Ulyett together, the score was raised to 50 after half-an-hour's play, but at 56 the latter ran out to drive Spofforth and was easily stumped. At 59 Lucas was snapped at the wicket, and one run later Studd was bowled with a bailer without scoring, and half the wickets were down for 60. Read joined Lyttelton, and just when the score reached the total of the Australian innings the latter was caught at the wicket. Barnes came in and scored a single and a four and was then bowled by a breaking ball. Steel became Read's partner and 26 runs were added before Steel pulled a ball into his wicket. Eight wickets were down for 96 when Hornby came in. Read made a cut for three runs and Hornby scored a single, bringing up the 100. With only one run added, however, Hornby's leg stump fell, and the innings closed about five minutes before the call of time.

Tuesday. Massie and Bannerman commenced the Australians' second innings at 12.10, the Colonists being 38 to the bad. Thirty went up after about 28 minutes' play, two bowling changes having been tried. At 12.45 the balance of 38 runs was knocked off. Barnes relieved Studd at 47, and from his first ball Lucas badly missed Massie at long-off, the batsman then having made 38. Fifty was hoisted after 40 minutes' play. It was not until the score reached 66 that loud applause greeted the dismissal of the great hitter, bowled leg stump by Steel. Massie had made 55 out of 66 in 55 minutes, and his hits consisted of nine fours, two threes, three twos, and seven singles. Bonnor took the vacant wicket, but at 70 his middle stump was knocked clean out of the ground, and Murdoch came in, but immediately lost Bannerman, caught at extra mid-off, with the total unchanged. Bannerman had played with great patience for an hour and ten minutes for his 13. Horan joined Murdoch, and the bowling was changed, with the result that the incomer was easily caught. Giffen, who took his place, was out in the same way, and the fourth and fifth wickets were down at 79. Blackham came in, and when the score had been hit up to 99 rain fell, and luncheon was taken.

Resuming at 2.45, after another shower, Blackham was well caught at the wicket without any addition to the score. Jones filled the vacancy and a single by Murdoch sent up the 100. At 114 Jones was run out in a way which gave great dissatisfaction to Murdoch and other Australians. Murdoch played a ball to leg, for which Lyttelton ran. The ball was returned, and Jones having completed the first run, and thinking wrongly, but very naturally, that the ball was dead, went out of his ground. Grace put his wicket down, and the umpire gave him out. Several of the team spoke angrily of Grace's action, but the compiler was informed that after the excitement had cooled down a prominent member of the Australian eleven admitted that he should have done the same thing had he been in Grace's place. There was a good deal of truth in what a gentleman in the pavilion remarked, amidst some laughter, that Jones ought to thank the champion for teaching him something. Spofforth partnered Murdoch, but was bowled middle stump at 117. Garrett came in, and very shortly after, a very smart piece of fielding on the part of Hornby, Studd and Lyttelton caused Murdoch to be run out at 122 for a very careful and good innings of 29. Boyle was last man in, but failed to score, and the tenth wicket fell at the same total at 3.25.

England, wanting 85 runs to win, commenced their second innings at 3.45 with Grace and Hornby. Spofforth bowled Hornby's off stump at 15, made in about as many minutes. Barlow joined Grace, but was bowled first ball at the same total. Ulyett came in, and some brilliant hitting by both batsmen brought the score to 51, when a very fine catch at the wicket dismissed Ulyett. Thirty-four runs were then wanted, with seven wickets to fall. Lucas joined Grace, but when the latter had scored a two he was easily taken at mid-off. Lyttelton became Lucas' partner, and the former did all the hitting. Then the game was slow for a time, and 12 successive maiden overs were bowled, both batsmen playing carefully and coolly. Lyttelton scored a single, and then four maiden overs were followed by the dismissal of that batsman – bowled, the score being 66. Only 19 runs were then wanted to win, and there were five wickets to fall. Steel came in, and when Lucas had scored a four, Steel was easily caught and bowled. Read joined Lucas, but amid intense excitement he was clean bowled without a run being added. Barnes took Read's place and scored a two, and three byes made the total 75, or 10 to win. After being in a long time for five Lucas played the next ball into his wicket, and directly Studd joined Barnes the latter was easily caught off his glove without the total being altered. Peate, the last man, came in, but after hitting Boyle to square leg for two he was bowled, and Australia had defeated England by seven runs.

Australia

A. C. Bannerman c Grace b Peate	9	– c Studd b Barnes	13
H. H. Massie b Ulyett	1	– b Steel	55
*W. L. Murdoch b Peate	13	– (4) run out	29
G. J. Bonnor b Barlow	1	– (3) b Ulyett	2
T. P. Horan b Barlow	3	– c Grace b Peate	2
G. Giffen b Peate	2	– c Grace b Peate	0
†J. McC. Blackham c Grace b Barlow	17	– c Lyttelton b Peate	7
T. W. Garrett c Read b Peate	10	– (10) not out	2
H. F. Boyle b Barlow	2	– b Steel	0
S. P. Jones c Barnes b Barlow	0	– (8) run out	6
F. R. Spofforth not out	4	(9) b Peate	0
B 1	1	B 6	6

1/6 (2) 2/21 (3) 3/22 (4) (80 overs) 63
4/26 (1) 5/30 (5) 6/30 (6)
7/48 (8) 8/53 (9) 9/59 (7) 10/63 (10)

1/66 (2) 2/70 (3) (63 overs) 122
3/70 (1) 4/79 (5) 5/79 (6) 6/99 (7)
7/114 (8) 8/117 (9) 9/122 (4) 10/122 (11)

Peate 38–24–31–4; Ulyett 9–5–11–1; Barlow 31–22–19–5; Steel 2–1–1–0; *Second innings*—Barlow 13–5–27–0; Ulyett 6–2–10–1; Peate 21–9–40–4; Studd 4–1–9–0; Barnes 12–5–15–1; Steel 7–0–15–2.

England

R. G. Barlow c Bannerman b Spofforth	11	– (3) b Spofforth	0
W. G. Grace b Spofforth	4	– (1) c Bannerman b Boyle	32
G. Ulyett st Blackham b Spofforth	26	– (4) c Blackham b Spofforth	11
A. P. Lucas c Blackham b Boyle	9	– (5) b Spofforth	5
†A. Lyttelton c Blackham b Spofforth	2	– (6) b Spofforth	12
C. T. Studd b Spofforth	0	– (10) not out	0
J. M. Read not out	19	(8) b Spofforth	0
W. Barnes b Boyle	5	(9) c Murdoch b Boyle	2
A. G. Steel b Garrett	14	(7) c and b Spofforth	0
*A. N. Hornby b Spofforth	2	(2) b Spofforth	9
E. Peate c Boyle b Spofforth	0	b Boyle	2
B 6, lb 2, nb 1	9	B 3, nb 1	4

1/13 (2) 2/18 (1) 3/57 (3) (71.3 overs) 101
4/59 (4) 5/60 (6) 6/63 (5)
7/70 (8) 8/96 (9) 9/101 (10) 10/101 (11)

1/15 (2) 2/15 (3) (55 overs) 77
3/51 (4) 4/53 (1)
5/66 (6) 6/70 (7) 7/70 (8)
8/75 (5) 9/75 (9) 10/77 (11)

Spofforth 36.3–18–46–7; Garrett 16–7–22–1; Boyle 19–7–24–2; . *Second innings*—Spofforth 28–15–44–7; Garrett 7–2–10–0; Boyle 20–11–19–3.

Umpires: L. Greenwood and R. A. Thoms.

Close of play: first day, England 101.

ENGLAND V AUSTRALIA, THIRD TEST 1885

August 11, 12, 13, 1884. Match drawn.

The Ashes were recovered in Australia the following winter before the Aussies returned to England in 1884. This was the first series to feature matches played away from The Oval, and so began the ground's tradition of hosting the final Test. The opening two Tests – the first to be played at Old Trafford and Lord's – left England one up as they arrived at The Oval.

The third and last of the three great matches arranged to be played against the full strength of England resulted in a draw, England wanting 120 runs to avert a single-innings defeat, with eight wickets to go down. The fact that three individual scores of over 100 runs each were scored on the first day rendered the match unique in the annals of the game. When stumps were drawn on the first day, the score stood at 363 for two wickets, Murdoch having scored 145, and Scott 101 undefeated, the pair having added 205.

Bannerman was out with the score at 15, and McDonnell at 158, but 205 more runs were added that day without further loss. On the Tuesday Scott was caught at the wicket after adding a single to his overnight score, but Murdoch was not dismissed until he had compiled 211, being the sixth batsman out with the total at 494. The remainder of the innings was alone remarkable for the success which attended Lyttelton's lobs. He went on for the second time when six wickets were down for 532, and took the last four wickets in eight overs for only eight runs.

McDonnell's very brilliantly-hit 103 consisted of 14 fours, two threes, nine twos, and 23 singles, and was made while 158 runs were scored. Scott was batting three hours and a half for his 102, out of 207 put on while he was in, and he gave one real chance in his splendid innings, and that was when he had made 60. His figures were one for 5 (four for an overthrow), 15 fours, three threes, seven twos, and 14 singles. Murdoch's magnificent innings of 211 consisted of 24 fours, nine threes, 22 twos, and 44 singles, and the celebrated batsman was at the wickets a little over eight hours, while 479 runs were scored. He gave three chances, all off Ulyett's bowling, when his individual score reached 46, 171, and 205 respectively.

The only innings on the England side calling for special notice were those played by Scotton and Read. The two batsmen became partners when eight wickets had fallen for 181 runs, of which number Scotton had scored 53, 21 of them having been made on the previous evening.

They were not separated until they put on 151 runs for the ninth wicket. Scotton was the first to leave, having been at the wickets five hours and three-quarters, while 332 runs were made. He never gave the slightest chance, and it is not too much to say that his splendid display of defensive cricket was the cause of England saving the match. The figures of his innings were nine fours, five threes, nine twos, and 21 singles. Read's 117 was a superb display of hard and rapid hitting of two hours and a quarter's duration, his hits being 20 fours, one three, 12 twos, and ten singles. One difficult chance to Spofforth was the only blemish in his innings.

Australia 551 (P. S. McDonnell 103, W. L. Murdoch 211, H. J. H. Scott 102; A. Lyttelton 4-19);
England 346 (W. H. Scotton 90, W. W. Read 117; G. E. Palmer 4-90) **and 85-2.**

ENGLAND V AUSTRALIA, THIRD TEST   1887
August 12, 13, 14, 1886. England won by an innings and 217 runs.

The 1886 Ashes followed the same schedule. On this occasion, however, England had already secured the series, winning in Manchester and at Lord's.

The third and last meeting between England and Australia had been robbed of a large amount of its interest by the poor form shown by the Australians, who had suffered defeat on each of the two previous occasions. Nevertheless there was a large company on the opening day at Kennington Oval, 11,368 persons passing through the turnstiles...

For the second time the Englishmen won the toss, and once more they took full advantage of their opportunity. Curiously enough the Australians were engaged for the whole day in getting down two wickets, just as they had been a fortnight before in the return match against Surrey. On the present occasion, however, the batting was not of such a high quality. Although Mr W. G. Grace made the highest innings he had ever scored against Australian bowling, it was pretty generally admitted that his cricket was more faulty than usual. He gave an easy chance to Scott at short slip when he had made six, when his score was 23 he hit a ball very hard back to Giffen, which was a possible chance to that bowler's left hand; when he had scored 60 he might perhaps have been caught in the long field, had Bruce started earlier for the ball, and when his total was 93 McIlwraith had a difficult one-handed chance of catching him at slip. Moreover, just before getting out, when his total was 169 he hit a ball straight back to Garrett, who failed to hold it. Still, these blemishes notwithstanding, the innings was a very fine one. He made the enormous proportion of 170 out of 216 during his stay, which lasted altogether four hours and a half, and his figures were 22 fours, four threes, 17 twos and 36 singles. In an hour and 52 minutes before luncheon Mr Grace made 40 runs, and consequently in two hours and 38 minutes afterwards he made 130.

This marked difference in the rate of scoring was certainly accounted for to a large extent by the state of the wicket, which was by no means perfect up to the interval, but which improved steadily as the afternoon wore on. Scotton batted with extraordinary patience even for him, and contented himself by keeping up his wicket while Mr Grace hit. The two batsmen put on 170 runs before they were parted, this being the largest number ever scored for the first wicket against an Australian team in England. Scotton's 34 – an innings of immense value to his side – occupied no less a time than three hours and three-quarters, and at one period the famous Notts left-hander was in an hour and seven minutes without making a single run. After the dismissal of Scotton and Mr Grace some beautiful cricket was played by Shrewsbury and Mr Walter Read. The two men became partners with the score at 216, and when time was called for the day, the score was 279 with only two wickets down, Shrewsbury being not out 42, and Mr Read not out 30. The weather for the most part of the day was dull and overcast, but there was not a single interruption by rain.

On the Friday there was another immense attendance, 9,786 persons paying for admission at the gates. As on Thursday, everything went in favour of the Englishmen, and at the close of the day's proceedings the Australians found themselves in a most hopeless position, wanting no fewer than 358 runs to avert a single innings defeat, and having ten wickets to fall. It must be stated, however, that the English team had all the best of the luck, for the rain which fell in London on the Thursday evening seriously damaged the ground, and the Australians had to play the cream of the English bowling on a wicket on which run-getting was a matter of great difficulty. The remainder of the English innings occupied from half-past 11 until ten minutes to four in the afternoon, the total ultimately reaching 434. It was generally thought that, as the Englishmen were in such a position that they could not lose, some of the batsmen threw their wickets away. Shrewsbury only added two to his overnight score, and after his departure Barnes, Mr Steel, Barlow, and Ulyett were dismissed in rapid succession, seven wickets being down for 320.

Then came a most brilliant display of cricket on the part of Mr Read and Briggs, who hit at a tremendous pace, and at one time made 56 in half an hour. Briggs was at last well caught at slip at 410 for a very dashing 53, composed of three fours, five threes, eight twos, and ten singles. When it seemed almost certain that Mr Read would reach his hundred he was out to a well-judged catch in the long field. Out of 202 runs scored while he was at the wickets, he made 94 by perfect cricket. He hardly gave a fair chance, and seldom seemed in the least difficulty with the bowling. He was batting for about three hours and a half, and hit eight fours, two threes, and 15 twos. It was surprising in so long an innings that Evans and Bruce were not put on more often to bowl. The batting of the Australians proved to be of the most disappointing description. The innings opened at ten minutes past four, and just before six the whole side were out for the wretchedly poor total of 68. Being assisted by the condition of the ground, Lohmann and Briggs bowled magnificently and carried all before them, only two men on the Australian side – Palmer and Trumble – showing the least ability to contend against them. The English fielding was exceptionally brilliant, and the catch with which Briggs dismissed Blackham deserves a special word of praise. Following their innings against the enormous majority of 366, the Australians scored eight runs without the loss of a wicket before the call of time.

The cricket on the concluding day needs but brief description. The Australians could not hope to avert defeat, and though Giffen and Palmer batted well, the total in the end only reached 149, and England was left with another decisive victory, by an innings and 217 runs. The only chance of saving the game was to stop in the whole of the day. Even with the ground in the best of condition this would have been a task to tax the powers of any eleven, but with the wicket still assisting the bowlers it was now practically out of the question. Lohmann and Briggs again proved by far the most successful bowlers, and in the whole match the young Surrey man obtained 12 wickets for 104 runs, while Briggs secured six for 58. All ideas as to the ability of the 1886 Australian eleven to meet the full strength of England were totally dispelled by this crushing defeat. In fairness to the Colonials it must be stated that, at The Oval at any rate, they had all the worst of the wicket; but they played throughout with a lack of the life and energy that have usually characterised Australian cricket.

England 434 (W. G. Grace 170, W. W. Read 94, J. Briggs 53; F. R. Spofforth 4-65);
Australia 68 (G. A. Lohmann 7-36) **and 149** (G. A. Lohmann 5-68).

ENGLAND V AUSTRALIA, SECOND TEST   1891

August 11, 12, 1890. England won by two wickets.

Another emphatic England victory followed at The Oval in 1888, but two years later the fixture produced a much tighter contest that adhered to the cricketing maxim of "a short game is a good game".

The colonial players had sustained so many defeats that it was unreasonable to expect the same amount of interest that had been excited in previous years by the meeting with England at The Oval, but when the Surrey ground the day before the match was saturated by rain, good judges, remembering what Turner and Ferris are capable of on a damaged wicket, confidently predicted a capital game, and their anticipations were more than realised. The opening day's play was just what might have been expected after the great amount of rain that had fallen. The ball beat the bat all through the afternoon, and between 12 o'clock and the drawing of stumps 22 wickets went down for an aggregate score of only 197.

The Australians, who won the toss, and of course took first innings, were batting nearly two hours and a half for a total of 92. This could only be pronounced a poor performance, for several showers had fallen during the morning, and the wicket was by no means so difficult as it afterwards became. A very fine display of batting was given by Trott, who stayed at the wickets an hour and 20 minutes for 39. He was out at last in a curious way, a ball that he played on to his pad running up his arm and being caught wide on the leg side by the wicketkeeper. Martin bowled wonderfully well on his first appearance for England, taking six wickets at a cost of 50 runs. Lohmann, who was inclined to pitch short, probably found the ground too slow for him. England on going in to bat started very badly, Grace being easily caught at slip from the first ball he received; Shrewsbury at the end of half an hour's cricket being finely taken at point with the score at 10; and Mr W. W. Read being bowled at 16. Cranston then joined Gunn, and if the latter batsman with his score at two had been caught at slip by Trumble – the ball going right past the fieldsman's hands to the boundary – the four best batsmen would have been out for 19 runs. As it was, Gunn and Mr Cranston did great service for their side, and had carried the score to 55, when the amateur foolishly started for a short run and lost his wicket.

With 70 on the board for four wickets, England looked to have much the best of the game, but on Charlton taking the ball from Turner at 77, the batting broke down completely, the innings being finished off for a total of 100, or only eight runs to the good. With the ground in a very difficult state, the Australians lost Barrett and Ferris in their second innings for five runs, and the second day they stayed in till 25 minutes to two, the last wicket falling for 102, which left England 95 to get to win. Trott again played much the best cricket on his side and Lyons hit vigorously for 21. Under ordinary circumstances the task of getting 95 runs would have been an easy matter for the England team, but with the wicket as it was it was impossible to feel over confident. Mr Grace ought for the second time in the match to have been caught from the first ball that he received, but Trott at point dropped a ball that was cut straight into his hands. Despite this lucky let-off, however, the four best England wickets fell for 32 runs, the interest then reaching a very acute point.

With 63 runs wanted to win, Mr Cranston was joined by Maurice Read, and the two batsmen made a splendid effort for their side. If, however, with the total at 63 and his own score at 17 Maurice Read had been caught by Murdoch at mid-on, the Australians would in all probability have won the game. As it was, the score had been taken to 83 – only 12 to win with six wickets to fall – when Maurice Read was caught at long-on for an invaluable 35.

On his dismissal there came a collapse that recalled the great match in 1882, Mr Cranston, Lohmann and Barnes being dismissed in such quick succession that with eight men out two runs were still wanted to win. Amid indescribable excitement Sharpe became Mr McGregor's partner, and five maiden overs were bowled in succession, Sharpe being beaten time after time by balls from Ferris that broke back and missed the wicket. Then at last the Surrey player hit a ball to cover point, but Barrett, who had a chance of running out either batsman, overthrew the ball in his anxiety, and a wonderful match ended in a victory for England by two wickets. Martin in the whole match took 12 wickets for 102 runs – a splendid performance.

Australia 92 (F. Martin 6-50) **and 102** (F. Martin 6-52);
England 100 (J. J. Ferris 4-25) **and 95-8** (J. J. Ferris 5-49).

Chapter 3

The Golden Age

T he beauty of The Oval having played a crucial part in over 170 years of sporting history is that you can find every major cricketing era represented. This is no truer than for the Golden Age of cricket that is commonly referred to as having occurred between 1890 and 1914.

With a decade of Test matches under its belt, The Oval confidently moved towards the new century, hosting iconic international performances from the likes of C. B. Fry, Gilbert Jessop, Wilfred Rhodes, George Hirst and Sydney Barnes. It was also the venue for a Test against South Africa in 1907, which was the first time England faced a team other than Australia beneath the gasholders.

On a domestic level, the concept of an official county competition was conceived at the start of the Golden Age, with The Oval playing host to the first great Surrey team. Captained by John Shuter and then Kingsmill Key, Surrey won the first official County Championship in 1890 and repeated the trick five more times over the course of the decade. A seventh title arrived in 1914, when Cyril Wilkinson led the county to a title that was decided in a Lord's committee room after the season was ended prematurely by the outbreak of war.

In 1899 Wisden chose its first Cricketers of the Year, an annual tradition which continues to be one of the game's most cherished honours. A number of great Oval characters were among the first to be awarded the title. George Lohmann was one of the six inaugural winners, while Tom Hayward, Tom Richardson, Jack Hobbs and Herbert Strudwick are among the 21 Surrey players honoured between 1890 and 1914, an indication of the dominance of the club at the turn of the century. Indeed, the Golden Age produced some remarkable individual performances from Surrey batsmen in particular, with Hayward, Walter Read and Bobby Abel all hitting triple-centuries.

Surrey v Oxford University — 1889

June 25, 26, 27, 1888. Match drawn.

Walter Read was one of Surrey's best batsmen of the late Victorian age, and his finest moment came in the match against Oxford University in 1888.

One of the most remarkable matches of the year, inasmuch as it produced the second-highest individual score ever obtained in a contest of first-class importance. Mr W. W. Read made 338 for Surrey, and thus fell short by only six runs of Mr W. G. Grace's record-innings in first-class matches – 344 for MCC against Kent in the Canterbury week of 1876. Mr Read went in shortly before half-past one on the first day with the total at 96 for two wickets, was not out 235 at the drawing of stumps, and ended his innings on the Tuesday afternoon, rain preventing any cricket on the second day until after luncheon. He was batting altogether for six hours and a half, the figures of his phenomenal score being one five, 46 fours, 14 threes, 29 twos and 49 singles. He gave two very hard chances of being caught and bowled when his score stood at 55 and 76 respectively, but his innings was a wonderful display of hard and brilliant hitting. Mr W. G. Grace, who has performed the feat twice, Mr W. L. Murdoch and Mr W. W. Read are the only batsmen who have played an innings of over 300 in a first-class match. Abel's 97 was a masterly innings. Surrey's total of 650 was, up to this time, the highest total ever obtained in England in a first-class match. Rain only admitted of 55 minutes' cricket on the Wednesday and Messrs Simpson and Gresson were batting two hours and a quarter.

Surrey 650 (R. Abel 97, W. W. Read 338; H. W. Forster 4-169); **Oxford University 47-0.**

GEORGE LOHMANN – CRICKETER OF THE YEAR · 1889

The great George Lohmann of Surrey took 150 wickets or more in seven successive seasons from 1886 to 1892, and in 1899 he became one of Wisden's *first Cricketers of the Year. As a bowler, he had much in common with Sydney Barnes, who was just eight years younger than Lohmann (though they never played together for England): both were medium-pacers who relied on their unerring accuracy and ability to seam the ball both ways using subtle variations. Of bowlers to have taken 100 Test wickets, this pair have the best averages – though Lohmann's 112 wickets at 10.75 stands well clear of Barnes's 189 at 16.43. Lohmann sadly died of tuberculosis aged 36, while Barnes lived to be 94.*

George Alfred Lohmann was born at Kensington, June 5, 1865, and first played for Surrey in 1884. He is by general consent admitted to be one of the best bowlers and most accomplished all-round cricketers ever seen, and he fairly challenged comparison with Turner by what he did during the season of 1888. Lohmann and Turner are, indeed, very much alike. They bowl with remarkable skill and judgment; their batting and fielding are invaluable to their side, and they both have that peculiar electrical quality of rising to a great occasion. It has often enough been said of cricketers of proved skill, when they have failed, that the match has been too big for them, but certainly no match was ever too big for George Lohmann or Charles Turner.

Tom Hayward was one of the first great Surrey batsmen, headlining the team that won six County Championships between 1890 and 1899. By the time he played his final game for Surrey in 1914, he had scored 36,171 runs for the club, a record surpassed only by Jack Hobbs.

Thomas Hayward was born at Cambridge on the March 19, 1871. He is a striking instance of hereditary talent for the game, being a son of Daniel Hayward and a nephew of the famous Thomas Hayward who, thirty-odd years ago, was by common consent the first professional batsman in England. Inasmuch as he was only five years old at the time of Hayward's death, the subject of our sketch could scarcely have seen his uncle play, but curiously enough he shares with him the distinction of having a beautiful style of batting. Getting his early cricket in connection with the Young Men's Christian Association Club at Cambridge, young Hayward in due course found his way to The Oval, and qualified for Surrey by the necessary period of residence. During the season of 1892 he played with brilliant success for the Surrey Club and Ground, and when in the next year he was ready for a trial in the county eleven great hopes were entertained of him. He soon made it clear that he was a batsman of no ordinary class, playing an innings of 100 against Leicestershire in his second county match. After this, however, he fell off to some extent, and before the end of June he had, for the time being, lost his place in the Surrey team. However, as several members of the eleven stood out of the return match with the Australians, he was tried again, and with scores of 53 and 20 made his position secure for the rest of the season. Surrey won the match after a desperately close fight by two wickets, Hayward's splendid defence against Turner on a very difficult pitch having a good deal to do with the result. After that the young batsman scored 112 against Kent, and altogether his work for Surrey in all matches during the season showed an aggregate of 637 runs with an average of 19.10. This was not, in a run-getting year like that of 1893, an exceptional record, but it was very good for a beginner, and everybody felt that barring illness or accident he was pretty sure to develop into a first-class batsman. No one praised him more warmly or formed a higher opinion of his ability than Mr John Shuter. Early last summer Hayward did not quite come up to expectation, but the ground he lost was more than recovered before the season came to an end. For Surrey against Somerset towards the close of July he scored 113 and not out 36, and on August 20 against Kent he made 142 – so far his highest score in a match of importance. In the Surrey averages in the County Championship he scored 618 runs with an average of just over 28, while in all matches for the county he stood third on the list with an aggregate of 873 runs and an average of 27.9. Well as he has done during his two seasons for Surrey, we look forward with confidence to his taking a far higher position than he has yet attained. Indeed, his method of play is so admirable that no distinction of the cricket field should be beyond his reach.

SURREY IN 1895

1896

John Shuter was the 12th captain of Surrey, leading the club to six consecutive Championship titles between 1887 to 1892 (the first three of which came before the competition was officially recognised). A year later he gave up the position due to business commitments. This short extract from the review of Surrey's 1895 season describes a presentation made to him by the club to show its gratitude.

The annual meeting of the Club, held in the members' dining-room at Kennington Oval on the 2nd of May, was of more than ordinary interest...

A presentation was made to John Shuter in recognition of his long and brilliant services as captain of the Surrey eleven... Only a silver salver was publicly given to Mr Shuter, but the present – valued altogether at £365 – included also a grand piano and a pair of guns...

Mr Shuter said that having been left a free choice by the committee he had selected a piano in order that the occasion might be associated as closely as possible with his wife.

SURREY V HAMPSHIRE 1896

September 2, 3, 1895. Surrey won by an innings and 20 runs.

Surrey's home match against Hampshire in 1895 drew a large crowd who were hoping to see the team win their fifth County Championship in the six years since the competition's formal establishment. This was a formidable Surrey side which included Bobby Abel, Tom Hayward, Bill Brockwell, Bill Lockwood, Walter Read and Tom Richardson.

As the result of their three defeats at the hands of Yorkshire, Lancashire and Somerset, the Surrey eleven despite all their splendid performances were in a very critical position at the end of the season, and in the improbable event of their being beaten by Hampshire, in this their last fixture, they would have lost the Championship. The game excited widespread interest, the Hampshire eleven having never before drawn such crowds to The Oval. The Surrey men did not cause their numberless supporters any anxiety, and on the second afternoon gained a single innings victory with 20 runs to spare. For this highly satisfactory result they were mainly indebted to Richardson and Maurice Read. With nothing in the condition of the ground to help him, the great fast bowler finished up his season's work for Surrey with a very fine performance, taking 15 wickets at a cost of 155 runs. Maurice Read, exceeding the hundred for the first time during the season in a big match, played in quite his best form. A. J. L. Hill and Barton batted finely for Hampshire, and the old Kent player, Wootton, punished Richardson's bowling severely.

Hampshire 182 (A. J. L. Hill 59; T. Richardson 6-85) **and 172** (V. A. Barton 57;
T. Richardson 9-70); **Surrey 374** (J. M. Read 131).

TOM RICHARDSON – CRICKETER OF THE YEAR 1897

Tom Richardson, Surrey's all-time leading wicket-taker, completed the extraordinary feat of taking well over 200 wickets in a season for three consecutive years from 1895 to 1897, during which time he was chosen as a Cricketer of the Year.

Thomas Richardson – beyond all question the most famous of contemporary bowlers – was born at Byfleet, in Surrey, on August 11, 1870. After making a considerable reputation at Mitcham, he first found a place in the Surrey eleven in 1892, the year in which Surrey, after seeming certain to only take second place, wound up by beating Notts for the Championship. It was not at first realised that Surrey had discovered the most deadly fast bowler since Freeman, but Richardson did enough in 1892 to make his future position in the county eleven pretty secure... The season of 1893 took him at once to the top of the tree and, as everyone knows, he has from that time to the present moment been the first of English bowlers. Lohmann's enforced absence from England through illness gave him in 1893 a great opportunity, and he emphatically made the most of it, taking in the County Championship matches for Surrey, 99 wickets for something over 14 runs each, and coming out in the first-class averages of the year with a record of 174 wickets at an average cost of 15.70. Since then he has never looked back, his greatest season being that of 1895, when in first-class matches he took the almost unprecedented number of 290 wickets for less than 14.5 runs each. Nearly all his work was done for Surrey, no fewer than 237 wickets falling to him in county matches alone... Last season Richardson did not equal his record of 1895, but on the dry wickets of May, June and July, he was as much as ever the best bowler in the country. When the rain came, however, he seemed a little overdone, and on some occasions – notably in Surrey's two matches against the Australians – he was less effective than might have been expected. His greatest feats last summer were certainly performed in the England matches at Lord's and Manchester. On the last day at Old Trafford, he bowled unchanged for three hours, and nearly won a match in which England had followed on against a majority of 181 runs. The characteristics of Richardson's bowling are too well known to require detailed description. It is generally agreed that no bowler with the same tremendous speed has ever possessed such a break from the off. Personally no professional cricketer in England enjoys greater popularity with the general public and among his brother players.

SURREY V LANCASHIRE   1899

August 18, 19, 20, 1898. Match drawn.

Tom Hayward was the first of five Surrey players who have hit 100 first-class centuries. The biggest of them came on his home ground: 315 not out against Lancashire in 1898.

For the fifth time during the month Key won the toss and Surrey made over 300 runs on the first day. Three wickets fell for 81, but after Holland's dismissal at 133, Jephson helped Hayward to put on 175, the score at the close being 361 for five wickets, Hayward not out 163. On the following day Hayward had the satisfaction of carrying out his best-ever hit for Surrey. He batted for six hours and three-quarters and hit two fives, 37 fours, seven threes, 29 twos and 78 singles. He had some luck but his driving on the off side was exceptionally fine. It was not until half-past three that the innings closed for 634 – the highest of all their scores – the delay in finishing the innings probably costing Surrey a victory. Lancashire lost four wickets for 39 runs but Baker and Eccles carried the score to 116, and on Saturday the visitors had not much difficulty in saving the game. In the follow-on they had to keep up their wickets for four hours and as Ward and Hallows, the first pair of batsmen, withstood the bowling for an hour and three-quarters there was never much likelihood of the game being played out.

Surrey 634 (T. W. Hayward 315*, D. L. A. Jephson 54, L. C. Braund 85);
Lancashire 173 (A. Eccles 51; T. Richardson 4-62, W. H. Lockwood 4-77)
and 210-4 (A. Ward 63*, J. Hallows 51).

SURREY V SOMERSET   1900

May 29, 30, 31, 1899. Surrey won by an innings and 379 runs.

Surrey's first-innings total of 811 against Somerset in 1899 remains the highest score posted by the county and included a landmark innings of 357 not out by Bobby Abel, another record that still stands.

For two reasons the Surrey and Somerset match will always be remembered. Surrey scored 811, the highest total ever hit on The Oval, and Abel carried his bat right through the innings for 357, the second-best individual score ever obtained in a first-class match. On the opening day, Surrey scored 495 for five wickets, and altogether their innings lasted just over eight hours and a half. As a matter of record it may be stated that Abel hit one six, seven fives, 38 fours, 11 threes, and 23 twos. He was from the start completely master of the weak Somerset bowling, and so far as could be seen his only mistakes were two chances of a stumping, the first at 224 and the second at 237. A collection on his behalf resulted in £33.3s being subscribed. Surrey won the match before half-past four on the third day by an innings and 379 runs. Though naturally overshadowed by Abel, Hayward and Crawford hit in brilliant style, Crawford making his first hundred in a big match.

Surrey 811 (R. Abel 357*, E. G. Hayes 56, T. W. Hayward 158, V. F. S. Crawford 129; G. C. Gill 4-170); Somerset 234 (W. Trask 70, J. Daniell 50; T. Richardson 4-77) and 198 (S. M. J. Woods 53; T. Richardson 4-59, W. Brockwell 5-76).

SURREY V YORKSHIRE
1900

August 10, 11, 12, 1899. Match drawn.

The visit of Yorkshire later that season produced yet more astonishing batting feats, with Abel again at the heart of it.

This was beyond question the most sensational of all the matches played at The Oval during the season, 1,255 runs being scored for the loss of only 17 wickets. The Oval has been the scene of many wonderful things in the way of run-getting, but nothing we fancy quite so startling as this. On each side there was an astonishingly successful partnership, Wainwright and Hirst putting on in three hours and a half 340 runs for Yorkshire's fifth wicket, and Abel and Hayward, with nothing but a draw to play for, staying together for six hours and a half, and in that time adding no fewer than 448 runs for Surrey's fourth wicket. Never before we should think in a first-class match have four such individual scores been made as 228, 186, 193, and 273. The batting, it need hardly be said, was wonderfully good and the wicket perfect. A curious incident occurred on the second afternoon, the Yorkshiremen contending that Hayward was bowled out by a ball from Haigh before he had made 70. The umpire, however, thinking the ball had come back off the wicketkeeper's pads decided in the batsman's favour. Yorkshire's 704 is the highest total ever hit against Surrey, and Wainwright and Hirst have never scored so heavily in a big match.

Yorkshire 704 (J. Tunnicliffe 50, F. Mitchell 87, E. Wainwright 228, G. H. Hirst 186; T. Richardson 5-152); Surrey 551-7 (R. Abel 193, T. W. Hayward 273; F. S. Jackson 4-101).

SURREY V WARWICKSHIRE   1900

September 4, 5, 6, 1899. Match drawn.

Surrey's first great era concluded in 1899 with a sixth Championship title in ten seasons, secured when Tom Hayward's century and a thunderstorm ensured a draw against Warwickshire.

Surrey entered on their last engagement under rather peculiar circumstances as defeat would have lost them the Championship. However, they were never in any anxiety on this point, for on the first afternoon they got Warwickshire out for 155 – Santall and Hargreaves putting on 77 for the last wicket – and then scored 73 without loss. On the second day Abel and Hayward made a long stand on a greatly improved wicket, and at the drawing of stumps Surrey's score stood at 462 with only six men out. The innings was declared closed the first thing the following morning and Surrey would no doubt have won the game easily enough, but after little more than an hour's cricket the ground was flooded by a terrific storm and at a quarter past two it was agreed to abandon the game. Hayward's 137 was not only the highest, but much the best innings in the match.

Warwickshire 155 (W. H. Lockwood 5-45) and 44-1; Surrey 462-6 dec (R. Abel 94, W. Brockwell 74, T. W. Hayward 137, W. H. Lockwood 76*).

47

ENGLAND V AUSTRALIA, FIFTH TEST   1903

August 11, 12, 13, 1902. England won by one wicket.

The Ashes series of 1902 featured arguably the strongest England and Australia teams ever. After the first two Tests produced draws, Australia claimed the series with victories at Bramall Lane and Old Trafford (the latter by just three runs). Nevertheless, the final Test at The Oval was one of the game's most famous matches, featuring the apocryphal 'we'll get them in singles' line which George Hirst is supposed to have said to his last-wicket partner Wilfred Rhodes, as well as a stunning 75-minute century by Gilbert Jessop which set up the chase.

Australia having already won the rubber, the fifth and last of the Test matches... produced a never-to-be-forgotten struggle and a more exciting finish, if that were possible, than the one at Manchester. In face of great difficulties and disadvantages England won by one wicket after the odds had been 50-1 on Australia. Some truly wonderful hitting by Jessop made victory possible after all hope had seemed gone, and Hirst and Rhodes got their side home at the close. In its moral results the victory was a very important one indeed, as no one interested in English cricket could have felt other than depressed and low spirited if all the Test matches played out to a finish had ended in favour of Darling's team... The wicket, though a trifle slow from the effects of recent rain, was in very good condition, and the Australians, staying in for the whole of the first day, made the highly satisfactory score of 324. At one time they did not seem likely to do nearly so well as this for, though Trumper and Duff scored 47 for the first partnership, there were four wickets down for 82 and five for 126. The change in the game was brought about by Hirst, who for a time bowled in quite his form of 1901. Duff was out to a marvellous catch by the wicketkeeper standing back, Lilley jumping a yard or more on the leg side and holding a ball that would have gone for four. Noble and Armstrong by putting on 48 runs considerably improved the Australians' position, but with seven wickets down for 175 the outlook was none too promising. However, all these disasters were so well retrieved that the three remaining wickets added 149 runs, an invaluable partnership by

Hopkins and Trumble putting on 81. The batting was very painstaking, but an unlucky mistake by Lilley at the wicket when Trumble had made nine had, from England's point of view, a deplorable effect on the game.

If the weather had kept fine the Englishmen would not on an Oval wicket have been afraid of facing a score of 324, but the bad luck that had handicapped them at Sheffield and Manchester still pursued them, heavy rain during the early hours of Tuesday morning making a great difference in the pitch. Under the circumstances they did not do at all badly to score 183, but apart from some bright hitting by Tyldesley there was nothing remarkable in the efforts of the early batsmen... Trumble bowled throughout the innings in splendid form and took eight wickets for just over eight runs apiece. Possessing such a big lead the Australians looked, when they went in for the second time, to have the match in their hands. They opened their innings with a great misfortune, Trumper throwing away his wicket in attempting a foolish run, and for the rest of the afternoon the batting was marked by such extreme care that at the drawing of stumps the score, with eight men out, had only reached 114...

On Wednesday morning Lockwood quickly obtained the two outstanding wickets, bringing the Australian innings to a close for 121, and then England went in with 263 wanted to win the match. Tuesday's cricket, while the turf was still soft after rain, had damaged the pitch to no small extent, and up to a certain point the batsmen were so helpless against Saunders and Trumble that the easiest of victories for Australia appeared in prospect. Three wickets fell to Saunders for ten runs and but for Gregory missing Hayward badly at short-leg there would have been four wickets down for 16. Even as it was, half the side were out for 48 and the match looked all over. At this point Jackson, who had gone in third wicket down, was joined by Jessop and a stand was made which completely altered the game. At first, however, Jessop's cricket was far from suggesting the wonderful form he afterwards showed. When he had made 22 Kelly missed stumping him and at 27 he gave a rather awkward chance to Trumper at long-off. At lunch time the two batsmen were still together, Jackson, who had played superb cricket, being 39 and Jessop 29. After the interval Jackson was far indeed from keeping up his previous form, being repeatedly in difficulties and giving a palpable chance to Armstrong at slip. Jessop, on the other hand, settled down at once, and hit as he only can. At one point he scored four fours and a single off successive balls from Saunders. The partnership had added 109 runs in 65 minutes when Jackson was easily caught and bowled. Jessop went on hitting for some little time longer, but at 187 he closed his extraordinary innings by placing a ball gently into short-leg's hands. He scored, in just over an hour and a quarter, 104 runs out of 139, his hits being a five in the slips, 17 fours, two threes, four twos, and 17 singles. All things considered a more astonishing display has never been seen. What he did would have been scarcely possible under the same circumstances to any other living batsmen. The rest of the match was simply one crescendo of excitement. Hirst played a great game and, after Lockwood's dismissal at 214, received such help from Lilley that victory gradually came in sight. The score was advanced to 248, or only 15 to win, and then from a good hard drive Lilley was finely caught at deep mid-off. Rhodes as last man had a trying crisis to face, but his nerve did not fail him. Once, however, he nearly lost his wicket, Armstrong at slip getting a catch in his hand, but, being partly overbalanced, dropping the ball. Hirst went on imperturbably, scoring again and again by means of cleverly placed singles, and at last he had the extreme satisfaction of making the score a tie. Then Rhodes sent a ball from Trumble between the bowler and mid-on, and England won the match by one wicket. Hirst's innings was in its way almost as remarkable as Jessop's. So coolly did he play that of his last 14 hits that scored, 13 were singles, whereas in the early part of his innings he had hit half-a-dozen fours. Darling is not often at fault in the management of his bowling, but he leaned too heavily on Saunders and did not make enough use of Noble. Trumble, bowling from the Pavilion End, was never changed during the match.

Australia

V. T. Trumper b Hirst	42	–	run out		2
R. A. Duffc Lilley b Hirst	23	–	b Lockwood		6
C. Hill b Hirst	11	–	c MacLaren b Hirst		34
*J. Darling c Lilley b Hirst	3	–	c MacLaren b Lockwood		15
M. A. Noble c and b Jackson	52	–	b Braund		13
S. E. Gregory b Hirst	23	–	b Braund		9
W. W. Armstrong b Jackson	17	–	b Lockwood		21
A. J. Y. Hopkins c MacLaren b Lockwood	40	–	c Lilley b Lockwood		3
H. Trumble not out	64	–	(10) not out		7
†J. J. Kelly c Rhodes b Braund	39	–	(11) lbw b Lockwood		0
J. V. Saunders lbw b Braund	0	–	(9) c Tyldesley b Rhodes		2
B 5, lb 3, nb 2	10		B 7, lb 2		9

1/47 (2) 2/63 (3) 3/69 (4) (123.5 overs) 324
4/82 (1) 5/126 (6) 6/174 (7)
7/175 (5) 8/256 (8) 9/324 (10) 10/324 (11)

1/6 (1) 2/9 (2) (60 overs) 121
3/70 (4) 4/79 (5) 5/75 (3) 6/91 (6)
7/99 (8) 8/114 (9) 9/115 (7) 10/121 (11)

Lockwood 24–2–85–1; Rhodes 28–9–46–0; Hirst 29–5–77–5; Braund 16.5–5–29–2; Jackson 20–4–66–2; Jessop 6–2–11–0. *Second innings*—Rhodes 22–7–38–1; Lockwood 20–6–45–5; Jackson 4–3–7–0; Hirst 5–1–7–1; Braund 9–1–15–2.

England

*A. C. MacLaren c Armstrong b Trumble	10	–	b Saunders		2
L. C. H. Palairet b Trumble	20	–	b Saunders		6
J. T. Tyldesley b Trumble	33	–	b Saunders		0
T. W. Hayward b Trumble	0	–	c Kelly b Saunders		7
Hon. F. S. Jackson c Armstrong b Saunders	2	–	c and b Trumble		49
L. C. Braund c Hill b Trumble	22	–	c Kelly b Trumble		2
G. L. Jessop b Trumble	13	–	c Noble b Armstrong		104
G. H. Hirst c and b Trumble	43	–	not out		58
W. H. Lockwood c Noble b Saunders	25	–	lbw b Trumble		2
†A. A. Lilley c Trumper b Trumble	0	–	c Darling b Trumble		16
W. Rhodes not out	0	–	not out		6
B 13, lb 2	15		B 5, lb 6		11

1/31 (1) 2/36 (1) 3/62 (4) (61 overs) 183
4/67 (5) 5/67 (3) 6/83 (7)
7/137 (8) 8/179 (9) 9/183 (6) 10/183 (10)

1/5 (1) (9 wkts. 66.5 overs) 263
2/5 (3) 3/10 (2) 4/31 (4)
5/48 (6) 6/157 (5) 7/187 (7) 8/214 (9) 9/248 (10)

Trumble 31–13–65–8; Saunders 23–7–79–2; Noble 7–3–24–0; . *Second innings*—Trumble 33.5–4–108–4; Saunders 24–3–105–4; Armstrong 4–0–28–1; Noble 5–0–11–0.

Umpires: C. E. Richardson and A. White.

Close of play: first day, Australia 324; second day, Australia 114-8 (Armstrong 21).

ENGLAND V AUSTRALIA, FIFTH TEST 1910

August 9, 10, 11, 1909. Match drawn.

During the 1909 Oval match, Australia's Warren Bardsley became the first man to score two centuries in the same Test. His second-innings opening partnership of 180 with Syd Gregory was an Australian record until 1993. Bardsley had to wait another 17 years for his next century against England!

At the start of the game Carr bowled with startling success, breaking through Gregory's defence at nine and getting Noble and Armstrong out leg before wicket at 27 and 55 respectively. When at 58 Barnes, with a ball that came off the ground at lightning speed, clean bowled Ransford the spectators were in a high state of excitement. However, with Ransford's downfall England's run of success came to an end. Bardsley, who from the first had played in magnificent form... hit finely all round the wicket, being especially strong past cover point and in front of short leg. When 30 he might have been caught at the wicket by Lilley and with his score at 77 he was palpably let off by MacLaren at second slip, but these were the only blemishes in a truly splendid display... On the third day the interest in the match declined, a draw always seeming inevitable... Still, though void of excitement, the day's cricket was memorable, Bardsley following up his 136 with 130 and thus performing the unprecedented feat in Test matches of getting two separate hundreds. Without making a mistake of any kind he withstood the English bowling for three hours and three-quarters. Up to the time he reached his hundred his cricket was delightful to look at, but after that, perhaps from fatigue, he became strangely slow, taking 80 minutes to score his last 30 runs... He and Gregory scored 180 together in two hours and a quarter for the first wicket. So complete was their command of the bowling that the partnership might have been indefinitely prolonged.

Australia 325 (W. Bardsley 136, V. T. Trumper 73, C. G. Macartney 50; D. W. Carr 5-146) and 339-5 dec (S. E. Gregory 74, W. Bardsley 130, M. A. Noble 55); England 352 (W. Rhodes 66, C. B. Fry 62, J. S. Sharp 105, K. L. Hutchings 59; A. Cotter 6-95) and 104-3 (W. Rhodes 54).

ENGLAND v SOUTH AFRICA, THIRD TEST 1913

August 12, 13, 1912. England won by ten wickets.

In 1912 The Oval hosted two matches in the triangular series involving England, Australia and South Africa. Sydney Barnes took ten or more wickets in three of England's six matches that summer, including his best haul of 13 for 57 against South Africa at The Oval.

As in four of their previous Test matches, the South Africans suffered an overwhelming defeat, England winning before lunch time on the second day by ten wickets... Winning the toss... the South Africans profited nothing by going in first... Barnes and Woolley divided the wickets equally, but Barnes looked by far the more difficult to play. He did not have the least bit of luck to help him, often beating the bat with balls that missed the stumps... [In South Africa's second innings] Barnes surpassed himself, bowling in even more deadly form than in any of the previous Test matches. He broke both ways and his length was irreproachable. The South Africans thought they had never faced bowling quite so difficult... Bowling unchanged from the Vauxhall End, Barnes took eight wickets and had only 29 runs hit from him. Considering the amount of work he got on the ball, his accuracy was astonishing. England only wanted 13 to win. Hearne was sent in with Hobbs, and from 27 balls the runs were obtained. The winning hit was a single by Hobbs, increased to four by an overthrow.

South Africa 95 (S. F. Barnes 5-28, F. E. Woolley 5-41) and 93 (S. F. Barnes 8-29);
England 176 (J. B. Hobbs 68; G. A. Faulkner 7-84) and 14-0.

NOTES BY THE EDITOR   Sydney Pardon, 1915

After a gap of 15 years, Surrey became county champions once again in 1914 – though not in the conventional manner.

It was pleasant to find Surrey winning the Championship, a distinction that had not fallen to them since 1899. Some people thought that when, in deference to public opinion – W. G. Grace himself was the chief spokesman – Surrey cancelled their last two matches, the Championship would have to remain in abeyance for the year, but this view received no countenance from MCC. It would have been iniquitous if Surrey had been robbed of the position they had so fairly won. When, at Surrey's own request, the question was brought before the MCC committee, the matter was promptly settled, Middlesex disclaiming any notion of objecting. Surrey had a fine eleven, but to make their side complete they needed a little more bowling. The enforced transfer to Lord's of the return matches with Kent and Yorkshire when, in the first days of the War, the military authorities took possession of The Oval, involved serious disadvantages. Indeed, the Kent match, as a benefit to Hobbs, was such a failure that the Surrey committee have decided not to treat it as a benefit. They will give Hobbs another match as soon as circumstances permit, his subscription list in the meantime remaining open. This generous action on Surrey's part – not hitherto made known – will please everyone. Hobbs is not only the best bat in England at the present time, but also the most attractive and popular.

Note: reports of some other Surrey matches played at The Oval during the Golden Age appear in chapters 6, 12 and 13.

Chapter 4

Gents and Players

The annual Gentlemen v Players match was a highlight of the Victorian age and continued until the abolition of amateurism in 1962. The Gentlemen all played the game at the highest level but required 'only' expenses to do so, while the Players were paid as professionals. It was a distinction based on social class.

In the era before the arrival of international cricket and a formal County Championship, these games drew large crowds. The first match was played at the old Lord's ground in 1806 and became a regular event at the ground's present site from 1819 onwards. The Oval first staged the fixture in 1857 and thus received its first mention in Wisden on page 70 of the inaugural edition of 1864. The printed scorecard recorded that John Wisden himself took eight wickets in the match.

However, early Wisdens do not include any match reports, with the first edition pointedly saying: "We of course make no comments upon the matches, leaving the cricketer to form his own opinion with regard to the merits of the men, since a great many of our readers are at least equal, if not superior, to ourselves in arriving at a right judgment of the play."

The matches at The Oval produced some of the finest performances by the game's leading players, including great Surrey men from George

Lohmann to Jack Hobbs. A number of the ground's statistical wonders also occurred in this fixture, such as Alex Kennedy taking all ten wickets for the Players in 1927 and both W. G. Grace and Bobby Abel hitting double-centuries, reports of which are included in this chapter.

By the 1930s, the busy county and international schedules made it harder to muster the best players for the Gentlemen v Players fixture. The last of these matches to be played at The Oval was in 1934, bringing to an end 77 years of tradition in some style as the Players registered their highest total and largest victory in the history of the contest.

Teams of Gentlemen or Players would also regularly use The Oval to play other representative matches, notably in 1878 when Edward Barratt took all ten Australian wickets. The feat was barely recorded by Wisden *save for one line printed in capital letters: "BARRATT'S BOWLING CAPTURED ALL TEN WICKETS – THREE STUMPED, SEVEN CAUGHT OUT."*

GENTLEMEN V PLAYERS
1870

June 24, 25, 26, 1869. Gentlemen won by 17 runs.

Wisden *produced its first full report of a Gentlemen v Players match at The Oval in the 1870 edition, an extract of which appears below. At the same time, it tried to make up for earlier omissions with highlights from some of the previous fixtures at The Oval. These included the 1868 match which, said* Wisden, *will be "famed for the 165 hit by Mr I. D. Walker". However, there is no mention of Mr D. Buchanan's nine wickets in the Players' second innings – proof that cricket has always been a batsman's game.*

This was the 13th Gentlemen v Players match played on The Oval, and both as to time and runs an excitingly close match it was. The weather, cool on the first day, was bright and genial the other two. About 15,000 visitors witnessed the three days' cricket; the pavilion seats were crowded each day, and the general attendance, both in numbers and quality, proved beyond doubt that this match is still *the* match of the Surrey season.

On wickets of surprising truthfulness Mr W. Grace and Mr Cooper at 12.15 opened the Gentlemen's innings; and at 20 minutes to five that innings was over for 200 runs. Mr Grace's 43 (out of 68 then scored) was a display of his best form. Mr Lubbock's 43 was obtained by first-class batting; and when a capital chance at slip ended Mr I. D. Walker's innings for 52, a spontaneous hearty burst of cheering from all (Players included) bore pleasing testimony to the very fine cricket that the Southgate gentleman had played. At five o'clock, Summers and Rowbotham began the Players' batting. Rowbotham left at 19 and Hearne at 33, *up to when not one run had been scored by Summers, who in fact was 35 minutes at the wickets before he did score.* Jupp was 20 minutes before *he* scored. But, when "time" was up, Rowbotham, Hearne, Summers and Jupp were all out – the Players score 106 for the four wickets; Silcock *not out* 12.

The second day Silcock, by as steady, true and good cricket as any played in the match, made his score 49, and when the Players' innings ended they had 33 runs the best of the first innings. At 20 minutes to four, Mr Grace and Mr Cooper commenced the Gentlemen's second innings; both were "in great form" and gave so much trouble to the pros that when Mr Cooper was out for 40, *the score was 105 for one wicket;* and at 139, Mr Grace left (second out) for 83 – an innings that fully merited the hurricane of applause that greeted the great batsman's return to the pavilion. Mr Pauncefote was third out, the score on 143, then, by top quality cricket, Mr I. D. Walker and Mr Lubbock played up to "time" – that day's cricket ending with the Gentlemen's score at 193 for three wickets; Mr Walker *not out* 23, Mr Lubbock *not out* 29.

The third day, as to weather, attendance and exciting cricket, was the most glorious of the three. With the score at 208, Mr I. D. Walker and Mr Lubbock both left and, as the other five wickets added but 58 more runs, the Players had 234 to score to win. It was 1.30 when they began that second innings, and so rapidly were a moiety of their wickets crumpled up, that when Emmett, Stephenson, Rowbotham, Jupp, and Hearne had been done with, *only 28 runs had been scored!* Summers and Silcock then added 60 to the score, when Silcock was "lbw", and at 108 another "lbw" got rid of Humphrey; at 135, Summers was eighth out, and at 172, Willsher was bowled. So with 62 wanted to win, Wootton (the last man in) faced Pooley, who hit freely, finely and fast.

Thereabouts the Gentlemen's fielding got all out of form; at 197 the wicketkeeper should have run out Wootton but did not, then an overthrow for four was (to the uproarious delight of the onlookers) backed up by a hit for four by Pooley, whereupon the score at 22 to win, and the time at 20 minutes to seven; when a four by Wootton drove the spectators half crazy with excitement, and then came "the end," Pooley being bowled (off his pad) for 52, so thus, within 15 minutes of time, after three days' hard, exciting, and evenly played cricket, and out of a gross total of 915 runs, the Gentlemen won this grandly contested match by 17 only.

Gentlemen 200 (I. D. Walker 52; T. Emmett 4-76) and 266 (W. G. Grace 83; T. Emmett 5-78);
Players 233 (D. Buchanan 4-97, C. A. Absolom 5-56) and 216
(E. W. Pooley 52; D. Buchanan 4-86).

GENTLEMEN V PLAYERS 1871

July 14, 15, 16, 1870. Match drawn.

The corresponding fixture of 1870 produced one of W. G. Grace's finest Oval innings.

The 513 scored by the Gentlemen, and the 215 by Mr W. Grace in this match are respectively the two largest innings yet played in a Gentlemen v Players of England match. The 16,000 visitors that during the three days visited The Oval evidenced the contest had lost none of its old attraction, and that it is still *the* match of the Surrey season. The Gentlemen played very strong, and scored 711 runs in their two innings. The Players played weak, and left off in a minority of 454 runs with six wickets to fall...

The Gentlemen began the batting; they lost Mr Dale with the score at three, and Mr W. Grace at 11. Mr Money then went in, and by batting of high-class stayed until the score was 147, when he was seventh out... Mr Green hit hard for 39 not out, and the innings ended for 198 runs.

In the Players' first innings, Daft was one hour and 23 minutes at the wickets for 27 runs, but Wootton made his 27 in 26 minutes, and at two o'clock on the second day the innings ended for 148, or 50 runs short of the Gentlemen's first.

The Gentlemen were admirably placed and fielded in excellent form; their bowling sums up 115 overs (58 maidens) for 145 runs from the bat. It was 23 minutes past two when Mr W. Grace and Mr Dale commenced the Gentlemen's second innings, and in the third over bowled Mr Grace was "nearly" had at short slip by Willsher. After dinner the two batsmen got well set; at four o'clock 60 was scored (Mr Grace 40), and at quarter to five the hundred was up (the Players fielding very indifferently); at five minutes past five the score was 130, and it rapidly rose to 160 (when Mr Grace had made his hundred), but shortly after Alfred Shaw bowled Mr Dale for 55, and thus at 25 minutes to six, *the first wicket went with the score on 164.*

Mr Ottaway took the vacant wicket and another great stand was made, the Oxonian playing cautiously, and Mr Grace hitting brilliantly, driving one ball from Wootton so grandly past the Racket Court that eight was run – seven for the hit and one for an overthrow. The cheers that rang out at this superb hit were almost deafening, and were repeated when the 200 was hoisted on the boards; Mr. Grace then having made 131, and so he went on hitting in his finest form till "time" was called, the second day's cricket closing with *the Gentlemen having made 264 runs for one wicket* – Mr Ottaway not out 26, Mr W. Grace not out 175.

On resuming play on Saturday the fourth ball delivered bowled Mr Ottaway for the steady and well played 26 he had made the preceding day. Then with the score at 264 for two wickets Mr Money commenced his great innings. By 12.30 Mr W. Grace and Mr Money had increased the score to 301, Mr Grace then having made his 200 exact, but when he had made 15 more runs Grace was third man *out* at five minutes past one on Saturday, the score then at 329. Of brilliant hitting this 215 was a grand display, and for judicious and successful "placing" of the ball the innings was a marvel. Being played on The Oval it can well be imagined how vociferously Mr Grace was "ovated".

Mr Money then had Mr Pauncefote for a partner, and so ably was the batting fame of the Universities maintained by the two captains, that by ten minutes past two they had increased the score from 329 to 400. Dinner was called at 2.30, with *the score at 428 for three wickets.* After dinner it was further increased to 445, when Willsher bowled

Mr Pauncefote for 48. At 488 Mr Walker was caught out at mid-off; before another run was scored Mr Green was wondrously well caught by Mr T. Humphrey at deep square leg (hit and catch alike very fine); and at 489 Pooley stumped Mr F. Grace. Mr Absolom was next man in, and at 12 minutes to five a rattling, ringing cheer greeted the hoisting of the 500 on the board (seven wickets down), *Mr Money then having made his hundred exact.* The remaining three wickets did but little, as at three minutes past five the innings finished for 513 runs. Mr Money *not out* 109.

So it will be seen that each of the first four wickets averaged considerably more than 100 runs per wicket, but the last five wickets added but 25 runs to the score. Mr Money's 109 *not out* was a superb display of defence and hit, he was greatly cheered; the occupants of the pavilion seats "rose at him" to a man, and gave him such a welcome as will not readily be forgotten…

It was 25 minutes past five when Jupp and T. Humphrey began the Players' second innings; they hit 40 runs in 23 minutes; at 46 Jupp was out for 20, and at 90 Humphrey was superbly "c and b" by Mr F. Grace for 48, brilliantly *hit in one hour*, four fives, two fours, one three, six twos and five singles. Silcock was third man out, the score 98; his 34 included so many as six fours, and when Pooley had played the ball hard on to his wicket, time was up and the match drawn, there having been 968 runs made, 34 wickets fallen and 2,217 balls bowled in three days. The wickets were wonders for truthful playing, and appeared to play as well on the third day as on the first.

Gentlemen 198 (W. B. Money 70) **and 513** (W. G. Grace 215, J. W. Dale 55, W. B. Money 109*; A. Shaw 6-99); **Players 148** (C. A. Absolom 4-68, G. F. Grace 5-38) **and 109-4.**

GENTLEMEN V PLAYERS   1884

June 28, 29, 30, 1883. Match tied.

A classic match was played out in front of the gasholders in 1883, when a Gentlemen side suffering the absence of W. G. Grace managed the first and only tie between these teams. Wisden's report reflects a tense encounter.

Favoured by exceptionally fine weather during the play, though heavy rain on Friday night made the wicket rather difficult on the third day, this great contest produced some grand cricket and ended in a tie, the only one recorded in the series of matches between the amateurs and professionals of England. The Players had a very strong team both in batting and bowling and were exclusively northerners; whilst the amateurs, for the first time since 1867, lost the services of Dr W. G. Grace. A large and appreciative concourse of spectators watched the play on each of the three days.

Thursday. The Players, having won the toss, commenced their first innings with Barlow and Ulyett to the bowling of Messrs Studd and Rotherham, and the score had reached 92 before Ulyett was caught at the wicket for a hard-hit 63, marred by but one chance, and including seven fours, three threes, and seven twos. At one time he scored 14 in one over from Mr Studd. Shrewsbury assisted to carry the total to 123, when he was bowled for 11, and two runs later Barlow was out for an admirably-played 47, which had taken him about two hours and a quarter to make, and which consisted of four fours, three threes, four twos, and 14 singles. The score advanced to 154, when Mr Rotherham commenced a series of successes by bowling Lockwood. Robinson was out at 171, and Barnes followed him at 173, having made 20. Flowers was c and b at 181; both Emmett and Peate fell at 199; and Sherwin, the last man, was bowled at 203, Mr Rotherham's six wickets having cost only 41 runs. The Gentlemen were first represented by Lord Harris and Mr Lucas, who were opposed by Peate and Barlow. At 42, Mr Lucas, who had played steadily for his eight runs, was unfortunately run out, and ten runs later Lord Harris was bowled for a freely-hit innings of 38, and just before time Mr Studd was taken at the wicket for a capital 30, the score being 92 for three wickets, Mr C. W. Wright, not out, 11.

Friday. The weather was very hot during this day's play, which was started by Mr Wright (the not out) and Mr Hornby. The latter was run out at 130, having contributed a well hit 20. Mr Steel came in, but lost the partnership of Mr Wright at 135, who had played steadily for 21. Messrs Steel and Forbes were not parted until the total had reached 178, when the Lancashire gentleman was bowled by Barnes for 21, and 11 runs later Mr Forbes also fell a victim to this bowler, having compiled 28 in excellent form. Mr Kemp, having made six, was out at 195, and

Mr Leslie followed at 214. The last wicket gave considerable trouble, and it was not until the score had reached 235 – 32 in excess of the Players' total – that Mr Frank was bowled. The Players started their second venture with Ulyett and Barlow, Messrs Studd and Rotherham being the bowlers. At 30 Ulyett was caught and bowled, and then Bates and Barlow took the score to 77 before the latter was caught. Shrewsbury and Lockwood then did little, and four wickets were down for 89; but Bates and Barnes hit hard and well, and added 63 runs to the total before the former was bowled for a magnificently free and dashing innings of 76, made without a chance, by 11 fours, two threes, seven twos, and 12 singles, *his last 30 runs being scored in eight hits.* The other five wickets fell for 29 runs, and the total score was only 181, thus leaving the Gentlemen an apparently easy task of getting 150 to win. It will be seen that Mr Steel's bowling was splendidly successful.

Saturday. Messrs Hornby and Lucas began the second innings of the Gentlemen, and were opposed by Peate and Flowers. Mr Hornby left at 18, smartly caught at mid-off. Mr C. T. Studd joined Mr Lucas, and the score was carried to 49 before the former was taken at long-off. During their partnership Mr Lucas, when he had scored eight, cut a ball to Lockwood at point, who held it and appealed for the catch. The umpires, however, were not in a position to give a decision and Mr Lucas resumed his innings. Lord Harris and Mr Wright were speedily dismissed, and four wickets were down for 50 runs. Then Mr Steel, by a freely-hit 31, brought the score to 92. Messrs Forbes, Leslie and Kemp were all out by the time the telegraph showed 115. With 35 runs to win, Mr Franks joined Mr Lucas, and by careful play the score was taken to 136, when a bailer beat Mr Franks. Fourteen runs were required when Mr Rotherham, the last man, came in. Six were put on, and then the incomer was badly missed by Bates at long-on, from a lofty drive. With the match at a tie, and the excitement at its highest point, Peate went on, and with his second ball clean bowled Mr Rotherham, leaving Mr Lucas to carry out his bat for 47, a grand display of defence and well-timed hitting, including four fours, three threes, and two twos. Flowers bowled extremely well.

Players 203 (G. Ulyett 63; H. Rotherham 6-41) **and 181** (W. Bates 76; A. G. Steel 7-43);
Gentlemen 235 and 149 (W. Flowers 6-40).

July 11, 12, 13, 1901. Players won by ten wickets.

The match of 1901 featured another memorable innings from the great Surrey batsman Bobby Abel and an impressive performance from the ageing Grace. However, the occasion was poorer for the unavailability of some key players, as was the case regularly in the coming years.

As has often been the case in recent years, the Surrey committee could not secure a representative team of Gentlemen. Every man on the side was an admirable cricketer, but with C. B. Fry, Ranjitsinhji, Mason, R. E. Foster, Jessop, L. C. H. Palairet and Frank Mitchell all away the title Gentlemen of England was something of a misnomer. On the other hand, the Players were very strong indeed, such capital cricketers as Wrathall and Victor Barton being the only men to whose presence exception could be taken. The Gentlemen were very weak in bowling, and the result of the match – a win for the Players by ten wickets – came in no way as a surprise. The game had one memorable feature, Abel making the biggest score ever hit in a Gentlemen v Players match. Previous to his 247, the highest innings for either Gentlemen or Players was 217 by W. G. Grace, in John Lillywhite's benefit match at Brighton, in 1871. In first on Thursday evening, Abel was out eighth at 464, his innings which included two fives and 27 fours having lasted six hours. When he had 78 he was nearly caught at extra mid-off, More, the fieldsman, indeed, appealing for a catch, but this was almost his only bad stroke. Having regard to the weakness of the bowling against him, the innings could not be classed with some he has played, but all the same it was a remarkable effort. Next to Abel's batting the best feature of the match was the fine bowling of Trott and Lockwood, who between them took 16 wickets. Though handicapped by lameness, W. G. Grace had the satisfaction of making the highest score for the Gentlemen – quite a triumph for him, seeing that he first took part in Gentlemen v Players matches 36 years before.

Gentlemen 283 (W. G. Grace 57, A. O. Jones 50; A. E. Trott 4-80) **and 213** (C. J. Burnup 50; W. H. Lockwood 4-51, A. E. Trott 5-87); **Players 474** (R. Abel 247; R. E. More 4-90) **and 23-0.**

HUNDRED YEARS OF SURREY CRICKET   H. D. G. Leveson-Gower, 1946

In his article marking Surrey's centenary in 1946, Oval grandee Henry Leveson-Gower told this story about persuading Grace to play for the Gentlemen in the twilight of his career.

There have been many extraneous games at The Oval, but most important of these were the long series of Gentlemen and Players which commenced in 1857 and continued well into the present century. The large programme of county matches and touring teams made it difficult for some little time before this contest was given up to get representative sides. One interesting fact in connection with this match: I was selecting the Gentlemen and Players sides at The Oval in 1906 and asked W. G. Grace to play; he was 58. He refused at first, but I told him I particularly wanted him to take part in the match, first because everyone would be delighted to see him at The Oval and, secondly, the days on which the match was being played included his birthday. To this W. G. replied, my birthday is on the third day and it may be finished in two days. Not if you play, I said. He consented and made 74; his first appearance in this match at The Oval had been 41 years previously...

SURREY V GENTLEMEN   1909

April 20, 21, 22, 1908. Surrey won by an innings and 41 runs.

The Gentlemen also played matches against Surrey, with the 1908 game notable for being Grace's last first-class appearance – 29 years after he made a century in the first-ever Test in England.

Contested in bitterly cold weather, this Easter Monday match possessed a sentimental interest inasmuch as it was the only first-class contest in which W. G. Grace appeared during the season. The famous veteran kept up his wicket for two hours on Tuesday and played very well indeed in the follow-on, but his side suffered defeat by an innings and 41 runs. Although Hobbs and Hayward failed, Surrey occupied the wickets for the whole of the first day, scoring 381 for the loss of eight batsmen.

Several members of the team shaped remarkably well considering the early period of the year. After seven wickets had fallen, Lees, in company with Busher, a Barnes Club amateur, hit up 97 out of 141 in just over an hour, bowlers and fieldsmen being greatly handicapped by the wintry conditions. In addition to scoring 52, Busher bowled in very promising form. Frank Crawford hit with great power in the first innings of the Gentlemen of England. Leveson-Gower – just elected as captain of Surrey – in fielding a ball had the misfortune to injure his thumb. Early on Monday morning The Oval was covered with snow.

Surrey 390 (A. Marshal 62, E. G. Hayes 56, F. C. Holland 56, S. E. Busher 52, W. S. Lees 97; J. J. Cameron 5-83); **Gentlemen of England 219** (V. F. S. Crawford 91, R. T. Crawford 55) and 130 (J. N. Crawford 4-21, S. E. Busher 4-41).

Gentlemen v Players   1928

July 6, 7, 8, 1927. Match drawn.

Despite waning public interest, games between Gentlemen and Players at The Oval continued most years after the First World War, with some of the great cricketers of the day still making the effort to turn out for their side. In 1927 the Players' swing bowler Alex Kennedy took ten for 37, one of seven occasions when a bowler has taken every wicket in a first-class innings at The Oval.

The great feature of the match came on Friday, when Hobbs having declared, Kennedy proceeded to dismiss the whole of the Gentlemen's team. On a drying pitch that showed signs of wear in places, Kennedy found a spot in line with the leg stump and, making the ball get up as well as turn a lot, he compelled eight batsmen to give catches while another was stumped, the ball on only one occasion hitting the stumps...

Despite the soaking it had received on Thursday, the pitch improved appreciably when rolled a second time and Falcon and Franklin withstanding the bowling during the last half hour, the Gentlemen managed to avoid defeat...

Players 424-9 dec (E. H. Hendren 150, C. P. Mead 54; M. Falcon 4-60); **Gentlemen 80** (A. S. Kennedy 10-37) **and 181-8** (T. F. Shepherd 4-20).

GENTLEMEN V PLAYERS   1935

July 11, 12, 13, 1934. Players won by an innings and 305 runs.

The final match at The Oval was in 1934, and the sullen tone of the reporter reflects a tradition that had grown tired.

The Surrey Club did not have to cancel the match through inability to get together representative sides as was the case in 1933, but the Gentlemen were weak and besides suffering defeat by an innings and 305 runs, provided the Players the opportunity to put together the record score for a match of this kind, the total of 647 at The Oval in 1899 being surpassed by four runs while only seven wickets fell…

The Players made 608 runs on Wednesday and in the morning Kennedy, the captain, declared directly he and Brooks had established the new record…

The Gentlemen were unlucky in having to bat in a poor light after rain had altered the state of a beautiful pitch and, but for Garland-Wells being missed in the slips when three, they would have fared far more disastrously… Rain again caused considerable delay on the third day and altogether the very moderate side of Gentlemen could regard themselves as unfortunate.

Players 651-7 dec (A. Sandham 65, J. Arnold 125, R. J. Gregory 51, H. S. Squires 119,
R. G. Duckfield 106, A. W. Wellard 91; A. D. Baxter 5-128); **Gentlemen 192**
(H. M. Garland-Wells 93; A. R. Gover 5-57, A. W. Wellard 4-60) **and 154** (J. Mercer 4-32).

Chapter 5

Surrey between the Wars

T he history of Surrey cricket is littered with great eras – but the interwar period is not one of them. This did not mean that the club was short of fantastic cricketers. Indeed, some of the grandest names of the day were regularly donning brown caps at The Oval.

From 1921 to 1931 Surrey were led by Percy Fender, a Cricketer of the Year in 1915. Fender was succeeded by Douglas Jardine, who captained the club for two seasons and is commemorated at the ground today with the Jardine Suite at the Vauxhall End.

Surrey's regular opening partnership consisted of Jack Hobbs and Andy Sandham. Hobbs has his own chapter in this book and somewhat overshadowed the deeds of Sandham, who scored the first Test triple-century and was a Cricketer of the Year in 1923. Surrey had five other Cricketers of the Year in these two decades, including Jardine, Errol Holmes and the dual cricket and football international Andy Ducat, whose 1920 citation said: "It is likely enough that for any other county than Surrey he would have earned an even bigger reputation than he now enjoys."

Freddie Brown, a spin-bowling all-rounder and future England captain, was honoured by Wisden in 1933, although he might have been irked by one line from the accompanying profile: "It would be idle to *pretend that Brown has fully realised the expectations formed of him when he was at Cambridge." The last to receive the accolade before the war was Alf Gover in 1937, after he became the first man in 39 years to take 200 first-class wickets in a season.*

Surrey may not have won the Championship between the wars, but a number of brief match reports from the period are included here to shed light on, among other things, the brilliance of Ducat, Fender and Sandham, as well as one of Surrey's largest victories.

Surrey v Oxford University

1920

June 26, 27, 28, 1919. Surrey won by an innings and 47 runs.

One of seven men to hit a first-class triple-century for Surrey, Andy Ducat's unbeaten 306 against Oxford University in 1919 helped earn him selection as a Cricketer of the Year.

Ducat played the highest innings of the season in first-class cricket. Oxford were quite outclassed, but their chance of making any headway against Surrey's high total was discounted by an accident to Donald Knight, who strained a muscle in his thigh while fielding and could not bat. Ducat scored his 306 not out in four hours and 40 minutes. He took nearly two hours to get his first hundred but after that he went at a terrific pace, knocking the weak bowling all over the field. At one time he made in successive scoring strokes, five fours, a five and four fours. On taking out his bat he was lifted shoulder high by the spectators before he could reach the pavilion. He found his best partner in W. J. Abel, 141 runs being added in 65 minutes by the two batsmen while together. Oxford gave a capital display of batting after following their innings, Gilligan hitting very hard before the game ended – in advance of lunch time – on Saturday.

Surrey 523 (A. Ducat 306*; P. W. Rucker 4-107); **Oxford University 126** (J. W. Hitch 5-48) **and 350** (F. C. G. Naumann 73, H. P. Ward 50, F. W. Gilligan 91).

Surrey v Northamptonshire 1922

June 8, 9, 1921. Surrey won by an innings and 341 runs.

Andy Sandham was the first man to hit a triple-hundred in Test cricket but never achieved the feat for Surrey. The closest he came was against Northamptonshire in 1921, when his captain declared with Sandham on 292 not out.

Surrey naturally found no difficulty in beating Northamptonshire, winning the game in two days by an innings and 341 runs. On the first afternoon they gave an extraordinary display of hitting. Fender was, of course, satisfied with a score of 616 for five wickets, and declared the first thing on Thursday morning. Sandham and Jeacocke opened the innings by scoring 266 together in just under two hours and a half; after Jeacocke left, Sandham and Ducat put on 247 runs in an hour and three-quarters. Sandham was lucky in being missed when he had made 22 but he played wonderfully well, his huge score including three fives and 23 fours. Though the wicket remained in first-rate condition Northamptonshire could gain no mastery over Surrey's bowling, and in the course of four hours and a quarter of actual play the match was finished off.

Surrey 616-5 dec (A. Jeacocke 138, A. Sandham 292*, A. Ducat 134);
Northamptonshire 128 (G. M. Reay 5-40) **and 147** (H. A. Peach 5-48, P. G. H. Fender 4-51).

Andy Sandham – Cricketer of the Year 1923

Sandham is best remembered as Jack Hobbs's opening partner for Surrey, and as the club's coach during the glory years of the 1950s. But he is one of Surrey's greatest players – the third-highest run-scorer in their history.

Andrew Sandham was born at Streatham on July 6, 1890, and thus plays for Surrey under the best of qualifications. His early cricket was played for Streatham United and afterwards he played for the Mitcham Club. He describes himself as a self-taught batsman, having imbibed all his ideas of correct play from watching Tom Hayward at The Oval. He certainly could not have chosen a better model. In two respects he recalls Hayward vividly – the beautiful straightness of his bat and his remarkable power of forcing the ball away off his legs. His play off his legs is indeed his most distinctive gift and it was never revealed more strikingly than when he scored 195 last season at The Oval against Cambridge University. Sandham came out for Surrey in 1911, and with scores of 53 against Cambridge and 60 against Lancashire proved at once that he was no ordinary colt. Good judges who noted his style felt sure he was a batsman with a future. Still he found no road to fame. In 1912 he played in only one county match, and in 1913, though he hit up a score of 196 against Sussex at The Oval, he could not get an assured place in the Surrey eleven. He had a most discouraging experience in the following year when, the season cut short by the outbreak of the war, he took part in five county matches and scored only 112 runs. However he kept up his form for the Second Eleven with an average of 53. The resumption of first-class cricket in 1919 marked the turning point of Sandham's career. Left out of the Surrey team at the height of the season he had a triumphant return early in August, scoring 175 not out against Middlesex at The Oval, and his anxieties were at an end. From that day till now he has only once looked back. In 1920 he finished up a good second to Hobbs in the Surrey averages but the season was far advanced before, apart from one innings, he found his form. Then in the last weeks of August he played as he had never played in his life, his success culminating with scores of 167 not out and 68 in the memorable match at Lord's which gave Middlesex the Championship. In 1921 Hobbs's accident and subsequent illness placed a heavy responsibility upon Sandham but he was equal to it.

SURREY IN 1922

1923

Percy Fender captained Surrey in 11 seasons from 1921 onwards. In 1920 he scored a century at Northampton in 35 minutes, which Wisden recognises as the fastest first-class century scored in uncontrived circumstances. His belligerence at the crease was regularly on display two years later.

In scoring 185 against Hampshire in May and 137 against Kent on the last day of July, Fender gave the two most astonishing displays of hitting seen at The Oval, or anywhere else, last summer. There has been nothing like his play in these two matches since Jessop was in his prime. Nearly all through the season Fender played in glasses, but as he hit just as well when, now and then, he took them off, there could not have been much amiss with his sight.

SURREY V GLOUCESTERSHIRE   1928

May 11, 12, 13, 1927. Match drawn.

The scores from Surrey's match against Gloucestershire in 1927 suggest that it was played on a very good pitch. Tom Shepherd did not waste the chance to hit a brilliant double-century, while the great Wally Hammond made a hundred in each innings for the visitors.

This was another match in which the bat beat the ball to an even greater extent than in Surrey's game with Hampshire, 1,357 runs being obtained for 28 wickets. Shepherd seized upon the occasion to put together the highest score of his career, making scarcely any mistake during a stay of four hours and three-quarters, and hitting three sixes, a five and 36 fours. He and Ducat, who also batted brilliantly, added 289 in two hours and three-quarters. Dipper and Hammond shared in a two hours' stand which yielded 226 runs. Dipper, beginning with far more freedom than usual, played splendid cricket. Hammond followed up an innings of 109 – ended by his first bad stroke – with one of 128. This was his third consecutive hundred in the course of four days and so admirably did he bat for two hours and ten minutes, 195 runs in all being added meanwhile, that, apart from a drive over mid-off's head, he made no stroke at all dangerous.

Surrey 557-7 dec (A. Sandham 50, T. F. Shepherd 277*, A. Ducat 142; C. W. L. Parker 4-122) and 31-1; Gloucestershire 406 (A. E. Dipper 186, W. R. Hammond 108; T. F. Shepherd 6-78) and 363 (H. Smith 67, W. R. Hammond 128, R. A. Sinfield 71*).

DOUGLAS JARDINE – CRICKETER OF THE YEAR 1928

Douglas Jardine is most famous for being the England captain who almost caused a diplomatic crisis in Australia during the Bodyline tour of 1932-33, which was sandwiched between his two seasons as Surrey skipper. By then he was firmly established as a correct, resolute batsman, as recognised by Wisden in 1928.

Douglas Robert Jardine, who provides a striking instance of heredity at cricket, was born on October 23, 1900, at Bombay, India... Standing fully six-feet high, and blessed with great power of wrist and forearm, Jardine has always possessed the qualifications essential to the making of a fine batsman, and to these he has added style and footwork the better to give effect to the mental gifts for cricket which he possesses in abundance. He is not a master of all the strokes; indeed, he is definitely restricted in his off-side play. But as to his strength on the on side and to leg, there can be no two opinions. Nobody plays with a straighter bat; few hit harder in defence whether in a forward or a backward stroke, and not often does he lift the ball. As with all really sound batsmen, fast bowling possesses no terrors for him. Above everything else stands out his splendid defence: the manner in which he watches the ball right on to the bat stamps him at once as an accomplished player. Provided he can spare the time, nothing appears more likely than that he will be in the next team that visits Australia.

SURREY V WARWICKSHIRE 1929

June 9, 11, 12, 1928. Match drawn.

Percy Fender was much more than an aggressive middle-order batsman, as he demonstrated with a stunning display of bowling on the first day of Surrey's home match against Warwickshire in 1928. He was backed up by centuries from Andy Ducat and Tom Shepherd, but the visitors held firm in their second innings.

Surrey, despite the absence of Hobbs and Sandham, enjoyed a great batting triumph, but could not force a win. Not until half-past two on Saturday could play be started and then, on a drying pitch, Fender, in his second spell of bowling, sent down ten overs for 12 runs and six wickets. Surrey on Monday had two men out for 37 and at 44 Ducat, when one, was missed at mid-on. Profiting by his luck, Ducat batted over four hours and, although offering chances at 126 and 172, gave a very fine display. Shepherd, hitting superbly, hit up 132 out of 199, added inside two hours for the fourth wicket. Peach, making 46 in 25 minutes, scored six fours in one over from Mayer – two straight drives, three pulls and an on-drive – before Fender declared. Warwickshire on Tuesday scored 363 runs and lost only three wickets. Kilner and Bates put on 112 and Kilner and Wyatt 144. Wyatt, setting himself to save the game, played admirable cricket for more than four hours.

Warwickshire 127 (P. G. H. Fender 8-24) **and 416-4** (N. Kilner 96, R. E. S. Wyatt 159*);
Surrey 490-8 dec (A. Ducat 179*, T. F. Shepherd 132; J. H. Mayer 5-137).

SURREY V KENT   1936

July 27, 29, 30, 1935. Kent won by ten wickets.

Andy Sandham's benefit match was the 1935 Championship game against Kent, for whom the great Frank Woolley produced his finest hour on the ground where his Test career had begun in 1909 and ended just the previous year.

Everything else in this match, which Kent won by ten wickets, was dwarfed by the innings of Woolley, who, after Ashdown and Fagg had led off with a stand of 136 before lunch, gave one of the finest displays of his long career. Woolley's second stroke was a six and when he fell to a yorker he had hit his 229 out of 344 in 190 minutes. Apart from a difficult chance to slip when 78, his batting was entirely free from fault and altogether he claimed four sixes and 30 fours. Fagg, very sure in driving to the on, hit 16 fours and with Woolley put on 133; Todd and Woolley added 106. Valentine getting three sixes and six fours, actually made his

71 in 35 minutes. Chapman declared at Saturday's total, and though Sandham, Gregory and Barling shaped well Surrey had to follow-on. Sandham in the second innings showed commendable enterprise, making his 93 in 110 minutes, and with Barling registering his first hundred of the season, Surrey round about three o'clock on Tuesday looked like saving the game, but subsequently the batting broke down.

Kent 579-8 dec (W. H. Ashdown 61, A. E. Fagg 111, F. E. Woolley 229, B. H. Valentine 71; A. R. Gover 4-144) and 80-0 (W. H. Ashdown 50*); Surrey 290 (R. J. Gregory 62, H. T. Barling 87; A. P. Freeman 5-99, C. S. Marriott 4-81) and 368 (A. Sandham 93, H. T. Barling 113; A. P. Freeman 4-137).

SURREY V SOMERSET
1940

May 6, 8, 9, 1939. Surrey won by six wickets.

In 1939 Alf Gover's ten wickets set up Surrey's early-season win over Somerset.

Two brilliant innings by Fishlock and one by Parker, coupled with deadly bowling on the first day by Gover, earned Surrey victory. Somerset declared in time to permit a tea interval so that their bowlers kept fresh for the vital last phase. Surrey wanted 197 in two and a half hours and they won with five minutes to spare. Fishlock hit 12 fours, five in one over from Andrews, and only ten runs were required when he was fourth out.

Somerset 157 (A. R. Gover 7-38) and 339-9 dec (F. S. Lee 59, H. Gimblett 53, E. F. Longrigg 60); Surrey 300 (L. B. Fishlock 90, J. F. Parker 111*) and 198-4 (L. B. Fishlock 101).

SURREY V SUSSEX
1940

May 31, June 1, 2, 1939. Surrey won by 388 runs.

Gover's good form continued with six first-innings wickets in the home game against Sussex later that month. Freddie Brown took six more on the final day as Surrey dismissed the visitors in 90 minutes to take victory.

Superior in every particular, Surrey finished the match dramatically by dismissing Sussex in an hour and a half. On the opening day Hammond accounted for Gregory and Fishlock at a cost of two runs, but Squires and Barling followed with a stand of 103, and free hitting by Parker, Garland-Wells and Brown gave Surrey a useful total. Despite an admirable display by John Langridge, who stayed until the total reached 206, Sussex were always struggling for runs. Again Surrey forced the pace, Squires playing another excellent innings, and when Sussex batted a second time, Brown found a worn pitch suited to his spin. He actually took six wickets for 14 runs in 33 balls.

Surrey 345 (H. S. Squires 97; H. E. Hammond 5-97) **and 314-6 dec** (R. J. Gregory 57, L. B. Fishlock 60, H. S. Squires 107*); **Sussex 208** (J. G. Langridge 108; A. R. Gover 6-60) **and 63** (F. R. Brown 6-21).

PERCY FENDER – OBITUARY   1986

One of the most recognisable faces of The Oval in the interwar period and beyond, Percy Fender died in 1985 and received a warm tribute from Wisden *the following year.*

Fender, Percy George Herbert, who died at Exeter on June 15, 1985, aged 92, was the last survivor of those who had played county cricket regularly before the Great War: more important, he was one of the most colourful figures in the cricket world for many years after it and was widely regarded as the shrewdest county captain of his generation. In a career of 26 years he scored 19,034 runs with an average of 26.66, took 1,894 wickets at 25.05, made 21 hundreds and caught 599 catches. Six times he did the double. But he was not a cricketer who could be judged on figures. *Wisden* has never been a slave to statistics and, when in 1915 he appeared as one of the Five Cricketers of the Year, it was after a season in which both his bowling and batting averages had been approximately 23 and he had not scored 1,000 runs nor taken 100 wickets. Yet the honour was fully deserved. Surrey had won the Championship and Tom Hayward had said that Fender was the making of their eleven...

Throughout his career Fender's policy was to hit fiercely, regardless of the state of the pitch, even of the quality of the bowling. He was a tremendous driver and also delighted in the pull, and he cut or slashed ferociously outside the off stump: he once slashed the ball over cover out of The Oval. It was difficult to set a field for him. His century in 35 minutes against Northamptonshire in 1920 remains a record, though it was equalled in farcical circumstances in 1983. His highest score, 185 against Hampshire in 1922, took 130 minutes and against Kent later that season he made 137 in an hour and a half, 52 of them off 14 consecutive balls...

His attitude to bowling was the same. His object was to get the batsman out, and the tactics fostered by the modern one-day game would never have suited him. He had at his command a great variety of pace, spin and swing and all were fully employed...

In 1921 he had succeeded C. T. A. Wilkinson as captain of Surrey, a position which he held until he handed over to D. R. Jardine after 1931, and it was generally recognised that it was his captaincy more than anything else that kept a side so deficient in bowling so high in the table: twice they were second and only in his last three seasons did they fall below fifth.

Note: reports of some other Surrey matches played at The Oval in the 1920s and 1930s appear in chapters 6 and 12.

Chapter 6

The Master

If you were to ask for one cricketer who represented The Oval, it would be hard to think beyond the immortal figure of Jack Hobbs.

Known simply as The Master, Hobbs has to be considered in any conversation about the greatest of all batsmen. His 199 first-class centuries – 29 more than anyone else – knock all other batsmen into a cocked hat. Realistically, it's a record that will never be broken. Bear in mind, too, that Hobbs did not play a first-class match between September 1914 and May 1919.

Hobbs is the only player to have received four citations in Wisden. He was a Cricketer of the Year in 1909, and in 1926 Wisden gave him a special portrait in place of its traditional individual awards after he broke W. G. Grace's record of 126 first-class centuries. Neville Cardus chose Hobbs as one of the Six Giants of the Wisden Century in 1963, and in the 2000 edition he was named as one of Five Cricketers of the Century.

Brought to the ground from the flats of Cambridge by Tom Hayward – himself a great batsman but one whose records were slowly ground into the dust – Hobbs first played for Surrey in 1905 at The Oval against a Gentlemen of England side captained by Grace. Twenty-five years later, he bid farewell to Test cricket on his home ground, a match remembered for *the 232 runs scored by the young Don Bradman, thus bookending Hobbs's career with a link between Grace and Bradman. The report for this match is included in chapter 7.*

Hobbs's 369th and final game at The Oval, where he scored 90 first-class centuries, was against Somerset in June 1934. In his final first-class match at the end of that summer – a scarcely credible 29 years after his debut – he captained the Players against the Gentlemen at Cheriton Road in Folkestone.

His influence lives on at The Oval. Entering the ground at the Pavilion End, you walk through the wrought iron Hobbs Gates that were installed in 1934 to mark his retirement and which were recently restored, while the Master's Club still meets at the ground every year on his birthday, December 16, to eat his favourite meal of roast lamb and apple pie.

JOHN BERRY HOBBS – CRICKETER OF THE YEAR Sydney Pardon, 1909

Hobbs was first honoured by Wisden *in 1909 under his Christian name, John, though he was always known as Jack. Editor Sydney Pardon clearly had an eye for a young talent.*

Few batsmen in recent years have jumped into fame more quickly than Hobbs. In his case there was no waiting for recognition, and no failure to show the skill he was known to possess... He joined the staff at The Oval in 1903 and, two years later, having completed the necessary period of qualification, he was tried in the Easter Monday match against a Gentlemen of England team got together by W. G. Grace... He scored 18 and 88, and ten days later in his first county match – against Essex [also at The Oval] – he made 28 and a magnificent 155, his long innings being only disfigured by one chance. These two matches made it clear that Surrey had found a first-rate man, and though as the season advanced he fell off in form, he obtained, in county matches alone, 1,004 runs – a remarkable achievement for a first year. From that brilliant beginning he has never looked back, and at the present time there is perhaps no better professional batsman in England, except Hayward and Tyldesley...

Among the many fine innings he has played for Surrey in the last four years I cannot recall a better one than his 162 not out against Worcestershire at The Oval in 1906. Surrey had 286 to get in the last innings, and four of the best wickets fell – all to Burrows' bowling – for 112 runs. The issue looked very much in doubt, but Hobbs and J. H. Gordon finished off the game in two hours and ten minutes, adding 174 runs without being parted. Hobbs gave one easy chance just before reaching his hundred, but this was literally his only mistake. Even this early in his career he showed that he had the nerve to face a crisis…

Very keen on the game and ambitious to reach the highest rank, he is the most likely man among the younger professional batsmen to play for England in Test matches at home in the immediate future.

SURREY V HAMPSHIRE   1910

May 6, 7, 8, 1909. Surrey won by an innings and 468 runs.

Surrey's second match of the 1909 season was notable both for a brilliant double-century from Hobbs and for the margin of victory, the second-largest in the club's history.

Scoring 645 in five hours and 20 minutes for the loss of four wickets on Thursday, Surrey, whose innings in all extended over six hours and 20 minutes, put together the highest total of the year and won after an hour's cricket on Saturday by no less than an innings and 468 runs. Strengthened by the assistance of C. B. Fry, Hampshire had hoped to acquit themselves in better form than is usual with that team when opposing Surrey at The Oval, but their bowling was punished with merciless severity and, apart from Fry, who played admirably in each innings, their batsmen cut a truly deplorable figure. Coming together on Hayward's dismissal at 59, Hobbs and Hayes actually put on 371 in two hours and three-quarters, the partnership being the sixth-highest in first-class cricket. Despite the tremendous pace at which he scored, Hobbs was so completely master of the bowling that he gave no chance. Hayes, whose cricket, though brilliant to a degree, was scarcely maintained at the same faultless standard as that of his partner, obtained his first 200 runs in three hours five minutes. Altogether, in making the highest individual score of the season, he batted for four hours and a half, among his figures being three fives and 33 fours. Crawford also hit with great power, getting his first 50 runs in half an hour. Fry and Bowell opened the Hampshire batting by making 63, but after they were separated Lees bowled to such purpose that the other nine wickets fell for 66 runs.

Surrey 742 (J. B. Hobbs 205, E. G. Hayes 276, J. N. Crawford 74; C. P. Mead 4-179);
Hampshire 129 (W. S. Lees 5-47) **and 145** (C. B. Fry 60; W. S. Lees 4-26).

SURREY V NOTTINGHAMSHIRE   1915
August 3, 4, 5, 1914. Match drawn

Another of Hobbs's finest performances for his county was the 226 he made against Nottinghamshire in 1914, a season in which Surrey were crowned champions.

Although putting together for the third time during the summer a total of more than 500, Surrey were denied even the satisfaction of taking points on the first innings. After the drawing of stumps on Tuesday, Notts, despite some desperately stubborn work, had lost half their wickets for 230, but next day so much rain fell that play was restricted to three-quarters of an hour. If thus disappointing in its concluding stage, the match furnished much enjoyment to a big crowd on the Bank Holiday, when nearly 15,000 people paid for admission. Surrey winning the toss, Hobbs seized the occasion to play his highest innings of the season, and at the call of time 472 runs had been obtained for the loss of five wickets. Going in first, Hobbs scored 226 in four hours and 20 minutes, being fourth man out at 375. From first to last he batted with wonderful skill and judgment, making runs all round the wicket in masterly fashion and giving no chance. He received admirable support from Knight who, playing himself in with commendable care, helped to put on 202 runs. Ducat shared in a partnership of 80 with Hobbs, and after this he and Bird punished the tired bowlers to such purpose that 90 runs were obtained in 50 minutes. The Notts attack suffered much from the absence of Wass, but Barratt bowled untiringly, and the fielding was excellent. Next day after Surrey's innings and been finished off, George Gunn and Hardstaff stayed together for two hours. So bad was the "barracking" at times that several of the offenders were removed by the police. Let off when ten, John Gunn afterwards batted in splendid form, and Carr hit well. Following upon the fall of the fifth wicket at 166, John Gunn and Payton, with Hitch unable to bowl, stayed together until the drawing of stumps.

Surrey 542 (J. B. Hobbs 226, D. J. Knight 67, A. Ducat 83; F. Barratt 4-139, W. Riley 4-153); **Nottinghamshire 283-6** (J. R. Gunn 88, W. R. D. Payton 51*).

SURREY V KENT 1920

August 18, 19, 1919. Surrey won by ten wickets.

A benefit match was held for Hobbs in 1914 but, with war breaking out, it failed to attract many through the gates. A second attempt five years later was far more successful.

Hobbs's benefit match brought county cricket at The Oval to an end for the season, and a glorious end it proved. Nothing quite equal to the cricket at the finish can be recalled. Surrey had 95 to get in less than three-quarters of an hour, and in 32 minutes, despite the disadvantage of bad light, Hobbs and Crawford hit off the runs, accomplishing in dazzling style a task that had seemed impossible. Crawford set the pace at first and put his side on good terms with the clock, Hobbs for an over or two being content with a few singles. Once set, however, Hobbs went even faster than his partner and to him fell the honour of making the winning hit. Naturally with such cricket in progress the crowd waited till the end, and when all was over there was a great scene in front of the pavilion.

Kent 218 (E. Humphreys 59, F. E. Woolley 55; J. W. Hitch 4-58) **and 184** (J. W. Hitch 4-64); **Surrey 308** (A. Ducat 76, H. S. Harrison 66; W. J. Fairservice 4-96) **and 96-0.**

SURREY V OXFORD UNIVERSITY

1927

June 23, 24, 25, 1926. Match drawn.

Showing no mercy against the students of Oxford, Hobbs and Andy Sandham racked up a Surrey record opening partnership in 1926.

Hobbs and Sandham, withstanding the Oxford bowling for just over five hours, put on 428 runs, and in so doing participated in what was the second-highest first-wicket stand ever recorded in a first-class match in this country. The record stands to the credit of the late J. T. Brown and John Tunnicliffe, who opened Yorkshire's innings against Derbyshire at Chesterfield in 1898 with a partnership of 554. Hobbs and Sandham, going in on Wednesday evening, scored 44 runs. On Thursday, before a storm burst over the ground at three o'clock and stopped play for the day, they raised the total to 276, and they were not separated until a quarter to one on Friday. Sandham gave no chance, but Hobbs was missed when 27, and again when 118. Hobbs, falling only five short of the highest score of his career, hit 30 fours. The performance of the two men was particularly remarkable, seeing that at times the ball rose awkwardly. For Oxford, who on Wednesday began by losing three wickets for 37, Taylor and Newman put on 141, Taylor playing practically faultless cricket for more than three hours. On Friday, Holmes and Fawcus both drove well.

Oxford University 273 (C. H. Taylor 105, G. C. Newman 66; H. A. Peach 6-84) **and 212-4** (C. L. D. Fawcus 70, E. R. T. Holmes 55); **Surrey 505-3 dec** (J. B. Hobbs 261, A. Sandham 183).

ENGLAND V AUSTRALIA, FIFTH TEST

1927

August 14, 16, 17, 18, 1926. England won by 289 runs.

Hobbs had been playing for more than 20 years before he made his first Test century at The Oval. But it was worth the wait, coming in a match against Australia that decided the destination of the urn.

After a wonderfully interesting struggle, the Fifth Test match – arranged, however long it might last, to be played to a finish – ended shortly after six o'clock on the fourth day in a splendid victory for England by 289 runs. Winning in this handsome fashion, the only one of the five Test games in which a definite issue was reached, the old country regained possession of the mythical ashes that Australia had held since the wholesale triumph over the English team led by John Douglas in the Commonwealth during the winter of 1920-21. Looked forward to with extraordinary interest, the contest underwent some truly dramatic changes. England, on the opening day, appeared to have jeopardised their chances by some strangely reckless batting, and yet left off on the first evening in distinctly the stronger position. On Monday, Australia played an uphill game to such good purpose, that they gained a slight lead. Tuesday brought with it some superb batting on a difficult wicket by Hobbs and Sutcliffe, and to wind up, came the collapse of Australia, who, when set 415 to win, failed so completely, that they were all out for 125 – their second-lowest total during the whole tour...

Chapman, winning the toss, secured first innings for England on a wicket which varied in pace at times, but otherwise played well. The start was full of hope, Hobbs and Sutcliffe settling down in excellent style, and in rather less than an hour, putting on 53 runs. Then, to the general amazement, Hobbs, who appeared to be in particularly fine form, was bowled by a full pitch. A googly dismissing Woolley, and Hendren pulling an off ball on to the wicket, there were three men out for 108 at lunch time. This poor beginning notwithstanding, Chapman, on resuming, hit out in vigorous fashion. Possibly he considered the position called for an endeavour to knock Mailey off his length. At any rate, he made 49 out of 87 in an hour and a quarter, but, following upon his departure, Mailey and Grimmett met with such poor resistance, that the last six wickets went down in an hour for the addition of 91 runs. Sixth out at 214, Sutcliffe batted admirably for three hours and a half, his clean off-driving and the certainty of his strokes on the leg side being the chief features of his play... The innings was all over in four hours and a quarter for 280. In a match unlimited as to time, the lack of restraint shown by several of the batsmen was difficult to understand...

While on Saturday the attendance did not exceed that of a popular county match – the public having been frightened away by prophecies of overcrowding and tales of all-night vigils outside the ground – the crowd on Monday was so large that the gates had to be closed shortly after noon... Australia, with six men out, were 158 runs behind, but Collins then found a splendid partner in Gregory. While his captain continued to bat with extreme caution, Gregory hit up 73 out of 107 in an hour and three-quarters, with ten fours as his chief strokes. Not only did Gregory bat so freely, but he showed rare judgment in picking the ball to hit. The stand completely altered the aspect of the game. Collins, who left directly after Gregory, withstood the England attack for three hours and 40 minutes. It was gratifying to notice that the excellence of the skill he displayed in trying to save his side was thoroughly appreciated by the crowd. Following Collins' departure came some capital batting by Oldfield and Grimmett, who not only headed the England total, but altogether added 67 for the ninth wicket in an hour and a quarter. Out at last for 302, Australia, at the wickets two hours longer than England, secured a lead of 22. Tate bowled with remarkable steadiness; indeed, except just before the tea interval, when Oldfield and Grimmett were together, the English attack always looked as though it wanted a lot of playing.

Exactly an hour remained for play when Hobbs and Sutcliffe entered upon England's second innings. As no object was to be served by forcing the runs, they proceeded quietly and if Hobbs took a little time to settle down, he and Sutcliffe at the close had raised the total to 49. This hour's steady cricket had, unquestionably, a big influence upon the later stages of the struggle.

The crux of the match came before lunch on Tuesday, when Hobbs and Sutcliffe excelled themselves. A thunderstorm, accompanied by a good deal of rain, had broken over south London on Monday evening, rendering the pitch slow and dead to begin with, and afterwards very difficult. The two batsmen, it is true, enjoyed the advantage of playing themselves in before conditions became distinctly awkward for them, but, admitting this, their performance during the last hour before lunch in withstanding all endeavours to separate them was an achievement of the highest order. While giving Hobbs and Sutcliffe all praise, those two famous men were fortunate in the fact that Richardson, while making the ball turn and rise quickly, stuck doggedly to the leg theory. He was awkward enough pursuing that method. He would probably have been deadly had he bowled over the wicket with something like a normally placed field, and point of course close in.

As it was, Hobbs and Sutcliffe added 112 runs in rather less than two hours and a half before lunch, but directly afterwards Hobbs, having just completed his hundred, was at 172 bowled by a ball that came back a little and touched the top of the off stump. He and his partner batted superbly for three hours and 40 minutes; indeed, his innings which included ten fours must be regarded as one of the most masterly displays of his great career. His hundred was his 11th three-figure innings for England against Australia, while the stand was the seventh of three figures he and Sutcliffe had made in Test matches with Australia. Woolley helped to put on 48, Hendren stayed while 57 runs were obtained, Chapman shared in a partnership of 39, and Stevens remained to add 57, but all the time interest of course centred chiefly on Sutcliffe. The Yorkshireman withstood Australia's bowling for rather more than seven hours and then in the last over of the day was bowled by a fine ball from Mailey. He gave no real chance, hit 15 fours and shared with Hobbs in a memorable piece of work...

Under the conditions which obtained, there never existed the slightest likelihood of Australia making the 415 runs required for victory, but no one could have been prepared to see a famous batting side collapse so badly. As matters went, an easy win for England was assured in 50 minutes, the first four wickets falling for 35 runs. The heavy roller brought up little moisture but Larwood made the ball fly, and Rhodes, directly he was tried, made it turn... Eight wickets were down for 87, and although Oldfield and Grimmett remained together half an hour to add 27, the side were all out for 125. Rhodes, with four wickets for 44, and Larwood with three for 34, had the chief share in the cheap dismissal of Australia, but all round, the bowling was excellent. Moreover, not a catch was missed nor was a run given away, the whole England side rising gallantly to the occasion. Naturally a scene of tremendous enthusiasm occurred at the end, the crowd swarming in thousands in front of the pavilion, and loudly cheering the players, both English and Australian.

England 280 (H. Sutcliffe 76; A. A. Mailey 6-138) **and 436** (J. B. Hobbs 100, H. Sutcliffe 161); **Australia 302** (H. L. Collins 61, J. M. Gregory 73) **and 125** (W. Rhodes 4-44).

ENGLAND V WEST INDIES, THIRD TEST 1929

August 11, 13, 14, 1928. England won by an innings and 71 runs.

Another Oval Test century followed two years later against West Indies.

The Third Test match took much the same course as that at Manchester, West Indies making a good start in batting, but being badly outplayed afterwards, and little cricket on the third day being required to finish off the game in a victory for England by an innings and 71 runs...

Glorious weather prevailing on Saturday, and the wicket being of a nice easy pace, West Indies, on winning the toss, had every chance of doing themselves justice... Being all out for 238... was thus so disappointing... Tate and Larwood bowled very well and, although three catches were missed, England on the whole fielded smartly. Duckworth kept wicket in capital form, giving away only two byes, and these off a ball on the leg side...

Hobbs and Sutcliffe gave England a splendid start, withstanding West Indies' attack for just over two hours, and raising the score to 155 before a yorker dismissed Sutcliffe. In so doing, the famous pair shared for the 11th time in Test match cricket in a three-figure first-wicket partnership. Sutcliffe began a little unevenly, and might have been caught off his glove in the slips for a single, yet he settled down in capital form, and Hobbs's play from the first was admirable. Skilful placing accounted for most of the runs, but Hobbs was always strong on the leg side, and drove hard on occasion, while Sutcliffe brought off some delightful strokes behind the wicket. Consequent upon the great heat, the batsmen turned very quiet for a time, but runs were coming with some freedom again when Francis broke up the partnership. Sutcliffe when 36 should have been caught high up behind the wicket, yet he played attractive cricket. Hobbs, making no mistake, left off not out, 89.

England's batting on Monday was not altogether satisfactory; indeed, some of it might fairly be described as disquieting, for after Hobbs and Ernest Tyldesley had added 129 runs in less than two hours, so raising the total to 284 before the second wicket fell, five men were actually dismissed – all by Griffith – in an hour for 49 more runs. For the moment England looked like being out for a score which, in view of the start given them by Hobbs, Sutcliffe and Tyldesley, must have severely damaged the reputation of the side, and although some spirited hitting produced 105 runs for the last three wickets, an aggregate of 22 for Chapman, Hammond, Hendren and Leyland left a distinctly uneasy feeling. Hobbs, too, was so far from reproducing his form of Saturday that he gave two chances before he had increased his figures from 89 to 100. Still he and Tyldesley, before rain drove the players from the field at 20 minutes past 12 and prevented further cricket until nearly half past two, put on 80 runs in as many minutes. When the game was resumed, the batsmen hit away without real restraint, and added 49 in half an hour before Hobbs brought his innings to an end by placing a ball into short leg's hands. Apart from the two chances in the 90s, and one or two wild strokes just at the finish, Hobbs played masterly cricket during a stay of four hours, putting together his eighth hundred of the season, and having 20 fours as his chief strokes.

Following upon Hobbs's departure at 284 came such a complete transformation that there were seven men out for 333... Altogether England batted rather more than six hours for their total of 438.

Entering upon their second innings 200 in arrear, West Indies, so far from repeating the fine commencement they had made on Saturday, lost three of their best wickets in an hour for 46 runs, and at the drawing of stumps, despite the stubborn defence of Martin, had four men out for 61. Thus, on Tuesday the tourists, with six wickets to fall, required 139 more runs to avoid a single innings defeat. At no time did they look like escaping that fate. Indeed, the six wickets went down in the course of 75 minutes for the addition of 68 runs, the side, after batting two hours and a half in all, being all out for 129. Martin alone offered any serious resistance, that player, who had gone in on the fall of the first wicket at 12, withstanding the England attack for an hour and 50 minutes. Seventh out at 102, he not only showed very skilful defence, but in the final stage of the contest made some capital hits. Tate had seven wickets in the match for 86 runs, Larwood five for 87, and Freeman six for 132, these three bowlers, moreover, scoring 105 runs between them. Only a few hundred people gathered to witness the finish, but during the three days more than 28,000 paid the two-shillings admission.

West Indies 238 (C. A. Roach 53; M. W. Tate 4-59) and 129 (A. P. Freeman 4-47);
England 438 (J. B. Hobbs 159, H. Sutcliffe 63, G. E. Tyldesley 73, M. W. Tate 54;
G. N. Francis 4-112, H. C. Griffith 6-103).

SURREY V SOMERSET   1930

July 17, 18, 19, 1929. Surrey won by an innings and 158 runs.

Now well into his forties, Hobbs hit another double-century in Surrey's Championship victory over Somerset in 1929.

Putting together their highest total of the season – 555 for four wickets – Surrey defeated Somerset by an innings and 158 runs. The issue was largely decided during the first hour of the match, when Allom bowled to such purpose that six wickets fell for 50 runs, the old Cantab's share being five for 24. Hunt and J. W. Lee added 64 for the last wicket. So completely did Hobbs and Sandham master the visitors' bowling that, despite brilliant fielding, they scored 142 before the drawing of stumps, and on Thursday Hobbs, who had made 150 not out against Kent at Blackheath two days previously, completed a magnificent innings of 204 in just over five hours. Third out at 409, Hobbs gave only one chance – when 134 – and hit 20 fours. Shepherd also batted with much freedom against an attack greatly weakened by the breakdown of Wellard. When Hobbs declared, Somerset made 101 for one wicket, but next day, apart from Lyon, they shaped indifferently. Lyon, handicapped by lameness, gave a most brilliant display of driving. Brooks made four catches behind the stumps on the last day – none of them easy.

Somerset 163 (G. E. Hunt 57; M. J. C. Allom 6-51) and 234 (M. D. Lyon 119; M. J. C. Allom 5-79);
Surrey 555-4 dec (J. B. Hobbs 204, A. Sandham 74, A. Ducat 63, T. F. Shepherd 131*).

May 27, 29, 30, 1933. Match drawn.

Age was no barrier for Jack Hobbs. Having turned 50 over the winter, he made 221 in his first appearance of the 1933 season against the touring West Indians.

There never existed much chance of a definite result, but a drawn match was notable for brilliant batting by Roach and Hobbs. Roach performed the rare feat of reaching three figures before lunch. Driving splendidly, besides cutting crisply and hooking with power, he hit 25 fours and after batting two hours 50 minutes he was second to leave at 285. Barrow helped in an opening partnership of 187, and with Wiles playing freely 98 runs came in 55 minutes. Roach gave four difficult chances but they were small blemishes in a magnificent display. Hobbs was masterly. For a man playing in his first match of the season at 50 years of age, his display was not only a triumph of skill, but no mean feat of physical endurance. Fifth out at 418, he withstood the bowling for six and a half hours. Although his innings contained only 17 fours it was abundant in beautiful strokes all round the wicket. His opening stand with Gregory yielded 117; Squires, Barling and Brown also rendered useful assistance. Owing to injury Sandham did not bat.

West Indians 460 (C. A. Roach 180, I. M. Barrow 62, C. A. Wiles 51; A. R. Gover 4-108) and 160-5 (O. C. Da Costa 58*); Surrey 470 (J. B. Hobbs 221, R. J. Gregory 55; F. R. Martin 4-53).

Chapter 7
The Don

There were many great cricketers from around the world who played beneath the Kennington gasholders, but none left their mark on the ground quite like Donald Bradman. In 11 first-class matches, including four Tests that spanned 18 years, The Don notched up six centuries at an average of 139.20 – on the very ground which would cruelly deny him a Test career average of 100 in his last match for Australia.

He began his Oval odyssey in May 1930 with an unbeaten 252 against a Surrey side containing Hobbs, Sandham, Fender, Jardine and Ducat, and his iconic 232 against England later that summer – Hobbs's last Test – ensured a famous Ashes win for the tourists. Even so early in his career, it seems that Bradman's brilliance was taken for granted, with Wisden noting: "As usual he scored well in front of the wicket but he obtained a large number of runs on the leg side, while from start to finish his defence was altogether remarkable." Another double-century followed in his next Oval Test four years later, as he and Bill Ponsford put on 451 for the second wicket to help Australia to victory in the match by 562 runs and in the series by the scoreline of 2–1.

Returning as Australia captain in 1938, Bradman put Surrey to the sword once more with 143 in a tour match in May. He was, as ever, a *central figure in the summer's final Test at The Oval – even though he did not bat in the match. With England batting first and Len Hutton playing one of the great Test innings, Bradman put himself on to bowl in an act of desperation. This was proved a disaster: in the middle of his third over, he fractured his ankle and took no further part in the game. Wally Hammond, the England captain, said later that he would not have declared at 903 for seven if Bradman had been fit. Thus was Test cricket denied the chance of its first innings-total of 1,000.*

War intervened, and Bradman's next visit to these shores was on his farewell tour of 1948. After hitting a century in both of the Oval tour matches against Surrey, he arrived at the ground for his final Test needing four runs to average 100. Famously, he was dismissed second ball for a duck and did not have another chance to bat in the game, his career average resting on the magical figure of 99.94.

SURREY V AUSTRALIANS   1931

May 24, 26, 27, 1930. Match drawn.

Bradman made an immediate impression in his very first innings at The Oval, hitting a double-century which augured well for the Test series which followed.

To a single day's cricket was the first of the Australians' two matches with Surrey restricted, the ground, owing to rain, being reduced to such a muddy condition that not a ball could be bowled on either Monday or Tuesday, but the one day's play produced some remarkable batting on the part of Bradman. The remarkable young Australian had previously put together huge scores at Worcester and at Leicester so this further success occasioned no great surprise. Still, the performance reached an exceptionally high standard of excellence. Going in first wicket down at 11, Bradman – at great pains to play himself in – took an hour and a half to reach 50, but doubled that score in less than an hour and then travelled so fast that he went from 100 to 200 in 80 minutes. Altogether, in five hours and 35 minutes, he made 252 out of 368 and was still unbeaten when rain caused stumps to be drawn five minutes before the usual hour. Scoring at first chiefly on the leg side, he afterwards employed the late cut to fine purpose and in the course of the day brought almost every stroke into play. Not until his figures stood at 207 did he make a real mistake – at that point he gave a chance to short-leg – and among his hits were 21 fours, ten threes and 26 twos...

Australians 379-5 (W. M. Woodfull 50, D. G. Bradman 252*) v **Surrey**

ENGLAND V AUSTRALIA, FIFTH TEST   1931

August 16, 18, 19, 20, 21, 22, 1930. Australia won by an innings and 39 runs.

The 1930 Test served as a passing of the torch from Jack Hobbs, playing his final Test, to Bradman, playing his first at the ground.

Australia won the rubber and so regained possession of the Ashes they had lost four years previously on the same ground. Each side having proved successful once and the other two games being drawn, the concluding Test match had to be played to a finish irrespective of the number of days involved. Including the Thursday when, owing to rain, not a ball could be bowled, the encounter was spread over six days – a longer time than had ever before been occupied by a Test match in England.

Australia won the match fairly and squarely, replying to England's first innings of 405 with a total of 695, and then getting the Englishmen out for 251, but just as rain had assisted England in the First Test Match at Nottingham, so it operated against them at The Oval. England had to play their second innings on a pitch so entirely suited to bowlers that in the circumstances they actually accomplished a good performance in scoring as many runs as they did on the last day. Still, Australia had outplayed their opponents on the first innings and, even if rain had not fallen they would, most probably, have won the match...

Once more Australia owed a great deal to Bradman who followed up his previous batting successes at Nottingham, Lord's and Leeds with an innings of 232. As usual he scored well in front of the wicket but he obtained a large number of runs on the leg side, while from start to finish his defence was altogether remarkable. All the same he did not play in anything like the attractive style he had shown at Lord's; indeed, there were periods when he became monotonous. Scoring so heavily as he did, Bradman again overshadowed everyone else, but his task was made the easier by the good work accomplished, before he went in, by Ponsford and Woodfull, who once more wore the bowling down by their workmanlike and steady cricket...

Wyatt winning the toss, England stayed in for the whole of the first day and scored 316 for five wickets but at one point – to be exact just before the tea interval – they were in a bad way, the fifth man leaving when the total was only 197. Then Wyatt went in and played well. To begin with, Hobbs and Sutcliffe put on 68 for the first partnership, Hobbs being caught at short-leg just before lunch, while at 97 Whysall left. Then came some delightful batting by Duleepsinhji who, driving, hooking and cutting in dazzling style, actually scored 50 out of the next 65 runs in 50 minutes. To some extent the situation had been retrieved but the quick dismissal of Hammond and Leyland threw England back again. After tea, Sutcliffe, who had been in four and a quarter hours for 66, batted beautifully and was not out 138 when play ceased. He and Wyatt had added 119 and before Sutcliffe was out on Monday morning at 367 the stand had realised 170 runs in two hours and 35 minutes.

Sutcliffe batted for six hours and three-quarters and scored exactly the same number of runs as he had done in the corresponding match four years previously. The situation compelled him to play a restrained game until he and Wyatt had definitely settled down together but from teatime on the opening day his cricket was first-class. Naturally, the Australian bowling had lost some of its freshness on the Saturday afternoon but that did not detract from the merit of the innings. Sutcliffe brought off some splendid hits to square leg and to the on, while his off-driving was admirable. As far as was seen he did not give a chance but just before the partnership ended Wyatt was missed at slip by Hornibrook. Eighth to leave at 379, Wyatt was in for three hours for a most valuable 64, in which he hit hard in front of the wicket. On the

Monday morning, five England wickets fell for 89 in about an hour and 50 minutes, the innings having lasted seven hours and 40 minutes.

Before lunch, Woodfull and Ponsford scored 36 but both should have been out, Woodfull being missed at the wicket when six and Ponsford at 23 giving a chance of stumping. Later on Ponsford, at 45, was let off again and for these mistakes England had to pay a heavy price. Altogether the two men scored 159 runs in two hours and 40 minutes before Ponsford was bowled third ball after tea. He batted extremely well, if not perhaps quite so skilfully as at Manchester, the manner in which at the start of the innings he dealt with Larwood clearly disproving the idea that he could not face the Notts fast bowler. Scoring at the start chiefly on the leg side, he afterwards cut and drove beautifully. Before Bradman reached the wicket there was a delay through defective light and a little while afterwards came a further break from the same cause. With the score up to 190, Woodfull was out, his stay having extended over three hours and a quarter. He hit only three fours but played a most valuable innings. When play ceased, Australia, with two men out for 215, were only 190 runs behind. In all, Bradman and Kippax added 73 for the third wicket. Then came the big stand of the innings, Bradman and Jackson not being separated until Wednesday at one o'clock, by which time they had put on 243 runs in four and a half hours. Jackson was nearly run out before he had scored and almost bowled when five, while Bradman, at 82, gave a chance at the wicket. Rain came on during lunch time on the Tuesday, the score then standing at 371 for three wickets, and, play being resumed soon after three o'clock, a further break through rain and bad light just about four o'clock occurred with the score at 402. It looked as though there would be no more cricket that day but the players went out at 25 minutes past six and in the five minutes one more run was obtained.

On the Wednesday morning the ball flew about a good deal, both batsmen frequently being hit on the body. The partnership might have ended at 458 had Leyland returned the ball to the right end and on more than one occasion each player cocked the ball up dangerously but always, as it happened, just wide of the fieldsmen. Caught, at length, at extra-cover point, Jackson played nothing like as well as those who we saw him in Australia knew he could. For the most part he was very restrained and, except that it helped in a record Australia stand for the fourth wicket, his innings was hardly worthy of his reputation. Bradman all this time had gone steadily on but when joined by McCabe was overshadowed, the latter driving brilliantly. Another 64 runs were added and then Bradman, at 570, was caught by Duckworth standing back. In seven hours he made 232 out of 411 with 16 fours, ten threes and 28 twos as his chief hits. McCabe, hitting nine fours, left at 594, but the tired England bowlers came in for further punishment, Oldfield and Fairfax putting on 76 in 65 minutes. In the end, Australia were all out just before half-past five, their innings having occupied 12 hours and five minutes. Fairfax was in for nearly two hours and a half. After tea the last three wickets fell in 35 minutes for 23 runs. Bowling 71 overs, Peebles took six wickets but had 204 runs hit from him. Although expensive he did fine work while Hammond – the only one who got real nip off the pitch – bowled much better than his record would suggest.

England, 290 behind, went in again at a quarter to six. When Hobbs and Sutcliffe reached the wickets, the Australians gathered round Hobbs and gave three cheers as a tribute to the great batsman playing presumably his last innings for England. A quiet start being made, Sutcliffe had scored only six out of the eight runs on the board when he was missed at the wicket off Fairfax. This was indeed a great piece of luck for England, but when the score reached 17 Hobbs played on. Defective light causing play to be stopped at a quarter past six, England, with nine wickets to fall and 24 runs scored, required 266 to save the innings defeat.

No play took place on the Thursday owing to rain. On Friday the sun shone and everyone realised that only a miracle could save England… With the last man in Hammond was missed at long-off by Bradman but three runs later he fell to a catch in the slips and at ten minutes to four the match was all over…

The Australian fielding in both innings was uncommonly good. Nobody did better than Bradman who, whether at fine leg or long-off, covered so much ground, picked up and returned so swiftly that many a possible four was turned into a single.

England

J. B. Hobbs c Kippax b Wall	47	– b Fairfax	9
H. Sutcliffe c Oldfield b Fairfax	161	– c Fairfax b Homibrook	54
W. W. Whysall lbw b Wall	13	– c Homibrook b Grimmett	10
K. S. Duleepsinhji c Fairfax b Grimmett	50	– c Kippax b Hornibrook	46
W. R. Hammond b McCabe	13	– c Fairfax b Homibrook	60
M. Leyland b Grimmett	3	– b Homibrook	20
*R. E. S. Wyatt c Oldfield b Fairfax	64	– b Homibrook	7
M. W. Tate st Oldfield b Grimmett	10	– run out	0
H. Larwood lbw b Grimmett	19	– c McCabe b Homibrook	9
†G. Duckworth b Fairfax	3	– b Homibrook	15
I. A. R. Peebles not out	3	– not out	0
Lb 17, nb 2	19	B 16, lb 3, nb 2	21

1/68 (1) 2/97 (3) 3/162 (4)   (171.2 overs) 405
4/190 (5) 5/197 (6) 6/367 (2)
7/379 (8) 8/379 (7) 9/391 (10) 10/405 (9)

1/17 (1) 2/37 (3)   (99.2 overs) 251
3/118 (2) 4/135 (4)
5/189 (6) 6/207 (7) 7/208 (8)
8/220 (9) 9/248 (10) 10/251 (5)

Wall 37–6–96–2; Fairfax 31–9–52–3; Grimmett 66.2–18–135–4; McCabe 22–4–49–1; Homibrook 15–1–54–0; *Second innings*—Wall 12–2–25–0; Fairfax 10–3–21–1; Grimmett 43–12–90–1; Homibrook 31.2–9–92–7; McCabe 3–1–2–0.

Australia

*W. M. Woodfull c Duckworth b Peebles	54	T. W. Wall lbw b Peebles	0
W. H. Ponsford b Peebles	110	P. M. Hornibrook c Duckworth b Tate	7
D. G. Bradman c Duckworth b Larwood	232		
A. F. Kippax c Wyatt b Peebles	28	B 22, lb 18, nb 4	44
A. Jackson c Sutcliffe b Wyatt	73		
S. J. McCabe c Duckworth b Hammond	54	1/159 (2) 2/190(1) (256.1 overs) 695
A. G. Fairfax not out	53	3/263(4) 4/506(5)
†W. A. Oldfield c Larwood b Peebles	34	5/570 (3) 6/594 (6) 7/670 (8)
C. V. Grimmett lbw b Peebles	6	8/684 (9) 9/684 (10) 10/695 (11)

Larwood 48–6–132–1; Tate 65.1–12–123–1; Peebles 71–8–204–6; Wyatt 14–1–58–1; Hammond 42–12–70–1; Leyland 16–7–34–0.

Umpires: W. R. Parry and J. Hardstaff, sen.

Close of play: first day, England 316-5 (Sutcliffe 138, Wyatt 39); second day, Australia 215-2 (Bradman 27, Kippax 11); third day, Australia 403-3 (Bradman 130, Jackson 43): fourth day, England 24-1 (Sutcliffe 8, Whysall 6); fifth day, no play.

ENGLAND V AUSTRALIA, FIFTH TEST   1935

August 18, 20, 21, 22, 1934. Australia won by 562 runs.

In 1934 a Bradman-inspired Australia scored an emphatic victory at The Oval, regaining the Ashes after losing them in the Bodyline series of 1932-33. This was the last Test played by Frank Woolley, one of the game's great all-rounders, who had made his international debut at the same ground 25 years earlier.

Each side having won once with two games left drawn, the fifth and concluding Test match was entered upon without any restrictions as to the time involved in reaching a definite result. As it happened, four days proved sufficient for Australia to win by 562 runs. Thus they regained the Ashes. Being successful in the rubber by two victories to one, they brought their number of wins in the whole series of encounters between the two countries to 52 as against 51 by England. Under conditions which, apart from the winning of the toss, favoured neither side unduly, the result was a fitting tribute to the superior all-round skill of Australia. They batted, bowled and fielded better than England and in every way thoroughly deserved what was, after all, a notable achievement...

The law of averages suggested that it was Woodfull's turn to win the toss. This he did and when Clark, coming on at 20, bowled Brown at 21 with the best ball sent down all day long, it seemed as though the England attack on a hard wicket was about to come into its own. Never were hopeful anticipations more rudely dispelled. Between them Ponsford and Bradman gave another glorious display of batting, staying together until nearly half-past six and engaging in a partnership which left that of Leeds far behind and produced 451 runs in five hours and a quarter. This time Bradman was the first to leave, hitting over his head at a bouncing ball and being caught behind the wicket at 472. McCabe went in and played out time, Australia, as the result of the first day's cricket, having 475 runs on the board with only two men out. It would be hard to speak in too high terms of praise of the magnificent displays of batting given by Ponsford and Bradman. Before Bradman joined him Ponsford had shown an inclination to draw away from the bowling of Bowes but he received inspiration afterwards from the example of his partner, who from the very moment he reached the centre and took up his stance was coolness and mastery personified.

The pitch did not help bowlers at all. Those with a command of spin found it extremely difficult to make the ball turn in the slightest and only by dropping it short could the fast bowlers make the ball rise above stump high. Clark tried leg-theory with a packed leg-side field but as, for the most part, he maintained a good length, his bowling, even if he now and again dropped the ball short, scarcely came under the category of what is known as bodyline. Incidentally Clark and the others tried all sort of theories but they had no effect on Bradman who, as the afternoon wore on, invested his batting with increasing daring. He drove and cut with the utmost certainty and power, and when the ball did bounce he just stepped back and hooked it. Included in his hits were a six and 32 fours and, having regard to the rate at which he, as well as Ponsford scored, a better display has rarely been seen. Ponsford was not quite so sure as Bradman and he frequently turned his back to the ball to receive blows on the thigh. All the same, he drove with great power and was clever in getting the ball away between the fieldsmen placed close in. Just after the new ball was brought into use at 200 the England bowling was at its best but generally speaking it never looked quite good enough for the task at hand and it was noticeable that scarcely a single yorker was sent down all day long while the bowlers of pace failed to keep their deliveries just that little bit short of a length to compel batsmen to play the forward defensive stroke. As during the day about 80 runs an hour were obtained it can be realised that too many long-hops and half-volleys were sent down. This great partnership meant that in consecutive representative encounters Bradman and Ponsford in two stands scored 839 runs in ten hours and three-quarters. Ponsford offered three very difficult chances and one when 115 comparatively easy; Bradman's batting, as far as was seen, was flawless.

On Monday England had further trouble before the innings which lasted nearly ten hours closed at 20 minutes to five for 701 runs – the second-highest in the history of Test matches between England and Australia... The England fielding fell much below the standard demanded in Test cricket. On the dry ground the ball sometimes shot off at an awkward angle but the catching was poor.

An hour and a half remained for cricket when England went in and anything might have happened, but Walters and Sutcliffe, scoring at a fine pace, made 90 together without being separated... Still, England were still 611 runs behind at the end of the day.

Tuesday was a black day for England and except for a superbly aggressive display by Maurice Leyland the batting proved deplorable...

Australia, 380 ahead, scored 186 for two wickets before the end of the day, Brown leaving at 13 and Ponsford at 42. [With Ames injured,] Woolley kept wicket and Gregory and McMurray of Surrey acted as substitute fielders. Incidentally the work of these two men was brilliantly accurate. Nobody on the England side, except Leyland, did so well in the outfield in any of the Test matches. Bradman and McCabe scored at a fine pace, making 144 together in 90 minutes. Light rain fell during the night but the wicket the next morning was not greatly affected. Ames was still away but Bowes returned and went on to bowl. He soon dismissed Bradman who, with McCabe, had added 150 in 95 minutes and then for the first time England's bowling got really on top so that, although the last partnership between Ebeling and O'Reilly produced 55 in 40 minutes, Australia were all out by half-past two for 327, the last eight wickets having produced 141 in two hours and ten minutes. Clark and Bowes shared the wickets, both bowling extremely well. Woolley kept wicket and made a catch standing back.

England were thus left with no fewer than 708 to get to win – only 34 short of the number England had set Australia in the first Test match at Brisbane during the 1928-29 tour. England made a shocking start, Walters leaving at one and Woolley at three but Sutcliffe and Hammond added 64 in 65 minutes. Hammond was fourth to leave after tea at 89 and following that it only became a question as to whether the match would be over or not before half-past six. Apart from an easy chance of stumping, Hammond certainly played very well but the tea interval proved his undoing. Leyland left at 109 and Wyatt at 122 and shortly before six o'clock with Allen stumped the innings was all over for 145 and, as was the case four years previously, Australia won the rubber on the anniversary of Woodfull's birthday. Grimmett bowled superbly.

Australia 701 (W. H. Ponsford 266, D. G. Bradman 244; W. E. Bowes 4-164, G. O. B. Allen 4-170) and 327 (D. G. Bradman 77, S. J. McCabe 70, Extras 50; E. W. Clark 5-98, W. E. Bowes 5-55); England 321 (C. F. Walters 64, M. Leyland 110) and 145 (C. V. Grimmett 5-64).

SURREY V AUSTRALIANS   1949

May 8, 10, 11, 1948. Australia won by an innings and 296 runs.

Ten years on from the extraordinary Oval Test of 1938 (see chapter 8), Bradman returned to England for his farewell tour. He made a hundred in each of two matches against Surrey, which seemed to bode well for his final Test at The Oval later that summer.

On their first appearance in London the Australians regained their batting form. They were fortunate to win the toss, for, after being easy-paced on the first day, the pitch became fast and dusty; nevertheless there was little excuse for Surrey's poor batting in the first innings. [For the Australians] Barnes and Morris opened with a stand of 136 and Barnes and Bradman added 207. Excelling with the cut and hook, Barnes hit 18 fours. He batted four and a quarter hours. Bradman, at his best, drove magnificently and made 146 in two and three-quarter hours. He hit 15 fours before being bowled by a fine ball. On the second day Hassett became the third century-maker. In a fine spell of 90 minutes Bedser dismissed Johnson, Lindwall and Hassett. With Lindwall quickly sending back Fletcher and Squires, Surrey were all out in three hours. Fishlock batted through the innings and never seemed in trouble, though Ian Johnson bowled off-breaks cleverly. When Surrey batted again Squires hit splendidly. The Australian fielding was grand, notably that of Harvey, who made three remarkable catches in the deep.

Australians 632 (S. G. Barnes 176, A. R. Morris 65, D. G. Bradman 146, A. L. Hassett 110, D. Tallon 50*; A. V. Bedser 4-104, J. W. J. McMahon 4-210); **Surrey 141** (L. B. Fishlock 81*; I. W. G. Johnson 5-53) **and 195** (H. S. Squires 54; W. A. Johnston 4-40).

SURREY V AUSTRALIANS   1949

June 30, July 1, 2, 1948. Australia won by ten wickets.

Bradman put Surrey in on winning the toss and two wickets fell for 14. Fishlock retired for a time following a blow on the head, but Parker (ten fours) played a fine innings, full of lusty pulls and drives, lasting nearly three hours. Fletcher helped him add 50 and Fishlock, returning, shared in a stand of 60. The Australians soon lost Hamence, who opened the innings because Brown split a finger while fielding, but Hassett and Bradman joined in a partnership of 231. Bradman (15 fours) obtained his sixth century of the tour in two hours 20 minutes and Hassett's 139, made in three hours, contained ten boundaries. Harvey hit hard to leg and Surrey faced arrears of 168. This time Fishlock gave a grand display of driving, making 61 out of 94 in 85 minutes with nine fours among his strokes. Parker again stayed three hours, he and Holmes adding 107 for the seventh wicket. The Australians needed 122 to win and Harvey and Loxton displayed such enterprise that they knocked off the runs in 58 minutes. Harvey hit two sixes and eight fours.

Surrey 221 (J. F. Parker 76) **and 289** (L. B. Fishlock 61, J. F. Parker 81, E. R. T. Holmes 54; C. L. McCool 6-113); **Australians 389** (A. L. Hassett 139, D. G. Bradman 128) **and 122-0** (R. N. Harvey 73*).

ENGLAND V AUSTRALIA, FIFTH TEST   Hubert Preston, 1949

August 14, 16, 17, 18, 1948. Australia won by an innings and 149 runs.

The 1948 Oval Test has gone down in cricketing folklore. Wisden's report does not mention the statistical relevance of Bradman's duck in his last Test innings, instead focusing on how The Don was moved by the ovation he received from the Oval crowd and the England team. Indeed, legend has it that he could not see the ball which bowled him because of the tears in his eyes.

Extraordinary cricket marked the opening day. So saturated was the ground by copious rain during the week that the groundsmen could not get the pitch into a reasonable state for a punctual start. The captains agreed that play should begin at 12 o'clock, and Yardley, having won the toss, chose to bat – an inevitable decision with the conditions uncertain and the possibility of more rain. As it happened, apart from local showers early on Sunday morning, the weather proved fine until England fared badly for the second time. All things considered, the Australians found everything favourable for them… This does not explain the lamentable collapse of England for the lowest score by either side in a Test at The Oval, apart from the 44 for which Australia fell in 1896, the last occasion on which W. G. Grace led England to victory…

The sodden state of the pitch, with sawdust covering large patches of turf nearby, made one doubt its fitness for cricket. Bowlers and batsmen found much sawdust necessary for a foothold. This supposed handicap did not seem to trouble the Australians, and reasons for the downfall of England in two hours and a half for such a meagre score were the splendid attack maintained by Lindwall, Miller and Johnston in humid atmosphere against batsmen whose first error proved fatal. Hutton, the one exception to complete failure, batted in his customary stylish, masterful manner throughout the innings, being last out from a leg glance which Tallon held with the left hand close to the ground as he fell – a great finish to Australia's splendid performance.

Lindwall, with his varied pace and occasional very fast ball, excelled. Always bowling at the stumps, he made the ball rise at different heights. Four times he clean bowled a hesitant opponent. Except that Watkins received a blow on the shoulder that destroyed his supposed value as a bowler, the batsmen escaped injury during a most pitiful display. After lunch Lindwall bowled 8.1 overs, four maidens, and took five wickets at a cost of eight runs!

Everything became different when Australia batted. Barnes and Morris, with controlled assurance and perfect strokeplay, made 117, and shortly before six o'clock Bradman walked to the wicket amidst continued applause from the standing crowd. Yardley shook hands with Bradman and called on the England team for three cheers, in which the crowd joined. Evidently deeply touched by the enthusiastic reception, Bradman survived one ball, but, playing forward to the next, was clean bowled by a sharply turning break-back – possibly a googly. As if to avenge the fall of these two wickets in an over, Morris twice hooked Hollies to the boundary and the score rose to 153, while on Monday it reached 226 before Hassett left – 109 for the third wicket. That those runs occupied two hours and a quarter testified to good bowling and fielding by a side in a forlorn position, and the next-best partnership was the sixth, which added 39.

Morris missed the special distinction of making 200 through his own ill-judged call for a sharp run, Simpson, fielding substitute for Watkins, with a good return from third man causing his dismissal for 196. Scoring these runs out of 359 in six hours 40 minutes, Morris hit 16 fours. His strokes past cover point were typical of the highest class left-handed batsman. His drives and hooks beat the speediest fieldsmen, and he showed marked skill in turning the ball to leg. He was eighth out, and Tallon got most of the 30 runs added before Bedser at last earned reward for steady bowling by taking the tenth wicket.

Facing arrears of 337, England lost Dewes with 20 scored, but Hutton and Edrich raised the total to 54 before bad light stopped play. The conditions remained anything but good on Tuesday, when the early fall of Edrich to a fine ball from Lindwall preceded the only stand of consequence, Compton and Hutton putting on 61 in an hour and 50 minutes before Lindwall, with his left hand at second slip, held a hard cut from Compton. Hutton maintained his sound form until a bumper from Miller struck Crapp on the head, soon after which the Yorkshireman gave Tallon a catch. Batting four hours and a quarter for 64 out of 153, Hutton was always restrained but admirable in defence.

After he left three wickets fell in deepening gloom for 25 runs. Evans, from the way he shaped without attempting a stroke, obviously could not see the ball which bowled him, Lindwall, with the pavilion behind him, sending down something like a yorker at express speed. The umpires immediately responded to the appeal against the light, and rain at four o'clock delayed the finish until Wednesday morning, when the remaining three wickets realised only ten runs in a sad spectacle for England. The usual scramble for the stumps and bails as Morris held a lofted catch from Hollies marked the close; but much happened subsequently. Mr. H. D. G Leveson-Gower on the players' balcony called for three cheers for Bradman and the victorious Australians. Responses over the microphone came in due course, the crowd of about 5,000 enthusiasts coming up to the pavilion to hear and see all that happened as a curtain to this series of Test matches in which Australia completely outplayed and conquered England.

England

L. Hutton c Tallon b Lindwall	30	–	(2) c Tallon b Miller		64
J. G. Dewes b Miller	1	–	(1) b Lindwall		10
W. J. Edrich c Hassett b Johnston	3	–	b Lindwall		28
D. C. S. Compton c Morris b Lindwall	4	–	c Lindwall b Johnston		39
J. F. Crapp c Tallon b Miller	0	–	b Miller		9
'N. W. D. Yardley b Lindwall	7	–	c Miller b Johnston		9
A. J. Watkins b Johnston	0	–	c Hassell b Ring		2
†T. G. Evans b Lindwall	1	–	b Lindwall		8
A. V. Bedser b Lindwall	0	–	b Johnston		0
J. A. Young b Lindwall	0	–	not out		3
W. E. Hollies not out	0	–	c Morris b Johnston		0
B 6	6		B 9, lb 4, nb 3		16

1/2 (2) 2/10 (3) 3/17 (4) (42.1 overs) 52
4/23 (5) 5/35 (6) 6/42 (7)
7/45 (8) 8/45 () 9/47 (10) 10/52 (1)

1/20 (1) 2/64 (3) (105.3 overs) 188
3/125 (4) 4/153 (2)
5/164 (5) 6/167 (7) 7/178 (8)
8/181 (9) 9/188 (6) 10/188 (11)

Lindwall 16.1–5–20–6; Miller 8–5–5–2; Johnston 16–4–20–2; Loxton 2–1–1–0. *Second innings*—Lindwall 25–3–50–3; Miller 15–6–22–0; Loxton 10–2–16–0; Johnston 27.3–12–40–4; Ring 28–13–44–1.

Australia

S. G. Barnes c Evans b Hollies	61	D. T. Ring c Crapp b Bedser		9
A. R. Morris run out	196	W. A. Johnston not out		0
'D. G. Bradman b Hollies	0			
A. L. Hassett lbw b Young	37	B 4, lb 2, nb 3		9
K. R. Miller st Evans b Hollies	5			
R. N. Harvey c Young b Hollies	17	1/117 (1) 2/117 (3)	(158.2 overs)	389
S. J. E. Loxton c Evans b Edrich	15	3/226 (4) 4/243 (5)		
R. R. Lindwall c Edrich b Young	9	5/265 (6) 6/304 (7) 7/332 (8)		
†D. Tallon c Crapp b Hollies	31	8/359 (2) 9/389 (9) 10/389 (10)		

Bedser 31.2–9–61–1; Watkins 4–1–19–0; Young 51–16–118–2; Hollies 56–14–131–5; Compton 2–0–6–0; Edrich 9–1–38–1; Yardley 5–1–7–0.

Umpires: H. G. Baldwin and D. Davies.

Close of play: first day, Australia 153-2 (Morris 77, Hassett 10); second day, England 54-1 (Hutton 19, Edrich 23); third day. England 178-7 (Yardley 2).

Chapter 8

Hutton at The Oval

S uch is the legacy of Len Hutton's world record innings in 1938 that, even as a Yorkshireman, he is more associated with The Oval than with his home ground at Headingley. Hutton's score of 364 in the 1938 Ashes Test may have since been surpassed but it remains the highest by an Englishman. Indeed, in nearly eight decades since Hutton's feat, Graham Gooch and John Edrich are the only England batsmen to have made a Test triple-hundred.

That innings will forever link Hutton and The Oval, but it would be remiss to forget that he went on to three more Test centuries at the ground. He made an unbeaten second-innings 165 against West Indies in 1939 and, ten years later, a double-hundred against New Zealand which "except for a slow period of three-quarters of an hour through the nineties," wrote Wisden, "could not be faulted in any way". Then, in 1950, Hutton rose "magnificently to the occasion" of the Oval Test against West Indies by carrying his bat for 202. Wisden was gushing: "Nobody who saw his effort of concentration and perfect strokeplay will forget the great attempt he made to save his country."

It was at The Oval in 1953 where Hutton led England to claim the Ashes for the first time in 19 years, and where he scored his 100th first-class hundred against Surrey two years earlier. Curiously, his first Oval century *had come in September 1937 during a match between champions Yorkshire and runners-up Middlesex. Wisden described it as a "Challenge Match" but didn't include a report or scorecard, nor an explanation for why it was played at The Oval.*

In retirement, Hutton moved to Surrey and became a great friend of the ground, helping to organise a fundraising campaign during a stretched financial period in the 1980s for which he was honoured with the erection of the Hutton Wall just inside the Hobbs Gates. It remains the only part of the ground named after a player who did not represent Surrey.

ENGLAND V AUSTRALIA, FIFTH TEST   1939

August 20, 22, 23, 24, 1938. England won by an innings and 579 runs.

Hutton was just 22 years old when he broke the record for the highest Test score, an innings which helped England to their biggest-ever victory margin.

No more remarkable exhibition of concentration and endurance has ever been seen on the cricket field than that of Leonard Hutton, the Yorkshire opening batsman, in a match which culminated in the defeat of Australia by a margin more substantial than any associated with the series of matches between the two countries. Record after record went by the board as Hutton mastered the bowling for the best part of two and a half days. At the end of an innings which extended over 13 hours, 20 minutes, this batsman of only 22 years had placed the highest score in Test cricket to his name, and shared in two partnerships which surpassed previous figures. Adding 382 with Leyland, he took part in a stand which was a record not only for England's second wicket but for any wicket for England, and his stand of 215 with Hardstaff established a new record for England's sixth wicket. As a boy of 14, Hutton at Leeds in 1930 had seen Bradman hit 334 – the record individual score in Test matches between England and Australia. Now on his third appearance in the series the Yorkshireman left that figure behind by playing an innings of 364.

This Test will always be remembered as Hutton's Match, and also for the calamity which befell Australia while their opponents were putting together a mammoth total of 903. First of all Fingleton strained a muscle, and Bradman injured his ankle so badly that he retired from the match and did not play again during the tour. Before this accident, England had established a supremacy which left little doubt about the result; indeed, Hammond probably would not have closed the innings during the tea interval on the third day but for the mishap to the opposing captain…

Hammond's fourth consecutive success in the toss was, of course, one factor influencing the result. Another was the way in which the Australian team was chosen. The risks taken by Bradman in going into the match with only O'Reilly, Fleetwood-Smith and Waite to bowl seemed to be inviting trouble… Whether Bradman, as was suggested, gambled upon winning the toss after three failures and so being in a position to call upon his spin bowlers when the pitch had become worn will probably never be known…

The first day's cricket brought about the overwhelming success of batsmen which, with the wickets easy-paced and true, it was natural to expect. Waite and McCabe, the opening pair of bowlers, were innocuous and although O'Reilly, soon after he went on, got rid of Edrich and so took his 100th wicket in Tests against England, that was the one success for Australia before stumps were drawn with 347 runs scored. Coming together at 29, Hutton and Leyland settled down to a partnership which surpassed all previous records for England…

With few bowlers of class at his call, Bradman had to conserve the energies of O'Reilly as much as possible. The field was set carefully for the saving of runs and although both the England batsmen scored numerous singles on the off side Australia gave a superb display in the field, Bradman inspiring the team with his fast running and clean picking-up. If the bowling lacked venom it was mainly accurate in length, particularly before lunchtime when 89 runs were scored. In a match with no time limit, Hutton and Leyland very wisely refused to take risks until after the interval; Hutton, in fact, never altered his cautious game. That the scoring-rate quickened was due mainly to the powerful driving and neat cutting of Leyland. Hutton used similar types of strokes in correct and fluent style and all the time his defence never faltered. At the close on Saturday, Hutton had scored 160 and Leyland 156 – the former having batted nearly six hours and Leyland 50 minutes less time. A curiosity of the day's cricket was that four times a no-ball led either to the wicket being hit or the ball being caught.

A heavy shower which fell shortly before Monday's play was due to begin caused 25 minutes' delay but this improved rather than spoiled the wicket. The first event of note was the passing of the record stand against Australia made by Hobbs and Rhodes, who in 1911-12 at Melbourne shared a first-wicket partnership of 323. Following the same steady lines as before, Hutton and Leyland carried on this magnificent batting until England were 411 runs up when the stand ended through a wonderful piece of fielding. Hutton drove a ball from O'Reilly hard to the off side, and Hassett fumbled it. Then he slung in a very fast return to the bowler's end and Bradman, sizing up the situation in an instant, dashed towards the wicket from mid-on, caught the throw-in and broke the wickets before Leyland could complete a second run. Out for 187 – his highest of seven three-figure innings against Australia – Leyland batted nearly six and a half hours and hit 17 fours.

Hammond was at the wickets to see his personal record of highest score for England in a home Test match surpassed by Hutton. It was a remarkable feature of the season's Test games that the 182 not out by Philip Mead at The Oval in 1921 which stood as the record for England against Australia in any home Test was beaten four times during the current series. At Nottingham Paynter made 216 not out, at Lord's Hammond excelled this with 240, Leyland followed with 187 and Hutton not only eclipsed their achievements but surpassed all individual records in Test cricket. Hammond stayed two hours, 20 minutes and helped to add 135 for the third wicket. He was much more defensive than usual, and although taking 12 off one over by Fleetwood-Smith, Hutton played no more than one boundary stroke during his last two hours at the wicket. Paynter's dismissal with one more run scored after Hammond left was a surprise. Misjudgment of a legbreak was the reason. Rain extended the tea interval to half an hour and Compton left immediately afterwards. By this time Hutton had entered upon the tenth hour of his innings, and he remained full of confidence even if becoming a little monotonous by reason of his grim, determined dominance of the bowling. Hardstaff, No. 7 in the order, batted very surely and after an ovation to Hutton when he passed the 287 made at Sydney in 1903-04 by R. E. Foster – before this match the highest innings hit against Australia – an appeal against the light led to stumps being drawn early. England at the end of two days had put together a total of 634 and only half their wickets had fallen.

Hutton claimed exactly 300 of the runs scored at this point and the 30,000 people who assembled at The Oval on Tuesday saw fresh cricket history made. The bowling and fielding of Australia looked more formidable than at any other time in the game and as Hutton carried his score nearer to the record Test innings, Bradman, the holder of it, brought several fieldsmen close in to the wicket for O'Reilly's bowling. Every run had to be fought for. As might be supposed, Hutton showed an occasional sign of strain and he completely missed the ball when with his total 331 he had an opportunity of beating the record by hitting a no-ball from O'Reilly. However, with a perfect cut off Fleetwood-Smith, Hutton duly reached his objective and the scene at the ground, with the whole assembly rising to its feet, and every Australian player, as well as Hardstaff, congratulating Hutton will be remembered for a long time by those who saw it. Hutton took nearly twice as long as Bradman did over as many runs eight years previously, but the Australian's big innings came during a Test limited in duration whereas Hutton played his innings on an occasion when time did not matter.

Before this memorable incident, Hardstaff hit with judgment without departing from the policy of all his predecessors in avoiding risks. The whole of the batting seemed to be inspired by a desire to build up a stupendous total. Hardstaff reached three figures in three hours, ten minutes and a little later Hutton lifted a stroke towards cover and Hassett held the ball easily low down. So a phenomenal innings, lasting from half-past 11 on the Saturday until half-past two on the Tuesday – the longest ever played in first-class cricket – came to an end. Only A. C. MacLaren, who hit 424 for Lancashire v Somerset at Taunton in 1895, has made a higher individual score in England. In addition to 35 fours, Hutton hit 15 threes, 18 twos and 143 singles.

England's total had reached 770 for the loss of six wickets and some spirited hitting by Wood came as a refreshing contrast to the stern batting which had gone before. Another three-figure stand resulted, Wood adding 106 in an hour and a half with Hardstaff, and shortly after these batsmen were separated there occurred the tragic accident to Bradman, who when bowling caught his foot in a worn foot-hole, fell prone and was carried off the field by two of his colleagues. During the tea interval, England's innings, which was the longest on record and produced the highest total for any Test-match innings and the highest for any first-class match in England, was declared closed. It was said that O'Reilly, who bowled 85 overs, wore the skin off a finger in imparting spin to the ball.

England

L. Hutton c Hassett b O'Reilly	364	†A. Wood c and b Barnes ... 53
W. J. Edrich lbw b O'Reilly	12	H. Verity not out ... 8
M. Leyland run out	187	B 22, lb 19, w 1, nb 8 ... 50
'W. R. Hammond lbw b Fleetwood-Smith	59	
E. Paynter lbw b O'Reilly	0	1/29 (2) (7 wkts dec, 335.2 overs) 903
D. C. S. Compton b Waite	1	2/411 (3) 3/546 (4)
J. Hardstaff not out	169	4/547 (5) 5/555 (6) 6/770 (1) 7/876 (8)

K. Farnes and W. E. Bowes did not bat.

Waite 72–16–150–1; McCabe 38–8–85–0; O'Reilly 85–26–178–3; Fleetwood-Smith 87–11–298–1; Barnes 38–3–84–1; Hassett 13–2–52–0; Bradman 2.2–1–6–0.

Australia

W. A. Brown c Hammond b Leyland	69	– c Edrich b Fames	15
C. L. Badcock c Hardstaff b Bowes	0	– b Bowes	9
S. J. McCabe c Edrich b Farnes	14	– c Wood b Farnes	2
A. L. Hassett c Compton b Edrich	42	– lbw b Bowes	10
S. G. Barnes b Bowes	41	– lbw b Verity	33
†B. A. Barnett c Wood b Bowes	2	– b Farnes	46
M. G. Waite b Bowes	8	– c Edrich b Verity	0
W. J. O'Reilly c Wood b Bowes	0	– not out	7
L. O'B. Fleetwood-Smith not out	16	– c Leyland b Farnes	0
D. G. Bradman absent hurt		– absent hurt	
J. H. W. Fingleton absent hurt		– absent hurt	
B 4, lb 2, nb 3	9	B 1	1

1/0 (2) 2/19 (3) 3/70 (4)	(52.1 overs)	201	1/15 (2) 2/18 (3) (34.1 overs) 123
4/145 (5) 5/147 (6) 6/160 (7)			3/35 (4) 4/41 (1)
7/160 (8) 8/201 (1)			5/115 (5) 6/115 (7) 7/117 (6) 8/123 (9)

Farnes 13–2–54–1 Bowes 19–3–49–5; Edrich 10–2–55–1; Verity 5–1–15–0; Leyland 3.1–0–11–1; Hammond 2–0–8–0. *Second innings*—Farnes 12.1–1–63–4; Bowes 10–3–25–2; Leyland 5–0–19–0; Verity 7–3–15–2.

Umpires: F. Chester and F. I. Walden.

Close of play: first day, England 347-1 (Hutton 160, Leyland 156); second day, England 634-5 (Hutton 300, Hardstaff 40); third day, Australia 117-3 (Brown 29, Barnes 25).

SURREY V YORKSHIRE 1947

July 27, 29, 30, 1946. Yorkshire won by eight wickets.

In his first match at The Oval after the war, Hutton made 101 out of a Yorkshire first-innings total of 197 in a low-scoring Championship game won by the visitors.

The torrential storm of Friday saturated the ground, delaying the start, and showers kept the pitch soft until the final stage when, with threatening clouds, the players went to lunch though only seven runs were required. The ball often got up shoulder high; Hutton received a blow on the right hand just before completing a perfect hundred, and he mishit the next ball, a "jumper", into cover-point's hands. He and Sellers added 104 in a rare struggle for runs; the other nine Yorkshiremen making only 22; Hutton hit seven fours in his polished display. Fishlock also played a great innings, including 11 fours, mostly drives, in his best left-handed manner. Robinson, bowling round the wicket from the Pavilion End, shared largely in Yorkshire's honours. Gover kept up a great pace, and Bedser, dismissing Hutton with the first ball and Yardley with the last ball of his first over, provided the final sensation on Monday, when the crowd numbered 16,432. Spectators, admitted free on Tuesday, saw Barber and left-handed Turner win the match after batting two hours 40 minutes for 105 runs.

Surrey 114 (E. P. Robinson 8-76) **and** 194 (L. B. Fishlock 99; E. P. Robinson 5-88); **Yorkshire** 197 (L. Hutton 101, A. B. Sellers 58; A. R. Gover 7-66) **and** 113-2 (C. Turner 51*).

SURREY V YORKSHIRE 1952

July 14, 16, 17, 1951. Match drawn.

Perhaps inevitably, one of Hutton's crowning achievements towards the end of his career came at The Oval, when he became the 13th man to hit 100 first-class centuries.

This match was memorable for the performance of Hutton in completing his century of centuries. After Surrey had broken down when the pitch gave little help to bowlers, Hutton and Lowson took charge and at the end of the first day their unfinished stand had realised 112. Hutton then wanted 39 runs for his hundred and on Monday 15,000 people turned up. They were not disappointed and Hutton achieved his objective with a stroke worthy of the occasion – a superb drive off Wait sped past cover-point to the boundary. Altogether the opening partnership produced 197 and Hutton, who batted faultlessly for four hours 40 minutes, hit 12 fours. Wilson drove finely, his not-out 114 containing three sixes and ten fours. Surrey looked in a hopeless position when they batted again 275 behind, but Yorkshire dropped vital catches and finally found themselves wanting 43 in 20 minutes. In a hectic scramble for runs, they paid the penalty for hitting recklessly at every ball, and although they raced to and from the pavilion gate the task was beyond them.

Surrey 156 and 317 (L. B. Fishlock 89; E. Leadbeater 4-112);
Yorkshire 431-3 dec (L. Hutton 151, F. A. Lowson 84, J. V. Wilson 114*) **and 30-6.**

ENGLAND V SOUTH AFRICA, FIFTH TEST
Norman Preston, 1952

August 16, 17, 18, 1951. England won by four wickets.

Later that summer, a short-but-sweet Test against South Africa contained the unusual spectacle of Hutton dismissed for obstructing the field.

This was the best match of the whole five. Full of surprises throughout the three days, it was fought on a pitch that provided a fair chance for both batsman and bowler. For once there was no batting paradise to fetter the bowlers, Compton's 73 was the highest individual score and South Africa's 202 the best total. Actually 36 wickets fell for 714 runs, an average of less than 20 a wicket, and it was a relief that no batting or bowling records were broken. The only thing new to Test cricket was the dismissal of Hutton for obstructing the field, a decision that had been given only four times previously in first-class cricket.

From England's point of view, the hero was Laker, the Surrey off-break bowler. He took ten wickets in the match for 119. Unafraid to pitch the ball well up to the batsmen, he attacked them persistently. Bowling round the wicket, he gave the ball plenty of air and his finger-spin whipped off the pitch across the bat towards his leg-trap of Hutton, Brown and Tattersall...

Athol Rowan drove and pulled cleanly, and he and his brother [Eric] scored 96 of South Africa's 202. Actually the last nine South African wickets fell in two hours.

Sixty-five minutes remained for play on this first day... Hutton and May looked set for a long stand when, in the last over, Hutton, playing back, fell lbw at 51. This was a great achievement for South Africa and the position became evenly balanced again...

When South Africa, who led by eight runs, batted [again]... Laker and Brown carried England to victory on Saturday, when the seven remaining South African wickets fell in two hours before lunch for 86. Laker took four for 29 and Bedser, by claiming two, raised his number of victims in 12 Tests since the previous December to 62, and equalled his feat of 30 wickets in the winter series against Australia.

The pitch was less difficult than on the first two days, for it was drier and the ball turned more slowly. England, wanting 163, began their task after lunch, and the two Yorkshiremen, Hutton and Lowson, batted with such ease and confidence that an easy victory seemed certain.

In 50 minutes they took the score to 53, and then came the Hutton sensation and calamity. A ball from Athol Rowan lifted abruptly and struck Hutton on the glove. It ran up his arm and, when he looked round, it appeared to him, as he afterwards explained, to be falling on to his wicket. In that split second Hutton never thought about the wicketkeeper making a catch. He flicked at the ball with his bat and missed it, but it fell neither on to his stumps nor into Endean's gloves. The wicketkeeper had been obstructed and the South Africans rightly appealed. Just as rightly, Dai Davies signalled Hutton out. Hutton did not wilfully obstruct the wicketkeeper, but he wilfully waved his bat, an action which prevented the wicketkeeper from getting to the ball. From his point of view it was a most unsatisfactory ending to his 100th innings in Test cricket...

Appropriately Laker made the winning hit by turning Rowan to long leg for three... It was England's first win at The Oval since they beat Australia in 1938.

South Africa 202 (E. A. B. Rowan 55; J. C. Laker 4-64) **and 154** (J. C. Laker 6-55); **England 194** (D. C. S. Compton 73; M. G. Melle 4-9) **and 164-6.**

ENGLAND V AUSTRALIA, FIFTH TEST   Norman Preston, 1954

August 15, 17, 18, 19, 1953. England won by eight wickets.

Huge national celebrations were triggered when Hutton led England to victory over Australia at The Oval in 1953, the year of Queen Elizabeth's Coronation. England had not held the Ashes since the Bodyline tour of 1932-33, losing five of the six series since. Hutton's contribution with the bat was key, top-scoring with 82 in the first innings.

England won by eight wickets and so won the Ashes for the first time since 1932-33. It was a most welcome victory in Coronation year and a triumph for Len Hutton, the first modern professional to be entrusted with the captaincy of England. Moreover, he led his team to success on the ground on which he made the world record Test score of 364 in 1938 – the last previous occasion England beat Australia in this country...

The absence of a genuine spin bowler proved a severe handicap to Australia. The issue was virtually decided on the third afternoon when Australia, 31 behind on the first innings, lost half their side to Laker and Lock for 61...

As in 1926, stories of long all-night queues frightened away many would-be spectators on the first day when the ground was comfortable with 26,300 people present. The news that Hassett had again won the toss was received gloomily by most England supporters, but by mid-afternoon, when seven Australian wickets were down for 160, pessimism changed to optimism...

Trueman, taking one of the longest runs known in cricket, covered a distance of at least 25 yards in 15 long strides and required 45 minutes to complete his first spell of five overs which cost 12 runs... Towards the end of [the first] hour Bedser broke the opening stand in his eighth over when his swerve deceived Morris, who, offering no stroke, turned his back and was leg-before... This success gave England timely encouragement, and within ten minutes Bailey claimed the dangerous Miller...

Now came Lindwall, and with only three wickets to fall he launched a hot attack, ably assisted by the left-handed Davidson. For an hour and 50 minutes Lindwall indulged in a magnificent display of clean hitting. His off- and cover-drives were of the highest class. The new ball at 210 did not halt him and... he was last out to the fourth catch of the innings by Evans. By adding 157 the last five wickets more than doubled the score, and in the circumstances no one could deny that Australia had made an excellent recovery...

Before bad light stopped the struggle at 6.17pm there was time for Lindwall and Miller each to send down one over, and England might well have lost Hutton in Lindwall's tearaway effort. The fourth and fifth balls were bouncers. The fifth flew off the handle of Hutton's bat and five slips surged forward for the catch which unexpectedly never arrived. The ball dropped short because it lost its pace in transit through striking Hutton's cap, which it removed. The cap just missed the stumps or Hutton might have been out hit wicket.

If Saturday belonged to England, Monday went to Australia, for the close of play found England 235 for seven – 40 behind with only three wickets left. The gates were closed long before play was resumed at 11.30am and thousands failed to gain admission. Upon England's batting this day everyone felt that the destination of the Ashes depended...

For a time England prospered. An early setback occurred when Edrich, having batted splendidly, left at 37, but there followed a grand partnership of 100 between Hutton and May, who were together two hours 20 minutes. When that was broken England went through a very bad time, chiefly because of the uncertainty of Compton.

Previously Hutton had been master of the situation, but when joined by Compton he added only six in the next half hour before being bowled by a well-pitched-up ball from Johnston which moved from leg and hit the middle stump. Third out at 154, Hutton made his 82 in three hours 40 minutes and hit eight fours. The departure of Hutton was a serious setback for England...

The way England pulled the game round on the third day was scarcely believable... To Hutton must be given the credit for bringing about Australia's subsequent collapse. He realised by the way Morris slammed Bedser past cover and Trueman to leg that the batsmen would thrive on pace bowling on this somewhat lifeless pitch for which Hassett had ordered the heavy roller. Hutton allowed Trueman only two overs and Bedser three before at 19 he introduced the Surrey spinners, Laker (right-arm off-breaks) and Lock (left-arm slow). That was the move that brought home the Ashes. The Australian batsmen had not settled down before they were confronted by spin, and their vulnerability to the turning ball as well as their fear of it led to their undoing. Suddenly a day which began so gloomily for England swung completely Hutton's way.

Laker started the Australian procession. Bowling round the wicket, he twice beat Hassett, and then with the last ball of his first over he got the Australian captain leg-before as he retreated into his wicket. One hour later half the Australia team were back in the pavilion for 61.

In one astonishing spell of 14 minutes, four wickets fell while only two runs were scored. Lock went over the wicket to the left-handed batsmen, but Hole threatened danger with free hitting at the expense of Laker. Again Hutton countered. He placed a deep extra cover as well as a long-on, and Laker with his very next ball got Hole lbw.

Lock never erred in length or direction from the Pavilion End, and as Harvey shaped to drive he knocked back his off stump. In the next over Trueman at short square leg hugged a sharp catch from Miller, and then Morris, playing back and trying to force Lock away, was leg-before. So on this gloriously sunny afternoon Australia found themselves confronted with impending defeat...

England, having dismissed Australia in two hours 45 minutes for 162, needed 132 to win with ample time at their disposal. They owed much to Lock. The pitch gave him little help, yet such was his finger-spin allied to skilful flighting and change of pace that he took five wickets for 45...

Fifty minutes remained on Tuesday when Hutton and Edrich began England's final task. Both produced some excellent strokes, but at 24 Hutton brought about his own dismissal. He hit Miller firmly to square leg and took the obvious single, but when De Courcy fumbled he tried to steal a second run and failed to get home. Hutton looked terribly disappointed as he walked slowly back to the pavilion. May stayed with Edrich for the last quarter of an hour and England finished at 38 for one wicket.

They now needed 94, and only rain and a sticky pitch were likely to deprive them of the victory so near their grasp. How those Australians fought to hold the Ashes! Johnston bowled tantalising slows from the Vauxhall End without relief and little help from the slightly worn pitch from 11.30am till 2.45pm...

At first Edrich and May made very slow progress... Only rarely did Lindwall risk a bumper; runs were too precious to be given away. Slowly the score crept to 88, and then Miller, having dispensed with his slips – five men were on the leg side for his off-spin – got May caught at short fine leg...

Earlier Edrich magnificently hooked two successive bumpers from Lindwall. Now he was joined by his Middlesex colleague, Compton, and they took England to victory. Compton made the winning hit at seven minutes to three when he swept Morris to the boundary.

At once the crowd swarmed across the ground while Edrich... fought his way to the pavilion with Compton and the Australian team. In a memorable scene both captains addressed the crowd, stressing the excellent spirit in which all the matches had been contested both on and off the field.

Australia 275 (A. L. Hassett 53, R. R. Lindwall 62; F. S. Trueman 4-86) and 162 (J. C. Laker 4-75, G. A. R. Lock 5-45); England 306 (L. Hutton 82, T. E. Bailey 64; R. R. Lindwall 4-70) and 132-2 (W. J. Edrich 55*).

Chapter 9
The Oval in Wartime

Throughout both World Wars, a new edition of Wisden continued to appear every year. Inevitably, without a great deal of cricket to write about, the main feature would be a long obituaries section telling stories of the many well-known cricketers who had lost their lives.

The Great War abruptly ended the 1914 season, which brought Surrey their seventh County Championship. Among the club's losses was Alan Marshal, an Australian batsman who played 98 first-class matches for the county between 1907 and 1910 and was named as a Cricketer of the Year in 1909. Marshal died six years later after contracting a fever in Gallipoli, where he was stationed with fellow Australian troops.

A brief mention of The Oval in the 1916 edition indicates that cricket was still played at the ground during the war, though Wisden did not provide reports of the matches, which "served a good purpose in helping to keep cricket alive during the war, but they were of no importance". These wartime editions were, of necessity, philosophical and crestfallen in tone.

The 1919 edition strikes a more positive note, making mention of four games the Surrey club played against leading public schools and reporting on the only match of first-class standard – though not officially recognised *as such – played at The Oval during the war. Well over 9,000 spectators turned up to watch an England XI including Hobbs, Woolley, Warner and Fender play a one-day match against a Dominions XI in August 1918. The event raised £1,000 for the Surrey branch of the Red Cross.*

The Oval was requisitioned during the Second World War, first as a searchlight site to spot Luftwaffe bombers at the time of the Blitz and then as a Prisoner of War camp (though it was never used). Parts of the ground were badly damaged by German airstrikes, and staging matches was impossible. However, Surrey arranged matches on Saturdays throughout the county in 1940, playing against clubs such as Esher, Richmond, Reigate Priory and Guildford. The 1941 Almanack also notes a testimonial held for A. W. 'Bosser' Martin, who had served as groundsman at The Oval for 51 years.

The 1943 edition mourns the death of Andy Ducat, one of Surrey's finest batsmen and a former Cricketer of the Year, who suffered a heart attack while batting for the Surrey Home Guard at Lord's. In his "Notes on the Season", R. C. Robertson-Glasgow wrote of Ducat: "His character was gentle and kind, but strong and clear. Nothing showy, insincere, or envious came near his nature. As an athlete, in his prime, he looked and was magnificent."

The end of the war enabled The Oval to stage a match against 'Old England' to celebrate the centenary of both Surrey and the ground in 1946 – albeit a year later than scheduled. The occasion attracted a large crowd, and among their number was King George, the club's patron. Given the damage inflicted on the ground over the previous six years, it was a remarkable achievement to put on such a high-profile event – not to mention host a full season of cricket.

NOTES BY THE EDITOR   Sydney Pardon, 1915

Turning to the past season, it was pleasant to find Surrey winning the Championship, a distinction that had not fallen to them since 1899. Some people thought that when, in deference to public opinion – W. G. Grace himself was the chief spokesman – Surrey cancelled their last two matches, the Championship would have to remain in abeyance for the year, but this view received no countenance from MCC. It would have been iniquitous if Surrey had been robbed of the position they had so fairly won. When, at Surrey's own request, the question was brought before the MCC committee, the matter was promptly settled, Middlesex disclaiming any notion of objecting. Surrey had a fine eleven, but to make their side complete they needed a little more bowling. The enforced transfer to Lord's of the return matches with Kent and Yorkshire when, in the first days of the War, the military authorities took possession of The Oval, involved serious disadvantages. Indeed, the Kent match, as a benefit to Hobbs, was such a failure that the Surrey committee have decided not to treat it as a benefit. They will give Hobbs another match as soon as circumstances permit, his subscription list in the meantime remaining open. This generous action on Surrey's part – not hitherto made known – will please everyone. Hobbs is not only the best bat in England at the present time, but also the most attractive and popular.

SURREY 1914–1918

From 1915: "For the first time since 1899 Surrey came out with the best record among the counties and so won the [1914] Championship. A brilliant season had a strange ending. As the military authorities required for about three weeks in August the use of Kennington Oval, the return match with Kent for Hobbs's benefit and the return with Yorkshire on the following days were, by permission of MCC, transferred to Lord's, and on August 31, public feeling against the continuance of first-class cricket during the War having been worked up to rather a high pitch, the Surrey committee at a special meeting decided unanimously to cancel the two remaining fixtures – with Sussex at Brighton, and Leicestershire at The Oval. It was in some ways a pity that this drastic step should have been found necessary, but in acting as they did the Surrey committee took a wise course."

    From 1917: "A good deal of cricket, largely military, was at The Oval during the [1916] summer, but no matches of importance were undertaken. The Surrey Club played three matches against schools."

From 1918: "Though The Oval was constantly used during the [1917] summer for school and military cricket, the Surrey Club only arranged for themselves a programme of three matches."

From 1919: "Though The Oval was constantly in use during the [1918] season, the Surrey Club's own activities were limited to four games with public schools, one of these fixtures having to be abandoned owing to rain."

ENGLAND XI v DOMINIONS XI   1919

August 5, 1918. Match drawn.

The game between England and a Dominions XI in August 1918 was the first significant match at The Oval in four years. A 9,000-strong crowd welcomed the sight of cricket under the gasholders, and Surrey's Percy Fender caught the mood with "an innings worthy of Jessop at his best".

This was the first time since the season of 1914 – abruptly cut short by the war – that Kennington Oval was the scene of a really interesting match, a third meeting between England and the Dominions being arranged for the August Bank Holiday on behalf of the Surrey branch of the Red Cross. Great success rewarded the experiment – 9,265 people paying their shillings for admission at the gates, and the game raising a profit of £1,000. Had the weather been kinder there would have been a still bigger crowd. The morning was very unpromising, and so much rain fell that before lunch play was in progress for barely an hour. During the afternoon the pavilion was a very pleasant place. Familiar faces were to be seen everywhere, and the delight felt at watching a good match on the old ground could not be disguised. The game had to be left drawn, but towards the end of the day the cricket was so full of incident as to work the crowd up to a high pitch of excitement. Winning the toss, the Dominions stayed in until nearly five o'clock, declaring their innings closed with nine men out for 194. H. W. Taylor, South Africa's star batsman at the present time – took the chief honours. In first and out fourth, he scored 63 of the 113 runs obtained during his stay. He was inclined to lift the ball rather dangerously, and when he had made 36 he ought to have been caught and bowled by Woolley, but for the most part he played very well, showing great resource. When their seventh wicket fell at 127 it did not seem likely that the Dominions would profit much from having had first innings, but Mellé and Docker, by very lively hitting, put on 49 runs for the ninth wicket, Mellé revealing a driving power of which no one had suspected him. Woolley bowled admirably, and Hardinge, though he met with no success, kept a fine length. England on going in had nothing to hope for but a draw, the ground being too slow to make the task of getting 195 in two hours and 20 minutes at all practicable. Still there was plenty of time to be beaten, and when the sixth wicket went down at 75, defeat seemed almost certain. At this point – 20 minutes to seven – Fender joined Douglas and played an innings worthy of Jessop at his best. He went for the bowling in uncompromising fashion, driving and pulling with equal power. One drive off Docker's fast bowling pitched it clean over the ring for six. When he had made 12 he gave a palpable chance, deep on the on side, but this was the only real blemish in an astonishing display. In rather less than three-quarters of an hour he scored 70 runs out of 87, being bowled at last by a slow full pitch. Needless to say he had a great reception at the pavilion. Stumps were drawn at half-past seven, England being 28 runs behind with two wickets to fall. While Fender was hitting Douglas kept up his end with great coolness and restraint.

Dominions 194-9 dec (H. W. Taylor 63; F. E. Woolley 6-68);
England XI 166-8 (P. G. H. Fender 70)

Surrey 1940–1947

From 1941: "The Oval was never available for matches [in 1940], and damage to the pavilion and other buildings will necessitate a large sum of money in repairs."

From 1942: "In December [1941] the Surrey Committee stated that… it was quite clear that very heavy expenditure would have to be faced before cricket could be resumed at The Oval, which had suffered severely from enemy bombers."

From 1944: "In an air raid in November 1940 the front of the tavern was badly hit, also the East Mound, and another bomb on the terrace in front of the long room brought down part of the balcony and roof, besides damaging doors and windows. The wall surrounding the ground suffered severely when a bomb fell in Harleyford Road, but this had been repaired to a certain extent. In May 1941 The Oval was bombed again, both the tavern and pavilion being knocked about. The committee hoped the War Damage Claims would cover the bulk of the repairs, but they estimated that the club would have to find a large amount. The turf in the centre of the ground remained in good order, but large areas of the outfield would require considerable attention. Experts who visited The Oval reckoned it would take 12 months to get it ready for cricket. Consequently Surrey may find themselves still temporarily homeless when the war ends."

From 1945: "A sum of £2,001 was transferred [in 1944] to the post-war repairs and redecoration fund, to which £2,659 was allocated the previous year. These large sums of money were not considered nearly adequate to put Kennington Oval in proper condition. The figure may go beyond £10,000. For many months the ground had been turned into a Prisoner of War cage and some hundred concrete posts were sunk into the turf besides concrete floors of huts."

From 1946: "Surrey celebrated the completion of 100 years at The Oval on August 21 [1945], but owing to the war the club could not fulfil the desire to play a match there on that date. Only four months previously the Prisoner of War camp, that was never used, was dismantled, but the pavilion and ground remained in a chaotic condition. Surrey marked the day by launching an appeal for £100,000 to carry out a big plan of reconstruction, the Duchy of Cornwall, their landlords, having agreed to extend the lease until 1984... During the year Surrey turned down another approach from Greyhound syndicates to establish a course at The Oval. This action supported the view of the Duchy of Cornwall, who, however, expressed the wish that the ground should be used for other recreations besides cricket and that it should not be closed for half the year."

From 1947: "Probably Surrey of all the counties resumed competitive cricket [in 1946] under the most severe handicaps. The

Oval suffered heavy damage during the six years of war; the playing area, apart from the pitch "table", required complete overhaul, and the pavilion was knocked about by bombing. Thanks to the wonderful efforts of the groundstaff a remarkable recovery was effected... The restoration fund received very good support, and nothing was more gratifying than the message from the South African Cricket Association that they would devote half their share of the net gate against Surrey during the 1947 tour as a donation to The Oval Centenary Appeal Fund."

SURREY V OLD ENGLAND 1947

May 23, 1946. Match drawn.

In May 1946 a match between Surrey and 'Old England' was played in the presence of King George VI to mark the centenary of The Oval and Surrey CCC, having been delayed a year because of the war.

The King and some 15,000 enthusiasts attended the one-day match arranged to celebrate the centenary of the Surrey County Cricket Club and of Kennington Oval as a cricket ground. Surrey faced a side comprised of ten old England players and Brooks, former Surrey wicketkeeper, the one member of the eleven without the honour of Test-match experience. Altogether the caps gained by the ten players and the umpires, Hobbs and Strudwick, numbered 370.

On one of the finest days of the summer, the cricket proved full of interest. Runs always came fast and there were three stands of over 100. Gregory and Squires put on 111 for Surrey; Woolley and Hendren hit up 102, and Hendren and Jardine 108 for Old England in a splendid effort to hit off the runs after Bennett, the new Surrey captain, declared.

Fender was prominent in the field, making a neat catch and taking two wickets with successive balls. The most exhilarating cricket came after the fall of Sandham and Sutcliffe for two runs. Woolley, at the age of 59, drove with the same ease that delighted crowds before and after the 1914–18 war. Hendren showed all his old cheery forcing play until just before time he lifted a catch off Surrey's most famous recruit, Alec Bedser, already marked for England honours.

To stay two and three-quarter hours and hit eight fours at the age of 57 was a great feat by Hendren. Douglas Jardine, wearing his Oxford Harlequin cap, was as polished as ever in academic skill.

The King, Patron of Surrey, accompanied by officials of the club, went on the ground, where all concerned in the game were introduced to him with the happiest of greetings. The band of the East Surrey Regiment was in attendance, and after the game a dance in the Pavilion Long Room completed the festive occasion.

In a letter to *The Times*, Mr P. G. H. Fender, captain of Old England, wrote: "May I express to the thousands of enthusiasts who gave Old England such a wonderful reception at The Oval the sincere heartfelt thanks of all those who were privileged to play in that side. There are many others who should have played, and we realise that we were the lucky ones, and that the tribute was to the game rather than to a few individuals.

"More than once while we were fielding a thought came to my mind that the warmth of the welcome, the size and the enthusiasm of the great crowd, and, above all, the presence of His Majesty, seemed to convey a message to the younger generation of cricketers, not only in this country, but all over the world. A message telling them that where cricket is concerned, public memory, of the old adage, is not short: a message to inspire all young cricketers, and urge them to achievements in the game greater even than their wilder dreams conjured up.

"Such a welcome as was given to Old England, collectively and individually, must surely be a public assurance that those who can carve for themselves a little niche in the greatest of games can always be sure of a warm place in the hearts of all lovers of cricket."

Surrey 248-6 dec (R. J. Gregory 62, H. S. Squires 68);
Old England XI 232-5 (F. E. Woolley 62, E. H. Hendren 94, D. R. Jardine 54).

Chapter 10

Surrey's Magnificent Seven

T he Oval was home to the most extraordinary achievement in English domestic cricket: Surrey's seven consecutive County Championship titles from 1952 to 1958.

This was a time when the public yearned for heroes to banish the horrors of the Second World War which were still fresh in people's minds. Surrey had a truckload of them, including Peter May, Alec Bedser, Peter Loader, Tony Lock and Jim Laker, with talented young players such as Ken Barrington and Micky Stewart coming into the team. Throughout the decade thousands would flock to Kennington to watch Surrey, led first by Stuart Surridge and then by May, produce a string of results which rate among the best in the history of British sport.

There may have been a number of exceptional individuals, but the team ethos was the key to success. Many of Surrey's big names were frequently on duty with England – who also enjoyed a purple patch in the 1950s – and so men such as Arthur McIntyre, Tom Clark, Eric Bedser (Alec's twin brother), Bernie Constable and David Fletcher all had vital roles to play. As many as 11 members of the side were made Cricketers of the Year between 1947 and 1966.

Wisden singled out three Surrey players for special praise during the miraculous seven-year run. The 1953 edition featured a paean to Alec

Bedser – "a giant among bowlers" – and in 1957 Neville Cardus wrote on "Laker's wonderful year", while former England and Surrey captain Douglas Jardine paid tribute to the man who started it all in "Stuart Surridge: Surrey's inspiration".

The selections in this chapter include a match from each title-winning year, chosen to highlight the contributions from a wide range of players, and an extract summarising each season. It also features the report of Laker's ten-wicket haul for Surrey against the Australians in 1956, a feat he would emulate in the Old Trafford Test later that summer.

Notes by the Editor   Norman Preston, 1953

In 1950 Surrey shared the Championship with Lancashire under the captaincy of Michael Barton, and two years later they won their first outright title since 1914. It was the first of Stuart Surridge's five seasons in charge and his impact was instant.

After an interval of 38 years Surrey finished champions [in 1952] and no one could challenge their right to the title. In W. S. Surridge, their new captain, they possessed an exuberant personality who by his own fine example in the field extracted the very best from all his men... Their enterprise was fully rewarded, as they equalled the feat of the brilliant Yorkshire pre-war team that gained 20 Championship victories in 28 matches in 1938 and 1939... It was significant that at the Surrey celebration dinner in December, Surridge thanked H. Lock, the groundsman, for providing pitches which gave the bowler a fair chance.

Surrey v Somerset   1953

July 2, 3, 4, 1952. Surrey won by an innings and 180 runs.

Of all the players to make contributions to the great Surrey era, Bernie Constable is among the least known. He made his highest score against Somerset in the season which kick-started Surrey's run of titles.

Fortunate to gain first innings, Surrey batted under favourable conditions before rain left the pitch in a treacherous state. The match was memorable for a superb display by Constable, whose not-out 205 was the best of his career and the highest of the season for Surrey. His square-cuts and drives were particularly fine, but he scored with equal facility all round the wicket, hitting two sixes and 25 fours, and altogether batted no more than four hours 50 minutes. Parker, too, played splendidly in a stand of 186, and Pratt, a left-hander, appearing in his first Championship match, stayed 50 minutes while 80 runs were added. Next day, when only one hour's play was possible, Somerset lost three men for 47, but Surrey were home by 3.30 on Friday with two hours 40 minutes to spare. Making the most of a soft pitch, they captured their 17 wickets in three hours ten minutes. A. V. Bedser, Lock and Laker were in their element, and as usual they were supported by really brilliant fielding, although in their eagerness Surrey missed some chances. Only once in the two Somerset innings did a bowler hit the stumps and altogether 18 catches were held.

Surrey 384-5 dec (B. Constable 205*, J. F. Parker 74);
Somerset 89 (A. V. Bedser 6-46) and 115 (J. C. Laker 5-48).

SURREY IN 1953   1954

Much like Adam Hollioake's team at the end of the century, the Surrey sides of the 1950s had great strength in depth which softened the blow of losing players to England. Surrey used 19 players in 1953, including a 22-year-old Ken Barrington in his debut season. Six bowlers took 44 wickets or more – four of them at an average of less than 17.

In carrying off the Championship for the second year in succession, Surrey achieved the distinction their superiority over all other counties merited... Possibly the main difference between Surrey and their chief rivals was the number of capable players they had in reserve. The club reaped the reward of their foresight of years ago in maintaining an adequate groundstaff at The Oval under the able coaching of Andrew Sandham. Also Surrey had the honour of giving four men to England when the Ashes were wrested from Australia in the final Test at The Oval... Undoubtedly the bowling was again the main strength and it was brilliantly supported by the close fielders – Surridge, Lock, May and Laker, as well as McIntyre, the wicketkeeper, and Constable at cover. While the three England men, A. V. Bedser, Lock and Laker, formed the main part of the attack, five others, Loader, McMahon, Surridge, Clark and E. A. Bedser, helped to maintain the high standard.

SURREY V WARWICKSHIRE 1954

May 16, 1953. Surrey won by an innings and 49 runs.

Surrey's 1953 campaign began with an extraordinary match which was completed in a day.

Members rose as one when the triumphant Surrey team walked from the field having begun their Championship programme with victory in a day. The last and only time that a first-class match had been completed in one day at The Oval was in 1857. Special applause was accorded to A. Bedser, who took 12 wickets for 35 runs, and Laker, who performed the hat-trick. Bedser bowled magnificently when play commenced at noon. Unable to obtain a proper foothold on the wet turf, he attacked the leg stump at below normal pace and, helped by fine catches, he equalled his previous best analysis of eight for 18. Surrey also found the pitch treacherous, but, chiefly through a sound innings by Constable, they took the lead with only two wickets down. The score then went from 50 for two to 81 for seven, and only the aggressiveness of Surridge, who hit three sixes in four balls from Hollies, Laker and Lock enabled them to gain a substantial lead. Lock became the second-highest scorer before a blow above the right eye led to a visit to hospital and his retirement from the game. Laker was called into the attack for the first time when Warwickshire batted again and he began the final rout by achieving the first hat-trick of the season. Warwickshire, batting for ten minutes of the extra half-hour, were all out in 70 minutes, five minutes less than their first innings. No Warwickshire batsman was bowled during a day in which 29 wickets fell for 243 runs – a fact that emphasised Surrey's excellent fielding.

Warwickshire

F. C. Gardner c Laker b A. V. Bedser	7	–	c Laker b A. V. Bedser	7
T. W. Cartwright lbw b A. V. Bedser	0	–	lbw b Laker	9
D. D. Taylor c Fletcher b A. V. Bedser	0	–	lbw b A. V. Bedser	20
†R. T. Spooner c Whittaker b A. V. Bedser	16	–	c and b Laker	0
*H. E. Dollery c Lock b A. V. Bedser	8	–	c Surridge b Laker	0
R. E. Hitchcock c Whittaker b Lock	3	–	c A. V. Bedser b Laker	0
A. Townsend c McIntyre b Lock	7	–	run out	0
R. T. Weeks not out	0	–	c Surridge b A. V. Bedser	0
C. W. C. Grove c Fletcher b A. V. Bedser	3	–	c Constable b Laker	10
K. R. Dollery c Brazier b A. V. Bedser	0	–	not out	0
W. E. Hollies c Laker b A. V. Bedser	0	–	c sub b A. V. Bedser	0
Lb 1	1		B 2, lb 3, nb 1	6

1/3 2/3 3/8 4/27 5/30   (26.5 overs)   45   1/20 2/22 3/26   (26.4 overs)   52
6/36 7/42 8/45 9/45 10/45   4/26 5/26 6/32
                                          7/32 8/49 9/52 10/52

A. V. Bedser 13.5–4–18–8; Surridge 6–1–17–0; Lock 7–3–9–2. *Second innings*—A. V. Bedser 13.4–7–17–4; Laker 13–6–29–5.

Surrey

D. G. W. Fletcher c Townsend b Weeks	13	*W. S. Surridge b Grove	19	
E. A. Bedser b K. R. Dollery	5	A. V. Bedser not out	5	
B. Constable c Grove b K. R. Dollery	37	G. A. R. Lock retired hurt	27	
T. H. Clark c K. R. Dollery b Hollies	2			
A. F. Brazier c Townsend b Hollies	6	Lb 4, nb 1	5	
G. J. Whittaker b K. R. Dollery	0	1/5 2/27 3/50 4/61 (39.1 overs) 146		
†A. J. W. McIntyre c and b K. R. Dollery	9	5/65 6/77 7/81 8/108 9/119		
J. C. Laker c H. E. Dollery b Hollies	18			

Lock retired hurt at 146-9.

Grove 10.1–3–29–1; K. R. Dollery 11–4–40–4; Weeks 8–1–24–1; Hollies 10–4–48–3.

Umpires: E. Cooke and L. H. Gray.

TONY LOCK – CRICKETER OF THE YEAR   Norman Preston, 1954

Tony Lock is one of the greatest left-arm spinners the game has seen. His performances at The Oval were so exceptional that he has a stand named after him at the ground. Operating in partnership with Jim Laker for club and country, Lock took 100 first-class wickets at 15.90 in 1953 as Surrey retained their title and England regained the Ashes at last.

The success of Surrey in reaching the top of the Championship three times in the last four seasons and the return of the Ashes to England have been due in no small way to the tenacious left-arm slow bowling of Graham Anthony Richard Lock...

He considers that, although he took eight wickets for 26 and five for 43 in Surrey's final match [in 1953] against Hampshire on a drying pitch at Bournemouth, his finest performance with the ball was at the beginning of June, the day after he had been chosen to make his first appearance for England against Australia at Trent Bridge. On an almost perfect Oval pitch, in the presence of F. R. Brown, chairman of England's Test selectors, Northamptonshire were dismissed for 160 and Lock's analysis was 31.2 overs, 17 maidens, 55 runs, six wickets...

While the leg-break is Lock's main weapon, he can introduce the top-spinner at will, and he also bowls the ball that goes with the arm into the batsman from the off. That brings many wickets, for there is no perceptible change of action and the victim plays for the non-existent turn the other way. He is also a master at varying flight and pace.

NOTES BY THE EDITOR   Norman Preston, 1955

Surrey were made to work harder for the third title in 1954, relying on a late surge to deny Yorkshire. It was one of the wettest summers in memory, but such was Surrey's bowling strength that they needed little time to dismantle their opponents.

By a desperate effort in the last month, Surrey overtook their rivals and won the County Championship for the third successive season. On July 27 [1954], they were eighth in the table, 46 points behind Yorkshire who had played two more matches. Then Surrey proceeded to win nine of ten matches – five in two days – the other yielding four points from a draw with Middlesex at The Oval. Superb bowling and fielding again gained Surrey success. The four England bowlers, Bedser, Laker, Lock and Loader, each took 100 wickets... The bowling of Laker and Lock during the last nine weeks was almost astonishing: Laker took 44 wickets, average 9.06 and Lock 43, average 8.83.

SURREY V WORCESTERSHIRE   1955

August 25, 26, 1954. Surrey won by an innings and 27 runs.

Surrey secured the 1954 Championship by brushing aside Worcestershire before lunch on the second day. Lock and Laker were unplayable on a drying pitch and, with bad weather around, Stuart Surridge was confident enough to declare at 92 for three on the first day.

Surrey won by an innings and 27 runs by half-past 12 on the second day, thus making sure of their third successive Championship. They won in little over five hours of cricket. Play began at two o'clock on Wednesday. In 100 minutes Worcestershire, sent in on a rain-affected pitch, were dismissed for the lowest score in first-class cricket since 1947. Against Laker and Lock, their last seven wickets fell for five runs. Surridge declared with an hour remaining and a lead of 67. His bowlers took two wickets for 13 overnight and next day they spent only an hour finishing the game. The aggregate of 157 runs was the smallest ever recorded in any completed Championship match. Lock's figures were remarkable.

Worcestershire 25 (G. A. R. Lock 5-2) and 40 (J. C. Laker 4-25); **Surrey 92-3 dec.**

THE COUNTY CHAMPIONSHIP IN 1955   1956

Alec Bedser, Tony Lock and Jim Laker took 368 Championship wickets between them in 1955 as Surrey saw off another Yorkshire challenge.

In winning the Championship outright for the fourth year in succession, Surrey equalled the records of Nottinghamshire and Yorkshire... Surrey took advantage of the weather to set up a new record for the number of points in the Championship table since the system of awarding 12 points for a win and four for a lead on first innings was introduced in 1938. The previous best was the 260 obtained by Yorkshire in 1939... Last season Surrey obtained 284 points, winning 23 games and leading on first innings in two of the five matches they lost. Not a single Championship match in which Surrey took part ended in a draw.

Surrey v Middlesex   1956
August 6, 8, 9, 1955. Surrey won by 39 runs.

In one of Tony Lock's finest games at The Oval, Surrey beat Middlesex on their way to a fourth consecutive Championship title.

After they had won the toss for only the fourth time in 21 Championship matches, Surrey lost four wickets for six runs against some admirable bowling by Warr and Moss, who exploited a green pitch and heavy atmosphere. Surrey fought back and a sixth-wicket stand of 92 by Barrington (he batted splendidly for three and a quarter hours) and Swetman gave them a sporting chance on a pitch that turned in favour of the spin bowlers on the second day. Lock revelled in the conditions, taking 13 wickets for the second successive match, but Dewes proved to be in his best form and he carried his bat for 101 in an innings lasting four hours. His leg-hitting and strong driving brought him most of his nine fours. Then Stewart showed the same determination for Surrey, who left Middlesex to make 166. Whereas Laker, troubled through his spinning finger becoming sore, accomplished little, Lock, supported by excellent fielding, again thwarted Middlesex, the turning point coming when he held a fierce return from Dewes, who was third out at 64.

Surrey 171 (K. F. Barrington 73) **and 193** (M. J. Stewart 60; J. A. Young 5-68);
Middlesex 203 (J. G. Dewes 101*; G. A. R. Lock 6-58) **and 122** (G. A. R. Lock 7-24).

Surrey in 1956   1957

Surrey's fifth title in a row was their last under Stuart Surridge, who retired at the end of the 1956 season to concentrate on his bat-making business. Once again the bowlers led the way, with Jim Laker enjoying the summer of his life.

Surrey, enthusiastically led by Stuart Surridge, and possessing an attack of international class in the Bedser twins, Loader, Laker and Lock, carried off the Championship for the fifth consecutive year, an achievement without parallel. Moreover, they accomplished another feat, and one which had not been performed for 44 years, when in the middle of May they defeated the Australians at The Oval by ten wickets... With the turf at The Oval giving much more help in recent years to bowlers... Surrey again thrived on a minimum quantity of runs. In all their 36 first-class matches, they reached 300 only six times.

SURREY V AUSTRALIANS 1957

May 16, 17, 18, 1956. Surrey won by ten wickets.

As if to underline their total mastery, Surrey thrashed the touring Australians in 1956, with Jim Laker taking all ten wickets in the second innings – a precursor to the 19 he famously took at Manchester just over two months later.

Surrey won by ten wickets, so becoming the first county for 44 years to triumph over an Australian team. There could be no doubt about their superiority in a sensational match, and Johnson, in presenting his cap to the Surrey captain, Surridge, admitted it freely.

To Laker belonged the great distinction of taking all ten wickets. Not since 1878 when E. Barratt, another Surrey man, did so for the Players, also at The Oval, had a bowler taken all ten wickets against an Australian side, and Laker was given the ball and a cheque for £50 by the Surrey Committee. He and, in the second innings, the left-handed Lock, fully exposed the weakness of the Australian batsmen against the turning ball.

Winning the toss appeared to have given the Australians a considerable advantage, and Burke and McDonald emphasised this view while scoring 62 in 95 minutes. McDonald, though enjoying two "lives", brought off many good strokes during a stay of three hours 35 minutes and he fell only 11 runs short of his second century in three successive innings. When he was taken at the wicket the total stood at

151 for four wickets, but Laker brought about such a series of disasters that five more batsmen were dismissed while the total rose by 48. Of these runs 12, including a drive for six, were hit by Davidson in one over from Laker and 16 came in three strokes by Crawford at the expense of the same bowler. Fortunately for the Australians, Miller, getting as much of the bowling as possible, scored briskly after a careful start, and he and Wilson put on 42 for the last wicket. Even so Laker, maintaining a splendid length in a spell of four hours and a quarter only broken by the lunch and tea intervals, exploited off-spin on the dry pitch so skilfully that he came out with this analysis: 46 overs, 18 maidens, 88 runs, ten wickets…

[In Surrey's reply,] Constable, cautious at first, gradually developed more freedom, but wickets fell steadily and six were down for 221. Then Laker attacked the bowling. He helped himself to 16, including a drive for six and two fours in an over from Johnson, and altogether hit 43 out of 57 added by the seventh partnership in 39 minutes, taking Surrey ahead… Surridge and Loader put on 34 for the last wicket, and so Surrey gained a lead of 88.

Next morning… matters went well enough with the Australians and an opening stand of 56 in 95 minutes by Burke and McDonald seemed to have made them reasonably safe from defeat.

Then the course of the game changed completely, for Lock, able by now to make the ball turn quickly and occasionally get up awkwardly from a dusty pitch, caused such a breakdown that in a further 95 minutes the innings was all over for another 51 runs. Lock, who took the first six wickets at a cost of 40 runs, finished with an analysis of seven for 49 – a marked contrast to his 0 for 100 in the first innings! Actually he achieved all his success from the Pavilion End – that from which Laker bowled in the first innings – in a spell of 23.1 overs, six maidens, for 36 runs. He owed something to smart fielding, the catch by which May at slip disposed of Davidson being first-rate.

Surrey required only 20 runs to win, but Lindwall and Crawford bowled so fast and accurately that they took 55 minutes to accomplish the task.

Australians 259 (C. C. McDonald 89, K. R. Miller 57*; J. C. Laker 10-88) and 107 (G. A. R. Lock 7-49); Surrey 347 (T. H. Clark 58, B. Constable 109; I. W. G. Johnson 6-168) and 20-0.

LAKER'S WONDERFUL YEAR

Neville Cardus, 1957

Against the Australians in 1956, J. C. Laker bowled himself to a prominence which might seem legendary if there were no statistics to prove that his skill did indeed perform results and deeds hitherto not considered within the range of any cricketer, living or dead.

No writer of boys' fiction would so strain romantic credulity as to make his hero, playing for England against Australia, capture nine first-innings wickets; then help himself to all ten in the second innings. Altogether, 19 for 90 in a Test match. If any author expected us to believe that his hero was not only capable in one chapter of a marvel as fantastic as all this, but also in another chapter (and in an earlier chapter, bowled a whole Australian XI out – 10 for 88), the most gullible of his readers would, not without reason, throw the book away and wonder what the said author was taking him for.

Yet as far back as 1950 Laker was hinting that he possessed gifts which on occasion were at any moment likely to be visited by plenary inspiration and accomplish things not only unexpected but wondrous. At Bradford, five miles from his birthplace, Laker, playing for England v The Rest, took eight wickets for two runs in 14 overs – a feat which probably the great S. F. Barnes himself never imagined within mortal bowler's scope – or even desirable. Against Nottinghamshire at The Oval in 1955, Laker took six wickets for five.

Between 1947 and 1953 he did the hat-trick four times.

Obviously the gods endowed him in his cradle with that indefinable power which from time to time generates talent to abnormal and irresistible achievement. And he has done his conjurations – they have been nothing less – by one of the oldest tricks of the bowlers' trade. Not by the new-fangled swing and not by googlies or Machiavellian deceit by flight through the air has Laker hypnotised batsmen into helpless immobility, but by off-breaks of the finger-spin type which would have been recognised by, and approved by, cricketers who played in Laker's own county of Yorkshire more than half a century ago...

Laker's actual finger-spin probably has seldom been surpassed on a sticky or dusty wicket, in point of velocity and viciousness after pitching. I can think only of Ted Wainwright, Cecil Parkin and Tom Goddard who shared Laker's ability to fizz the ball right-handed from the off-side...

Any great performer needs to be born at the right time. If Laker had begun to play for Surrey in the 1930s, when wickets at The Oval and on most large grounds were doped and rolled to insensibility, he might have made one or two appearances for Surrey, then vanished from the scene. Or maybe he would have remained in Yorkshire where pitches were never absolutely divorced from nature and original sin...

There is sometimes an air of indolence in his movements, as he runs his loose lumbering run, swinging his arm slowly, but with the flick of venom at the last split second. At the end of his imperturbable walk back to his bowling mark he stares at the pavilion as though looking for somebody, but looking in a disinterested way. He is entirely what he is by technique – good professional technique, spin, length and the curve in the air natural to off-spin...

His bowling is as unassuming as the man himself and on the face of it as modest. That's where the fun comes in; for it is fun indeed to see the leisurely way Laker sends his victims one after another, as though by some influence which has not only put the batsmen under a spell, but himself at the same time. Somebody has written that all genius goes to work partly in a somnambulistic way. Jim Laker is certainly more than a talented spinner.

SURREY V SOMERSET   1957

June 2, 4, 5, 1956. Surrey won by an innings and nine runs.

An outstanding display of batting from Somerset's Peter Wight could not deny a rampant Surrey another innings victory on their way to title number five.

The honours of the match went to Wight, who on a rain-affected pitch scored 62 out of the 159 in Somerset's first innings and 128 out of 196 in the second. Staying for three and three-quarter hours for his 162, he batted altogether for eight hours without being dismissed, showing an extraordinary calm in difficult circumstances. Surrey were fortunate to bat on a firm pitch and, given a sound start by Fletcher and Clark, they shaped consistently, but against some accurate left-arm slow bowling by McMahon, their former colleague, they did not reveal much freedom until 6pm. Then Surridge hit boldly, making 52 out of 75, including two sixes and six fours in half an hour. The value of his enterprise was emphasised when Surrey were able to enforce the follow-on and press home their advantage thanks to some keen bowling, especially by Loader, who took ten wickets in the match.

Surrey 364-7 dec (T. H. Clark 80, B. Constable 58, W. S. Surridge 52*; J. W. J. McMahon 5-105); **Somerset 159** (P. B. Wight 62*; G. A. R. Lock 4-53) **and 196** (P. B. Wight 128*; P. J. Loader 7-56).

STUART SURRIDGE: SURREY'S INSPIRATION   Douglas Jardine, 1957

Wisden *introduced its celebratory feature on Surrey's greatest captain with the following words: "Surrey, under the bold leadership of W. S. Surridge, broke all county cricket records by winning the Championship outright for five consecutive years. Here, Douglas Jardine, whom many people regard as England's shrewdest captain since the turn of the century, pays tribute to Surridge. Jardine himself played for Surrey and captained the side for two seasons, 1932–33."*

Inspiration is the operative word.

Exactly what inspiration may mean varies too much for exact definition or analysis. Leave it, therefore, that most people would claim to recognise it when they see it, and what is quite as important, everyone appreciates the difference between being at the sending or at the receiving end of inspiration.

Having got his inspiration, Mr Stuart Surridge was able not only to digest it, but to pass it on to each and every Surrey side from 1952 to 1956. In this, rather than in changing personnel, can be summed up the difference between the sides of 1948 to 1951.

To some extent Surridge's advent as leader may, from his own point of view, be considered to have been fortunately timed. It is no secret that during the years from 1948 to 1951 there was a very general conviction among players and members alike that there was present in the team, in good measure, all the ability and talent needed to win the County Cricket Championship. But the title continued to elude the county's grasp. The ability was never quite harnessed, or the talent fully and firmly exploited.

It is improbable that many recognised Surridge's inspiration for what it was. Few, however, could fail to appreciate his enthusiasm and the tautened determination springing naturally from it. The fielding had never been bad; no Oval crowd would tolerate that. But there was, nevertheless, a world of difference between the good workmanlike stuff served up before Surridge and the dynamic current with which he has charged it for the last five years. Don't drop a catch and you won't lose the match is an old and tired adage. It would be no great exaggeration to say that the majority of catches missed by Surrey were chances only because they were made into possibles by the fieldsmen. Surridge supplied the electricity close in on the off side, while Lock did as much on the leg side. To the unfortunate who had made nought in the first innings and was looking for a chance to get off the mark in the second innings, the Surrey infield must have offered anything but an alluring prospect...

Thus in due course we come to the question of wickets at The Oval, nursed and produced by the most successful groundsman in England, Bert Lock. From a batsman's point of view no wicket has changed more radically since 1939 than that at Kennington Oval. Before 1939 centuries in the second innings were a commonplace; since then they have been rare indeed...

Lock, at Kennington, has more nearly than anyone else achieved the four-fold ideal facing groundsmen today. That consists of producing a wicket which, while fair to batsmen, lends itself to definite results in three days while encouraging both speedy and spin bowlers. Neither Bedser nor Loader nor Laker nor Lock object to bowling on their home pitch.

In these four bowlers, backed by Surridge himself, lies the mainspring of Surrey's success, for like it or not, it is bowling, not batting which in the main wins Championships. Where the majority of county captains were too often wondering whom they could or should put on next, Surridge was faced with the pleasanter but not necessarily easier problem of whom to take off in order to give 'X' a chance.

By contrast with the Surrey bowling, the batting has been all too often unimpressive, to say the least of it. But the change of wickets is accountable for much of this. No side including P. B. H. May, and with a tail whose policy it was to hit and not poke its way out of a mess, could be other than dangerous opponents to tackle.

So let us return to Surridge at the summit of his success. The temptation to go on for just one more year must have been well-nigh irresistible; yet he has resisted it, and we can only applaud his voluntary breaking of his wand as he takes his bow with a peerless record as a county captain.

One may regret that he never had the honour of captaining the Gentlemen against the Players at Lord's; still more that he was never entrusted with the task of taking, and bringing on, an England A Team overseas. But Surridge was ever a county man, first and last, and as such can have few if any regrets.

SURREY IN 1957   1958

In 1957 Surrey had a new captain in Peter May but the transition was seamless, with the team spirit fostered by Surridge still very apparent as the club romped to the most emphatic of their seven titles.

For the sixth successive year incomparable Surrey carried all before them. Their high skill, ruthless efficiency, matchless team spirit and appetite for quick runs left no reasonable doubt that their record run of Championship victories would be extended. Once they had taken the lead theirs was a lonely supremacy, and in the final table they were separated from Northamptonshire, the runners up, by the wide margin of 94 points. On August 16 they clinched the title, a date which equalled Warwickshire's post war record, set in 1951, of winning by the earliest date. Surrey's policy of persistent aggression from the first ball to the last never wavered, even in the rare threat of defeat. As many as nine of their 21 Championship victories were gained inside two days. Nor was it a coincidence that they scored faster than any other side – an example of their dynamic approach to the game... Surrey's achievements undoubtedly entitle them to be considered the greatest county combination of all time. Though it was yet another glorious record of uninterrupted success the season marked a new chapter in Surrey cricket. After five triumphant years Stuart Surridge retired and the captaincy passed to P. B. H. May, England's captain since 1955. As May was an automatic choice to lead the national side again, there were fears that his dual responsibility, and his absence in many county fixtures – he missed nine – would react unfavourably against Surrey. May's services to England virtually meant his sharing the Surrey captaincy with his newly appointed deputy, senior professional, Alec Bedser... Bedser was a brilliant deputy. His wide experience, deep technical knowledge, shrewdness and willingness to encourage the new members earned him a new stature in English cricket... Captain and vice captain shared the credit for the maintenance of Surridge's legacy of a great team spirit. It was a spirit born of success, and thrived because, by habit and practice, Surrey played as a side and not as a collection of brilliant individualists.

ARTHUR McINTYRE – CRICKETER OF THE YEAR
L. N. Bailey, 1958

In an era of famous names that have passed into legend, Arthur McIntyre is one of the least heralded Surrey cricketers of the 1950s – yet he was a vital member of the team. A metronomic wicket-keeper, McIntyre was a permanent presence behind the stumps and was denied an England career only by the brilliance of Godfrey Evans.

One of the main reasons for Surrey's record run of six County Championships has been the superb close-to-the-wicket fielding. Four players last season [1957] accounted for no fewer than 264 wickets. In the centre of all this snapping up of what to many other counties would not even be chances was Arthur John William McIntyre, for ten years regular wicketkeeper to the county champions.

Competent and consistent, McIntyre has missed most of the big honours of the game through being contemporary with Godfrey Evans, whose sustained brilliance has made him always first choice for England since the first season after the war. McIntyre has only three England caps, two received when Evans was injured and one in his own right – as a batsman against Australia at Brisbane in 1950 – but for years he has been to more than one selection committee the keeper in the shadow team for home Tests...

McIntyre has always been a useful batsman in the middle of the order for Surrey, where his aggressiveness has brought him more than 10,000 runs. He passed that milestone during last summer. Of his quick scoring McIntyre recalls the match against Nottinghamshire at Trent Bridge in 1955 when he scored 189 runs for once out. In the first innings he made 110, taking only 108 minutes over his century, helping K. F. Barrington in a stand of 177. In the second innings he made 79 not out, which included four sixes and nine fours, and helped Peter May put on 149 runs in 57 minutes.

PETER LOADER – CRICKETER OF THE YEAR Ebenezer Eden, 1958

Peter Loader was a genuinely quick bowler who complemented the guile of Bedser, Lock and Laker, his more illustrious colleagues. In 1957 he took 101 Championship wickets at 14.73.

The initial P in the name of Peter James Loader might well represent perseverance, so prominent a part did this sterling quality play in his advance from club to county and Test-match cricket. Last season he reached the peak of his achievements and earned fame by performing the hat-trick in the Fourth Test match with West Indies – a feat never previously accomplished by an England player in a home Test. In five successive years he helped substantially in the carrying off by Surrey of the County Championship. His pace, ability to make the ball move late in its flight, and his skill in disguising the occasional slower delivery placed him in the forefront of present-day fast bowlers...

Between July 8 and July 17 [in 1953] he enjoyed such a phenomenal spate of success that in three matches he took 34 wickets, average 7.97. At Birmingham he dismissed eight batsmen – seven of them bowled – in the first Warwickshire innings for 72 runs; he followed with nine for 28 – the other man was run out – in Kent's first innings at

Blackheath; eight for 21 v Worcestershire at The Oval and six for 70 on the opening day of the meeting with Gloucestershire at Bristol.

SURREY V GLOUCESTERSHIRE   1958

June 19, 20, 1957. Surrey won by an innings and 149 runs.

In a typical display of dominance in 1957, Surrey scored a telling victory over Gloucestershire after dismissing them for 68 in the first innings. Centuries from Bernie Constable and Ken Barrington set the game up before Alec Bedser, captain in May's absence, ran through the opposition.

The largely inexperienced Gloucestershire side were outplayed so completely that the match was all over half an hour before teatime on the second day. After risking first innings on a "green" pitch, Emmett alone faced Surrey's formidable attack with assurance, scoring 33 out of 42. Gloucestershire were all out 20 minutes after lunch and Surrey's batting was in such dominant contrast that by tea they led by 22 with nine wickets standing. Constable spent three hours over his first century of the season and Barrington played a most attractive innings, full of excellent drives and pulls which brought him four sixes and 12 fours. Going in again on a pitch showing signs of wear, Gloucestershire had no hope of withstanding A. Bedser in the conditions, though Mortimore played admirably for over an hour.

Gloucestershire 68 (P. J. Loader 4-30, G. A. R. Lock 4-7) **and 104** (A. V. Bedser 6-49); **Surrey 321-3 dec** (M. J. Stewart 59, B. Constable 107, K. F. Barrington 124*).

THE COUNTY CHAMPIONSHIP IN 1958   1959

May led by example once more in 1958 as the only Surrey batsman to pass 1,000 Championship runs. The bowlers, as usual, did the rest. Surrey were champions for the seventh time in seven seasons; they would manage it just once in the next 41 years.

Surrey, warding off a determined challenge from Hampshire, emerged once more as the champion county, their seventh success running... Surrey's total of 212 points was 100 less than in 1957, for which the weather must be blamed to a large extent... Whereas Surrey finished strongly, Hampshire fell away so much that they gained only four points from their last four matches. Hampshire, 13th in 1957, finished second, the highest position in their history. Somerset, similarly, had never previously been as high as third, except for the early days when the Championship was restricted to a few counties.

SURREY V WARWICKSHIRE   1959

May 17, 19, 20, 1958. Surrey won by an innings and 80 runs.

With a 40-year-old Alec Bedser moving towards retirement, Surrey were increasingly reliant on the raw speed of Peter Loader. His dominant performance against Warwickshire in 1958 put the club on course for the last title in their magnificent streak.

With M. J. K. Smith, their captain, playing for MCC, Warwickshire were no match for Surrey, and in particular Loader. On a pitch giving the batsmen at least an equal chance, Loader brought the game to a close before lunch on the third day by taking nine second-innings wickets for 17 runs, his best figures. Whether such an analysis also reflected his best performance is doubtful, for the batsmen possessed neither the skill nor the fight to combat intelligent pace bowling. The limitations of the recognised batsmen were seen clearly in the first innings when the tailenders contributed 95 of the 162 runs. In between, Surrey also found runs difficult to score against bowlers inclined to pitch a shade short, though May gave another excellent display, notably to the off, once he had his eye in. He was finally run out through splendid fielding in the covers by Horner.

Warwickshire 162 and 63 (P. J. Loader 9-17); Surrey 305-9 dec (B. Constable 59, P. B. H. May 73, G. A. R. Lock 56; Khalid Ibadulla 4-43).

Chapter 11

Things Get a Bit Shorter

T he Oval has always been at the forefront of cricketing innovations, and the ground played its part in the creation of what is now known as "white-ball cricket". The first one-day county competition was introduced in 1963 but it wasn't until the following year that Surrey played their first limited-overs match at home, when Micky Stewart's side took on Gloucestershire in May – the same month in which Bobby Moore led West Ham to their first FA Cup.

Amid the growing popularity of the new format, The Oval staged three matches in the first Cricket World Cup in 1975 and went on to feature in the tournaments of 1979, 1983 and 1999, and more recently in the Champions Trophy. The thrilling final of the 2004 competition between England and the West Indies is the only time a major international one-day trophy has been handed out at The Oval – but the ground is due for a repeat when the 2017 tournament concludes in Kennington.

Things got even shorter after the turn of the century, when the ground attracted a large crowd to watch Surrey play Middlesex on June 13, 2003, the day on which the world's first professional Twenty20 matches were played. Around this time, a series of explosive Surrey teams produced a number of extraordinary white-ball records at The Oval.

Twenty20 cricket at The Oval has been one of the great recent success stories of English domestic cricket, regularly drawing sell-out crowds for the first time in decades.

SURREY V GLOUCESTERSHIRE, GILLETTE CUP 1965

May 27, 1964. Surrey won by 46 runs.

The first one-day match at The Oval pitted Surrey against Gloucestershire in the knockout Gillette Cup.

Better all-round play and superior strategy brought Surrey deserved victory. They were given a splendid start by Edrich and W. A. Smith who shared in an opening partnership of 105. Edrich hit 12 fours and two sixes. In contrast to the defensive field-setting favoured by Graveney, Stewart went all out in attack. The Gloucestershire opening batsmen were restricted to seven runs in the first seven overs. When Gloucestershire forced the pace they lost wickets steadily. Edrich was adjudged the man of the match by F. R. Brown.

Surrey 268-6 (60 overs) (J. H. Edrich 96); **Gloucestershire 222** (59.5 overs).

SURREY V MIDDLESEX, GILLETTE CUP SEMI-FINAL 1966

July 14, 1965. Surrey won by five wickets.

The following year's domestic semi-final took the form of a London derby.

The meeting of two London rivals produced some of the best cricket seen at Kennington for some time, with an aggregate of 502 runs. Middlesex, after scoring only 77 for three from 32 overs, hit furiously. The Man of the Match award went to Edwards, who in ten hectic overs with Barrington added 92 runs. Edwards hit nine fours. The crowd numbered 8,000…

Middlesex 250-8 (60 overs) (W. E. Russell 70, J. M. Brearley 60);
Surrey 252-5 (56.2 overs) (J. H. Edrich 71, K. F. Barrington 68*, M. J. Edwards 53*).

September 7, 1973. West Indies won by eight wickets.

The first one-day international took place in Australia in 1971, and less than three years later The Oval made its own ODI debut.

West Indies not only gained quick revenge for their narrow defeat at Leeds, but also won the [Prudential Trophy] by virtue of their faster scoring-rate over the two games.

Under conditions ideal for quick scoring, England's total of 189 was completely inadequate and their bowlers were harshly treated by Fredericks. In an inspired display he hit one six and ten fours and with Kallicharran added 143 for the second wicket in 30 overs. Long before Fredericks had competed his century off 111 balls, England's fate was sealed.

That England got as many runs as they did was due to Fletcher, who picked up a faltering innings so effectively that 109 runs were made off the last 20 overs. He improvised some remarkable strokes but was unable to repair all the damage done earlier.

England, who brought in Jameson, David Lloyd and Arnold for Boycott (unfit), Hayes and Hendrick, began well enough with a partnership of 38 in 12 overs by Jameson and Smith. Then Clive Lloyd, who bowled because Sobers was not playing, dismissed Smith with his first ball and had Denness lbw with his fourth. Jameson and David Lloyd, both on trial for winter tour places, then struggled through 15 overs while 20 runs were scored. No attempt was made to attack Gibbs who conceded only 12 runs in his 11 overs while removing Jameson. Greig, Old and Arnold helped Fletcher in fruitful partnerships despite brilliant ground fielding.

England 189-9 (55 overs) (K. W. R. Fletcher 63); **West Indies 190-2** (42.2 overs) (R. C. Fredericks 105, A. I. Kallicharran 53*).

AUSTRALIA V SRI LANKA, WORLD CUP   1976

June 11, 1975. Australia won by 52 runs.

The first Cricket World Cup was in England in 1975, and Australia took on underdogs Sri Lanka in one of three matches at The Oval.

Australia won by 52 runs, but their victory did not gain them many admirers. Facing a total of 328, the Sri Lanka batsmen, most of them short in stature, put up a brave show against the hostile Australian bowlers. They cut and hooked the short balls with marked skill and accuracy, but Thomson caused two to retire hurt. The tiny Mendis was struck on the head when he ducked into a rising ball and Wettimuny played another riser on to his body and now assisted by a runner was hit on the right instep by the next ball. As he staggered in and out of his crease, Thomson threw down the wicket appealing for a run-out that was disallowed. Both batsmen went to St. Thomas's Hospital and soon recovered. Sri Lanka never gave up and the captain, Tennekoon, and Tissera like their predecessors got behind the line of the ball and refused to be intimidated.

Earlier, Turner, whom Laurie Fishlock nominated Man of the Match, hit one gigantic six over long-on and nine fours in reaching 100 out of 178 off the fifth ball of the last over before lunch. McCosker played steadily in a profitable opening stand of 173 and later Greg Chappell and Walters put on 117 in 19 overs with a splendid array of strokes against a mediocre attack.

Australia 328-5 (60 overs) (R. B. McCosker 73, A. Turner 101, G. S. Chappell 50, K. D. Walters 59); **Sri Lanka** 276-4 (60 overs) (S. R. D. Wettimuny 53*, M. H. Tissera 52).

ENGLAND V AUSTRALIA, THIRD ONE-DAY INTERNATIONAL   1978

June 6, 1977. Australia won by two wickets.

A 55-over game between England and Australia in 1977 featured superb centuries from Dennis Amiss and Greg Chappell as well as a tight finish played out in less than ideal conditions.

The final stages were played in heavy rain against a blinding low sun at the Vauxhall End with pools of water in the middle. So Australia avenged their defeats at Old Trafford and Edgbaston thanks almost entirely to brilliance of their captain, Greg Chappell, who made 125 not out. He received splendid help from Robinson in a stand of 148. Just as this pair contributed so much with the bat for Australia, so did Amiss (108) and his captain, Brearley (78), for England at the beginning of the exciting contest. Their opening stand extended to the 38th over and produced 161 runs out of a final total of 242.

Despite a forecast of bad weather and a gloomy morning, Chappell, winning the toss, sent in England to bat and soon a large Bank Holiday crowd were entertained with some brisk batting which yielded 44 from the first ten overs. Thomson and Pascoe concentrated more on length and direction than excessive pace but, apart from a difficult chance by Brearley when 23 off Pascoe to Thomson at first slip, the batsmen generally played soundly with attractive cover-drives and strokes past midwicket.

The stand ended when Brearley moved far out of his crease to drive O'Keeffe and left Robinson a simple stumping. Only 17 overs remained, but apart from Old the other batsmen did not try to settle down before attempting to hit. Amiss went on to complete his second Prudential hundred against Australia and was seventh out in the 50th over.

It was significant that except for putting himself on for the last over, Chappell preferred to reserve his energy for batting and how wise this proved. So far the threatened rain had held off and with some sunshine the light had been good; moreover it was a good pitch for batting, unlike those in the two previous one-day internationals.

Australia suffered a setback at 33 when McCosker was leg before in the tenth over, but Robinson had begun soundly and Chappell lost no time in finding a powerful range of strokes, and one over by Old cost 16. Both men drove well and Robinson hooked Lever for six, but with the total 83 for one teeming rain held up the match for an hour. As the weather cleared the captains agreed to complete the match that evening (if possible), which was sensible seeing the morrow was Jubilee Day.

Underwood put in a grand spell at the crisis, but though he removed Walters, and twice saw Chappell lift him perilously near mid-on, Australia slithered to a well-deserved victory.

England 242 (54.2 overs) (J. M. Brearley 78, D. L. Amiss 108); Australia 246-8 (53.2 overs) (R. D. Robinson 70, G. S. Chappell 125*).

ENGLAND V NEW ZEALAND, WORLD CUP   1984

June 9, 1983. England won by 106 runs.

The Oval staged one of the first round of fixtures in the 1983 World Cup, a match in which England posted what was then considered a huge 60-over total to beat New Zealand.

England won by 106 runs, a convincing victory over a New Zealand side who had beaten them five times during the winter. Once Lamb and Gatting, coming together at 117 for three, had made 115 in 16 overs, there was no doubt that England would score enough runs. Lamb's 102 was made off only 103 balls and the last 25 overs produced 203 runs. New Zealand's disappointing bowling was followed by a poor start to their innings of 62 for four, and although Crowe made 97 before being last out, they had lost sight of victory long before.

England 322-6 (60 overs) (A. J. Lamb 102); New Zealand 216 (59 overs) (M. D. Crowe 97).

SURREY V WORCESTERSHIRE, NATWEST TROPHY SEMI-FINAL   1995

August 9, 1994. Worcestershire won by seven runs.

The one-day game had proved a great success in county cricket, attracting both crowds and the television cameras. Although its popularity began to wane towards the end of the century, this tense NatWest Trophy semi-final of 1994 was a reminder of its appeal.

Moody began the revels with a blistering innings and wrapped them up with a magnificent catch to win a match full of records. He and

Curtis set the tone with an unbroken third-wicket stand of 309, the highest partnership for any wicket in limited-overs cricket. Moody's unbeaten 180 came from 160 deliveries, with three sixes and 25 fours; once he reached his half-century, his strokeplay went from the audacious to the outrageous. It was the highest innings for Worcestershire in any one-day competition and the highest against a first-class county in the history of this tournament. The often dour Curtis was hardly less potent, hitting 136 in 180 balls. However, Surrey seemed undaunted at the prospect of having to make the highest-ever total by a side batting second. Darren Bicknell provided the anchor whilst first Thorpe, then Brown kept their hope alive. Later, Hollioake, who hit 60 off 36 balls, and, improbably, Benjamin hammered the score past 300. In the final over, with 22 runs required, Benjamin thrashed two enormous sixes, nailing another record – the highest aggregate of runs, 707, in a limited-overs match. He was trying for a third six when Moody stretched out his long arm to pluck the ball and the tie away from Surrey with one delivery to spare. The one man to take no pleasure from the occasion was Tony Murphy, Man of the Match in the quarter-final, who was left out by Surrey. He cleared his locker and left the club.

Worcestershire 357-2 (60 overs) (T. S. Curtis 136*, T. M. Moody 180*);
Surrey 350 (59.5 overs) (D. J. Bicknell 89, A. D. Brown 52, A. J. Hollioake 60;
G. A. Hick 4-54).

SURREY V NOTTINGHAMSHIRE, SUNDAY LEAGUE   1998
June 26, 1997. No result (abandoned).

A Sunday League match in 1997 was scheduled to be the first official day-night game in English domestic cricket; the weather had other ideas.

What was scheduled to be the first day-night match in a major English competition was called off owing to torrential rain over the previous 24 hours. The temporary floodlights had already been positioned around the boundary, however, and the soggy turf was badly cut up as they were driven off in heavy lorries.

SURREY V GLAMORGAN, C&G TROPHY 2003

June 19, 2002. Surrey won by nine runs.

The Surrey teams of the late 1990s and early 2000s played a powerful and charismatic brand of cricket in the image of their captain, Adam Hollioake. Those traits were fully on show during a Cheltenham and Gloucester Trophy match in 2002 which turned out to be one of the most extraordinary games ever played at The Oval.

This sensational match left a trail of broken records in its wake. Thanks to a belter of a pitch and a 60-yard boundary under the gasometers, it was a batsman's – and statistician's – delight. At its heart was Ali Brown's brilliant, scarcely credible world-record 268, yet this was no one-man show. Perhaps most astonishing was that Glamorgan, not given a prayer by anyone after conceding 438, so nearly won. Robert Croft, acting-captain while Steve James tended his sick daughter, led a never-say-die fightback with a captain's innings that was also a phenomenal feat of pinch-hitting. He smacked Bicknell's first five balls for four as he sprinted to 50 in 22 balls. His hundred came up in 59 minutes off 56 balls, whereas Brown's first hundred had taken 98 minutes and 80 balls. Hemp, the game's third centurion, got there in 85 balls and kept the run-rate near the required 8.78; off the last ten overs, Glamorgan needed a just-about feasible 103. Thomas made amends for haemorrhaging 12 runs an over by cracking an unbeaten 71 off only 41 balls. But wickets were falling at the other end, mainly to Hollioake who, with ten runs needed off two balls, bowled Cosker to complete a wonderful contest. The honours, though, went to Brown for his second – and only the sixth-ever – one-day double-hundred, following his 203 in a Sunday League game against Hampshire in 1997. His brutal innings contained 192 in boundaries, including 12 sixes, one short of Ian Botham's world record, and his 268 came off only 160 balls, at a strike-rate of 167. His pulling, especially, was perfection, but he also hit 22 fours and two sixes through or over the covers, driving off the back foot as well as the front. "I'm in the best

Birth of the Ashes: the notice printed in the *Sporting Times* after England's shock defeat at The Oval in 1882.

In Affectionate Remembrance
of
ENGLISH CRICKET,
Which Died at the Oval on
29th AUGUST, 1882,
Deeply Lamented by a Large Circle of Sorrowing Friends and Acquaintances.
R.I.P.
N.B.—The Body will be Cremated and the Ashes taken to Australia.

Death of English cricket: a scene from the 1882 Test which led to the famous mock obituary.

Surrey giants of the Golden Age: (right to left) Tom Richardson, Tom Hayward, Bobby Abel and (standing, far left) Bill Brockwell in front of the Oval pavilion.

We'll get them in singles: England openers Archie MacLaren and Lionel Palairet walk out to bat during the helter-skelter Ashes Test of 1902.

Below: "Jumping Out": George Beldam's iconic photograph of Australian batsman Victor Trumper at The Oval.

Left: Matchmaker: Surrey secretary Charles Alcock was a key figure in arranging the 1880 Oval Test – the first played in England.

Below: Testing the tourists: South Africa slip to defeat against Surrey during their first Test tour of England in 1907.

NO 1 TOTAL. NO 3
232 428 0
WICKETS 1
BOWLER 4 **BOWLER 10**
CAUGHT
2 LAST PLAYER 183
LAST WICKET FELL AT 428

Above: The inseparable couple: openers Jack Hobbs (left) and Herbert Sutcliffe during their match-turning partnership at The Oval which sealed the 1926 Ashes.

Left: Striking a pose: Hobbs (left) and Andy Sandham after their Surrey record partnership against Oxford University in 1926.

Below: Marathon effort: Len Hutton leaves the field during the 1938 Oval Test in which he made 364, still a national record.

Left: Runs on the board: England's total in 1938 is the second-highest in Tests. In the foreground stands legendary Oval groundsman Austin "Bosser" Martin with his heavy roller ("Bosser's Pet").

Right: National service: The Oval was turned into a POW camp during the Second World War, though it was never used.

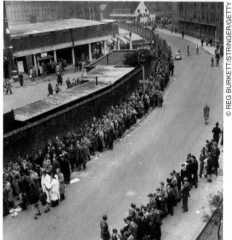

Spot the difference: the Bedser twins, Eric (left) and Alec.

Crowd-puller: spectators queue outside The Oval in 1948 to see Don Bradman appear in his last Test match.

Hats off: the England players salute Bradman as he arrives in the middle to play his final Test innings, in 1948.

© CENTRAL PRESS/STRINGER/GETTY

© CENTRAL PRESS/STRINGER/GETTY

Left: End in tears: an emotional Bradman is bowled by Eric Hollies for a duck, giving him a final Test average of 99.94.

Below: National heroes: Denis Compton and Bill Edrich part the crowd following England's Oval victory in 1953 which secured the Ashes for the first time in 19 years.

© CENTRAL PRESS/STRINGER/GETTY

Quick out the blocks: Fazal Mahmood leads his team off the field after bowling Pakistan to their first Test victory in England on their maiden tour of 1954.

Below: Four and counting: Stuart Surridge (far right) leads the balcony celebrations in 1955 during Surrey's peerless run of seven consecutive titles. In the foreground (wearing a tie) is Peter May, his successor as captain.

Six of the best: champions again in 1957 under Peter May, who would lead Surrey to a seventh straight title the following summer.

Triple-centurion: The Oval stands to applaud Fred Trueman for becoming the first bowler to take 300 Test wickets at the end of the 1964 Ashes.

Pitching in: spectators join the mopping-up operation which allowed England just enough time for a dramatic victory in 1968.

Sign of things to come: Ajit Wadekar (in blazer) and B. S. Chandrasekhar celebrate India's maiden Test win in England which sealed the 1971 series.

Lucky charm: Bella the elephant patrols the boundary during India's famous Oval victory in 1971. The animal was loaned to Indian supporters from Chessington Zoo to honour a Hindu festival.

Below: Feeling at home: jubilant West Indies supporters roar their delight after England were defeated in 1973, a Test that marked the start of a Caribbean era of dominance.

Whispering death: Michael Holding delivers another thunderbolt during his 14-wicket match-haul in the rout of England at The Oval in 1976.

Below: Scorcher: Viv Richards carves his way to a magnificent 291 in 1976, when a roasting summer had left The Oval's outfield parched.

The 366-run bat: Lancashire's Neil Fairbrother is all smiles in 1990 after breaking the record for the highest first-class score at The Oval.

History-maker: Devon Malcolm leaves the field after a devastating display of fast bowling that ripped through South Africa in 1994. His 9-57 is an Oval Test record.

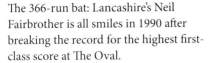

Bamboozled: John Crawley is bowled by Muttiah Muralitharan, one of Murali's nine second-innings wickets – and 16 in the match – which set up victory for Sri Lanka in 1998.

Back in English hands: Alec Stewart raises the Wisden Trophy in 2000 after England won a Test series against West Indies for the first time in 31 years.

Champions again: Surrey celebrate back-to-back titles in 2000.

Brothers unite: Adam (left) and Ben Hollioake during their 84-run partnership in the 2001 B&H final against Gloucestershire at Lord's, which Surrey won by 47 runs. Ben, who died in a car crash less than a year later, was Man of the Match for a dazzling 73.

Below: Bowing out: Alec Stewart leaves the field after his final Test innings, against South Africa in 2003. England won the match to level the series.

Below: Go England: Kevin Pietersen basks in the glory of his match-saving 158 on the fifth day of the 2005 Test. England thus regained the Ashes for the first time since 1987.

Great times: Captain Michael Vaughan lifts the urn, prompting national celebrations to begin.

Finishing on top: Ricky Ponting ends his first-class career with a hundred for Surrey during his brief spell with the club in 2013.

Tiny but precious: captain Alastair Cook kisses the urn as England retain the Ashes despite defeat at The Oval in 2015.

Local hero: Surrey's Jason Roy raises his bat after a scintillating 162 in the 2016 ODI against Sri Lanka.

© EVENING STANDARD/STRINGER/GETTY

Ground invasion: crowds spill onto the pitch during a match at The Oval in the 1970s. The undeveloped ground is stark by comparison with its appearance today.

Modern view: The ground as it looked in 2013, with the addition of the Bedser Stand, OCS Stand and a grand new frontage for the Pavilion.

© ANTHONY DEVLIN/PA ARCHIVE/PA IMAGES

form of my life", he said later. Asked to name his best shots, he chose "the sixes I hit when Darren Thomas pitched it short". Ward made an admirable 97 off 95 balls with four sixes and helped add 286 for the first wicket but he, like everyone else, was eclipsed by Brown.

Surrey 438-5 (50 overs) (I. J. Ward 97, A. D. Brown 268); **Glamorgan 429** (49.5 overs) (R. D. B. Croft 119, D. L. Hemp 102, S. D. Thomas 71*; A. J. Hollioake 5-77).

ENGLAND v WEST INDIES, CHAMPIONS TROPHY FINAL   S. Rajesh, 2005

September 25, 2004. West Indies won by two wickets.

The 2004 Champions Trophy was largely disappointing – until England and West Indies served up a classic final on a chilly late-September evening at The Oval.

A tournament full of insipid, forgettable moments ended with one of the most memorable finals in recent years, as West Indies scripted a soul-stirring fightback to put paid to England's hopes of winning their first one-day tournament of any significance. For a region devastated by various opponents on the cricket field, and by Hurricanes Ivan and Jeanne off it, this was a victory to savour. The reactions of the players immediately after Bradshaw struck the winning boundary told the story – the entire West Indian party roared on to the field in semi-darkness, hugging, kissing, and screaming, ecstatic yet bewildered by their achievement.

None of those wild celebratory scenes looked even remotely possible when West Indies slumped to 147 for eight in their quest for 218. The top-order batsmen had all perished – Chanderpaul the last of them for a dogged 47 – and England moved in to finish off the formalities as Bradshaw joined Browne. About the only thing in the batsmen's favour was the asking-rate, which was less than four and a half an over. Browne and Bradshaw – both from Barbados, although Browne was born just round the corner in Lambeth – capitalised on that, initially looking for no more than nudges and pushes. But a stand which started off as nothing more than irritant value for Vaughan slowly assumed more ominous proportions.

Sensing a shift in momentum, Vaughan turned to Harmison, his chief weapon through much of the summer. It seemed an unequal battle: Harmison hurtling down his deliveries at 96mph in dubious light against batsmen of little repute. Not only did they see him off – Browne even cracked a magnificent square-drive in his penultimate over – they also quelled the venom of Flintoff, who had earlier ripped apart the heart of the West Indian middle order. The other bowler who might have been a force, Gough, had a strangely lacklustre day, and suddenly Vaughan had run out of attacking options. In cold and overcast conditions, he had preferred seam to spin throughout, and as crunch time approached, he stuck to his guns, opting for Wharf over Giles, who did not bowl at all. Wharf went for only two in the 47th over. But with 12 needed from the last two, West Indies clinched it in style – Browne thumped Wharf over gully for four, before Bradshaw found the third-man fence to seal an unbelievable win.

The statistically minded in the England camp should have had a whiff of defeat the moment Trescothick struck his eighth one-day century – this was the fifth to end in a losing cause. Trescothick, though, was the only one among England's specialist batsmen who solved the mystery of getting runs on an unusually bowler-friendly Oval pitch. Solanki and Vaughan were consumed early in the piece by Bradshaw, before West Indies found an unexpected hero in the middle overs. Exploiting the conditions to the hilt, Hinds kept a tight leash on the runs, and picked up three crucial middle-order wickets as well. Lara's alacrity at short midwicket had a huge hand in two of those, though – a fierce pull by Flintoff was scooped up left-handed and inches from the ground to give Lara his 100th catch in one-day internationals, while Jones's heave was intercepted with a perfectly timed leap. Trescothick stuck to his task, however, and with Giles chipping in with a valuable 31, England had put together a competitive total of 217.

That seemed more than sufficient when Harmison and Flintoff got in on the act with the ball. Solanki kept up the high level of fielding with a one-handed, leaping effort which took care of Hinds. A sharp return catch by Harmison dismissed Gayle, while Sarwan and Lara both perished off the outside edge. Chanderpaul offered stout resistance, but when he left, so did many West Indian supporters, believing the game to be over. Little did they realise that they would be missing the best part.

England 217 (49.4 overs) (M. E. Trescothick 104); West Indies 218-8 (48.5 overs).

Surrey v Gloucestershire, Friends Provident Trophy   2008
April 29, 2007. Surrey won by 257 runs.

A powerful Surrey side piled on a record 50-over total during a league match in the 2007 Friends Provident Trophy.

Ali Brown and James Benning launched an astonishing assault on the Gloucestershire attack to help Surrey pulverise the record for a 50-over total. Surrey were in the mood: the day before, they had fallen just 36 short of a target of 503 against Hampshire in the Championship. Now Brown and Benning put on 294, the fourth-highest opening stand in List A matches – and the highest between two first-class counties. Brown, who five years earlier hit a world-record 268 against Glamorgan in the same competition on the same ground, smashed 176 from 97 balls, with eight sixes and 20 fours – a total of 128 coming in boundaries. He reached his fifty from 32 balls and took just 18 more to reach three figures – his 19th hundred in limited-overs cricket. By comparison, Benning was restrained, making 152 from 134 deliveries, with four sixes and 15 fours. (It was just the fourth instance in List A cricket of an innings containing two scores of 150-plus, and the first outside the Indian subcontinent.) Most ferocious of all was Clarke, who crashed 82 from 28 balls, six of which disappeared for six and nine for four. All told, Gloucestershire conceded 69 boundaries, including 22 sixes. In reply, they stumbled to 65 for five before Hardinges and Adshead added a face-saving 114. Even so, they crumbled to lose by 257 – another record for games between first-class counties. Mohammad Akram, who claimed four wickets, and Schofield (three) were the only bowlers in the match to go for less than a run a ball; Hardinges had earlier gone for more than 12 an over.

Surrey

J. G. E. Benning c Ali b Ireland	152	R. J. Hamilton-Brown not out.		6
A. D. Brown b North	176	Lb 6, w 4, nb 6		16
Azhar Mahmood c Ali b Hardinges	35			
R. Clarke not out	82	1/294 (2) 2/365 (1)	(4 wkts, 50 overs)	496
†J. N. Batty b Kirby	29	3/409 (3) 4/477 (5)		

M. R. Ramprakash, ˚M. A. Butcher, S. J. Magoffin, C. P. Schofield and Mohammad Akram did not bat.

Noffke 10–1–89–0; Ireland 8–0–74–1; Kirby 10–0–91–1; Fisher 8–0–90–0; Hardinges 6–0–77–1; North 5–0–41–1; Gidman 3–0–28–0.

Gloucestershire

Kadeer Ali lbw b Mohammad Akram.	18	I. D. Fisher b Schofield.		4
C. M. Spearman b Azhar Mahmood.	28	A. A. Noffke c Ramprakash		
M. J. North c and b Azhar Mahmood.	2	b Mohammad Akram.		33
C. G. Taylor c Azhar Mahmood		S. P. Kirby c Hamilton-Brown b Clarke		6
b Mohammad Akram.	1	A. J. Ireland not out		3
˚A. P. R. Gidman c Ramprakash		Lb 4, w 9, nb 14		27
b Mohammad Akram.	6			
M. A. Hardinges c Hamilton-Brown		1/44 (1) 2/52 (2) 3/53 (4)	(34.1 overs)	239
b Schofield.	57	4/61 (3) 5/65 (5) 6/179 (7)		
†S. J. Adshead c Clarke b Schofield	54	7/188 (6) 8/195 (8) 9/210 (10) 10/239 (9)		

Azhar Mahmood 6–0–37–2; Mohammad Akram 6.1–1–36–4; Magoffin 7–0–57–0; Hamilton-Brown 4–0–41–0; Schofield 7–0–38–3; Clarke 4–0–26–1.

Umpires: G. I. Burgess and V. A. Holder.

SRI LANKA V WEST INDIES, WORLD TWENTY20 SEMI-FINAL   2010

June 19, 2009 (day/night). Sri Lanka won by 57 runs.

The first World Twenty20 was held in South Africa in 2007 and two years later it was England's turn, with The Oval staging nine games, including the semi-final between Sri Lanka and West Indies.

The received wisdom was that, if Gayle were at the crease come the final ball, he would have guided his side to victory. Gayle was there at the end all right, but was surrounded by the mangled wreckage of the West Indian innings as he became the first to carry his bat in Twenty20 internationals. Needing a gettable if tricky 159, West Indies began catastrophically, thanks to an astounding opening over by Mathews, who hit the stumps with his second, fourth and sixth deliveries. All three victims played on, though Simmons was unlucky that the ball ricocheted down from the bottom of his thigh pad into leg stump. Gayle hit with awesome power, but those early blows knocked the sense out of his side. Batsman after batsman fell to reckless swings, swipes and swishes when the primary aim should have been to give Gayle the strike. Sri Lanka had also relied on the brilliance of an opener: Dilshan came within a shot of becoming only the second player, after Gayle, to hit a hundred in Twenty20 internationals. He took advantage of a diet of full tosses as the bowlers struggled to find a yorker length. He allowed only 15 dot balls, and scored 20 singles and eight twos to go with his 14 boundaries.

Sri Lanka 158-5 (20 overs) (T. M. Dilshan 96*); **West Indies 101** (17.4 overs) (C. H. Gayle 63*).

SURREY V GLAMORGAN, CLYDESDALE BANK 40 LEAGUE   2011
August 4, 2010 (day/night). Surrey won by 39 runs (D/L method).

Surrey continued to break records in limited-overs cricket. This 2010 encounter with Glamorgan was curtailed by two overs for rain, but it didn't stop the hosts from hitting the biggest 40-over total.

Driven on with zeal by their young captain Hamilton-Brown, who faced just 69 balls, Surrey went 11 runs beyond the world-record 40-over total they set at Scarborough in 1994 under Alec Stewart. And they did so in only 38 overs against a poor Glamorgan attack – matched by shoddy outfielding and catching – who must have regretted Jamie Dalrymple's decision to bowl in such easy batting conditions. A storm reduced Glamorgan's task to a still-formidable 227 in 20 overs; Mark Cosgrove, in a fifth consecutive half-century, slammed 88 before holing out, attempting his fourth six, from his 55th ball.

Surrey 386-3 (38 overs) (R. J. Hamilton-Brown 115, S. M. Davies 88, M. R. Ramprakash 85*,
M. N. W. Spriegel 56*); **Glamorgan 187-5** (20 overs) (M. J. Cosgrove 88,
J. W. M. Dalrymple 54*).
Glamorgan's target was revised to 227 in 20 overs.

ENGLAND v NEW ZEALAND, FIRST TWENTY20 INTERNATIONAL

Andrew Alderson, 2014

June 25, 2013 (day/night). New Zealand won by five runs.

With Twenty20 internationals becoming a feature of English summers, The Oval produced a superb game in 2013.

Three of New Zealand's younger brigade set up their victory, although old hands Brendon McCullum thumped an important 68 and Taylor pulled off a match-changing catch. Rutherford got the innings off to a rollicking start, batting as if he were playing rounders and peppering the fence between mid-on and backward square. Then, as New Zealand defended their highest Twenty20 total away from home, Corey Anderson sent down a tight final over. It started with 16 required, which shrank when Stokes hit the first ball for six – but the last five deliveries produced only four runs. The third relative newcomer, Latham, was all action behind the stumps, catching Wright and running out Buttler to atone for a missed stumping off Hira when Hales had 31. England had begun quickly, reaching 50 in 3.3 overs, but then Nathan McCullum yorked Lumb and the rate slowed. Still, at 134 for two in the 14th over England seemed on course, but Taylor's one-handed leap disposed of Morgan and justified the brave decision to keep a slip in. The Barmy Army serenaded the new batsman with a chant of "Oh, Ra-vi Bo-pa-ra", to the tune of the White Stripes' "Seven Nation Army", but he couldn't quite repay them with a victory. Earlier, Boyd Rankin had taken a wicket with the fourth ball in his first international for England, after 52 caps for Ireland.

New Zealand 201-4 (20 overs) (H. D. Rutherford 62, B. B. McCullum 68);
England 196-5 (20 overs) (L. J. Wright 52).

ENGLAND v NEW ZEALAND, SECOND ONE-DAY INTERNATIONAL

Andrew Alderson, 2016

June 12, 2015 (day/night). New Zealand won by 13 runs (D/L method).

As the skills learned for Twenty20 cricket started spilling over to the 50-over game, so run-rates began to soar. England's match with New Zealand in

2015 broke the record for most runs scored in a one-day international in this country.

New Zealand levelled the series thanks to another mammoth first-innings total, but they were grateful for a little meteorological help. Rain struck with England on 345 for seven, needing 54 runs from 37 balls, and an enterprising stand between Rashid and Plunkett already worth 70. But when play resumed the equation became an even more testing 34 from 13. Both batsmen fell in the same over, bowled by Nathan McCullum – a remarkable relay catch between Southee and Boult to dismiss Rashid on the long-on boundary sealed the game.

England's highest total batting second (despite facing only 46 overs) was little consolation. New Zealand's top seven had all contributed to a daunting 398 on a pitch that offered all the seam movement of a tennis ball on tarmac. The upshot was 40 fours, 13 sixes and their second-highest one-day total, behind 402 for two against Ireland at Aberdeen in 2008. Williamson, with 93 from 88 balls, and Taylor, who made an unbeaten 119 from 96 after being dropped by Roy at backward point on seven, stood out. England chased competitively after Roy and Hales began with 85 inside 13 overs and, at 259 for four after 32, might even have been favourites. But Buttler was caught behind off Boult, later ruled out of the tour with a back injury. Then Morgan – who looked set for England's fastest one-day century – scythed McClenaghan to deep point to depart for a swashbuckling 88 from 47 balls. Billings followed quickly, before Rashid and Plunkett threatened to turn the game. New Zealand closed it out for their 300th ODI win; it had taken 684 matches, more than the seven other sides to have reached the mark.

New Zealand 398-5 (50 overs) (M. J. Guptill 50, K. S. Williamson 93, L. R. P. L. Taylor 119*);
England 365-9 (46 overs) (A. D. Hales 54, E. J. G. Morgan 88).
England's target was revised to 379 in 46 overs.

Surrey v Glamorgan, NatWest T20 Blast   2016
May 15, 2015 (day/night). Glamorgan won by 25 runs.

The Oval witnessed yet more record-breaking in Surrey's opening Twenty20 match of 2015.

The tournament began in spectacular style with 455 runs; the highest aggregate for a domestic Twenty20 match in England. Surrey regretted giving Colin Ingram a life – they caught him off a no-ball when he had nine – as he and fellow South African left-hander Jacques Rudolph went on to hammer 141 off 72 deliveries. On his county debut, Wahab Riaz conceded 29 from the 19th over, which included three sixes by an inspired Chris Cooke (also born in South Africa). Surrey's batsmen made a spirited attempt, with Steven Davies and Zafar Ansari scoring at a brutal rate.

Glamorgan 240-3 (20 overs) (J. A. Rudolph 62, C. A. Ingram 91);
Surrey 215 (19.3 overs) (S. M. Davies 58, Z. S. Ansari 67*; D. A. Cosker 4-30).

ENGLAND V SRI LANKA, FOURTH ONE-DAY INTERNATIONAL   Dean Wilson, 2017
June 29, 2016 (day/night). England won by six wickets (D/L method)

Playing on his home ground, Jason Roy smashed a stunning 162 off 118 balls in a one-day international between England and Sri Lanka in 2016.

On his home ground, Jason Roy came within a hit of overhauling England's long-standing individual record score. But, having pillaged a spectacular 162, he aimed a tired hoick at Pradeep Fernando, and was bowled. It meant the record remained Robin Smith's unbeaten 167, made against Australia at Birmingham in 1993, though it would fall before the summer was out. Roy faced 118 balls, and hit 13 fours and three sixes. Just as impressive was his work-rate: he scampered 16 twos and 54 singles. By the time he fell in the 38th over of a game restricted to 42 a side by the weather, England were in sight of a series-clinching victory. After Moeen (promoted to open because Alex Hales had jarred his back) went cheaply, Root helped pile on 149 in 18 overs, an England record for the second wicket against Sri Lanka. Then Morgan and Bairstow sat back and let Roy run riot; the pick of his innings was a massive straight strike off Prasanna that sailed into the pavilion. Earlier, Sri Lanka had produced their best batting performance of the series on a flat Oval track, easing past 300 following an interruption for rain in the 19th over. England's target was swelled slightly to 308 – but it was nowhere near enough, and they sailed to their second-highest successful run-chase with 11 balls to spare.

Sri Lanka 305-5 (42 overs) (M. D. Gunathilleke 62, B. K. G. Mendis 77, L. D. Chandimal 63, A. D. Mathews 67*); England 309-4 (40.1 overs) (J. J. Roy 162, J. E. Root 65). *England's target was revised to 308 in 42 overs.*

Note: reports of some other one-day matches at The Oval appear in chapters 15, 17 and 18.

Chapter 12

Visitors from the East

Fittingly for a ground that is situated at the heart of one of the world's most diverse communities, The Oval inspires glorious memories in every cricketing corner of the earth. This is particularly true in the game's modern commercial centre of south Asia.

India and Sri Lanka have enjoyed landmark Test victories at The Oval, while Pakistan have an intrinsic connection with the ground through both the performances of the national side and the presence of some wonderful Pakistani players in the Surrey team over the last 50 years.

Six of Asia's greatest cricketers – Zaheer Abbas, Sunil Gavaskar, Javed Miandad, Sanath Jayasuriya, Rahul Dravid and Younis Khan – have made Test double-centuries at The Oval. Of the bowlers, Pakistan's Fazal Mahmood and Abdul Qadir have each taken ten or more wickets in an Oval Test, while 16 of Muttiah Muralitharan's 800 Test wickets came in Sri Lanka's famous victory in 1998.

Then there was the one that got away. In the 2011 Oval Test, Sachin Tendulkar was just nine runs from completing his 100th international hundred for India when he was adjudged lbw. Had he reached the milestone, the ground would have surely been guaranteed blessed status in India.

The Oval may have been deprived of Sachin's century of centuries, but the ground has been the setting of plenty of special moments for Asian cricket over the years.

ENGLAND V INDIA, THIRD TEST   1937

August 15, 17, 18, 1936. England won by nine wickets.

The first time India visited The Oval to play a Test was in 1936. It turned out to be a baptism of fire, largely due to the efforts of Wally Hammond, who scored 217, and Gubby Allen, who took seven wickets in the second innings.

At no time did India threaten to make a close fight and England won the rubber with ease. The gaining of first innings on a perfect pitch meant no inconsiderable advantage to the Englishmen, who had 422 runs on the board when their fourth wicket fell and declared first thing on Monday. As at Manchester, Merchant and Mushtaq Ali gave India a good start, but England's slow bowling paralysed several of India's batsmen and the last six wickets fell for 37, involving India in a follow-on 249 behind. In the second innings, the pace of Allen, who took seven wickets for 80 runs, proved the telling factor. By close of play on Monday, three of the most dependable India batsmen were out, and despite a gallant innings after a painful injury by Nayudu, England were left the modest task of making 64 runs to win.

England 471-8 dec (W. R. Hammond 217, T. S. Worthington 128; M. Nissar 5-120) **and 64-1**;
India 222 (V. M. Merchant 52, S. Mushtaq Ali 52; J. M. Sims 5-73) **and 312**
(Dilawar Hussain 54, C. K. Nayudu 81; G. O. B. Allen 7-80).

SURREY V INDIANS   1947

May 11, 13, 14, 1946. India won by nine wickets.

An otherwise regulation tour match at The Oval in 1946 was enlivened by an extraordinary last-wicket partnership in India's first innings.

A record-breaking last-wicket stand between Sarwate and Banerjee featured in India's first victory of the tour. Although Merchant and Gul Mahomed put on 111 for the third wicket, nine men were out for 205 when the last pair came together. They were not separated for three hours ten minutes, their partnership of 249 being the highest ever recorded for the last wicket in England. Never before in history had Nos. 10 and 11 in the batting order each scored a century in the same innings. Both Sarwate and Banerjee gave masterly displays and neither at any time appeared in difficulties. Fishlock drove well for Surrey, who collapsed badly before the Indian spin bowlers. Nayudu, dismissing Fishlock, Bennett and A. V. Bedser, performed the hat-trick. Following on from 319 behind, Surrey made a better fight. Fishlock, again in good form, and Gregory opened with a stand of 144, but next day the slow bowlers were again on top. Sarwate followed his fine batting by clever variation of spin, and India were left to get only 20 runs for victory. Gregory batted just short of three hours. Surrey were handicapped by an injury to Gover, who could not bowl again in the match after straining a tendon in his heel before lunch on the first day.

Indians 454 (V. M. Merchant 53, Gul Mohammad 89, C. T. Sarwate 124*,
S. N. Banerjee 121; A. V. Bedser 5-135) **and 20-1; Surrey 135** (L. B. Fishlock 62)
and 338 (R. J. Gregory 100, L. B. Fishlock 83; C. T. Sarwate 5-54).

ENGLAND v PAKISTAN, FOURTH TEST
Leslie Smith, 1955

August 12, 13, 14, 16, 17, 1954. Pakistan won by 24 runs.

India played their debut Test at Lord's in 1932 but had to wait nearly 40 years before their first victory in England. On the other hand, Pakistan managed the feat on their first visit to the UK with this dramatic win at The Oval.

Just before half-past 12 on the fifth day of the final Test, Pakistan achieved the greatest moment of their short career as a cricket country by beating England and so sharing the rubber. Their success was well deserved, for they showed great fighting spirit when victory seemed beyond their grasp. To Fazal Mahmood, the medium-paced bowler, went chief credit, his six wickets in each innings causing the batting failures of England. Others who played leading roles in the triumph were the late batsmen, particularly Zulfiqar Ahmed, Wazir Mohammad, Shujauddin and Mahmood Hussain...

The events of the first day did not suggest that England were in for such a struggle. Overnight and morning rain prevented a start until half-past two, and Pakistan, who won the toss, soon found themselves in trouble. The pitch did not become difficult, but the ball occasionally did the unexpected. Weak batting mainly accounted for seven wickets falling for 51 runs...

A Pakistan recovery began after tea. Kardar stayed seventy minutes before Evans held his third catch of the innings. The last two wickets added 56, Zulfiqar, Shuja and Mahmood Hussain playing the bowling with surprising ease, Shuja batted almost two hours for 16 not out. Tyson and Loader took seven wickets between them, making satisfactory Test debuts.

Only two overs could be bowled in England's innings before the close. Next day a cloudburst in the ten minutes between 11.50am and noon put the ground under water and prevented cricket. The Oval presented an astonishing sight with miniature lakes and pools over it. Naturally the pitch suffered and next day England underwent a nasty experience. The ball often rose awkwardly from a length and Fazal and Hussain made the most of the conditions. The English batsmen tried unsuccessfully to hit their way out of trouble. Compton made a gallant attempt, staying two hours 20 minutes, but he was missed three times. Pakistan celebrated the seventh anniversary of their Independence Day by gaining a lead of three runs. Fazal bowled throughout the innings and his figures, six for 53, would have been much better but for dropped catches. For all that, every England batsman was caught.

The pitch, drying out, was more in favour of spin when Pakistan went in again, but although Wardle bowled cleverly, McConnon failed to seize his opportunity. Shuja opened the innings with Hanif and again batted steadily, but Pakistan lost four wickets for 63 by the close. The early stages of the fourth day suggested an early victory for England. Pakistan at one stage were 82 for eight, but again they came back strongly. The last two wickets doubled the total, Wazir

Mohammad and Zulfiqar adding 58 for the ninth. Wazir, who spent half an hour over his first run, played a defiant innings of two and three-quarter hours. Wardle finished with the impressive figures of seven for 56.

England needed 168 to win and appeared keen to get the runs in the two hours 35 minutes available that evening. Simpson and May put on 51 in 40 minutes for the second wicket. May batted beautifully for 53 and when he left victory for England seemed near, only 59 runs being needed with seven wickets to fall. Then came a surprising decision, Evans being sent in, presumably to attempt to force a win in the half an hour which remained. Evans failed and so did Graveney, and when Compton fell just before the close, Pakistan were on top. With all the recognised batsmen gone and McConnon having to bat with a dislocated finger – the result of a fielding accident – England began the last day needing 43 to win with four wickets left. In 55 minutes the match was over, the cautious methods of the remaining England batsmen proving of no avail. Fazal, who this time took six wickets for 46, was helped considerably by the safe wicketkeeping of Imtiaz, who held seven catches in the match.

Pakistan 133 (F. H. Tyson 4-35) **and 164** (J. H. Wardle 7-56); **England 130** (D. C. S. Compton 53; Fazal Mahmood 6-53, Mahmood Hussain 4-58) **and 143** (P. B. H. May 53; Fazal Mahmood 6-46).

ENGLAND V PAKISTAN, THIRD TEST   Norman Preston, 1968

August 24, 25, 26, 28, 1967. England won by eight wickets.

The 1967 Oval Test was dominated by two contrasting centurions: England's Ken Barrington, who made his first Test hundred at the ground, and Pakistan's Asif Iqbal, who was batting at No. 9 and sparked a pitch invasion when he reached three figures.

Everything else in this match was dwarfed by a wonderful innings of 146 from Asif Iqbal but it did not save Pakistan from defeat. Still, it provided a rare treat for the Bank Holiday crowd. When Asif arrived at the crease Pakistan had slumped to 53 for seven wickets and the match seemed bound to finish before lunch as they still needed 167 to make England bat again.

He found a staunch ally in Intikhab and they indulged in a partnership of 190, a new record for the ninth wicket in Test cricket. Asif's 146 was the highest score by a No. 9 Test batsman... Hitting boldly, Asif excelled with the drive and hook. He raced to 50 out of 56 and Higgs, Arnold and Underwood, so supreme at one stage, all suffered during his drastic punishment. Intikhab's share when the stand reached three figures was 28. A sparkling off-drive from Higgs gave Asif his 14th four and took him to his first Test century in two hours 19 minutes.

An amazing scene followed. Hundreds of Pakistanis raced to the wicket and hoisted Asif shoulder high. The game was held up for five minutes and when a squad of police rescued him, the poor fellow was bruised and battered.

The team manager received him with a drink and he celebrated his great day by striking Higgs for five more boundaries in two overs... Asif spent three hours ten minutes for his 146 out of 202 and he hit two sixes and 21 fours. Intikhab, last out, followed in the next over, bowled by Titmus for a noble 51 included six fours...

Barrington held the stage on the second day when he made his first Test century at The Oval... moreover he became the only cricketer to reach three figures for England on each of the six home Test Match centres... For two and a half hours in the middle of the day the crowd, basking in the sunshine, saw cricket at its best while Barrington and Graveney put on 141. Graveney, who hit ten fours, gave an artistic display. Barrington placed his off-drives with marked skill and he hooked strongly...

[Pakistan] left England only 32 to win, and before the finish Asif crowned a great personal triumph by disposing of the two England opening batsmen, Close and Cowdrey, so that Barrington was left to make the winning hit, a cover-drive for four from Hanif, the match being completed by ten minutes past five with a day to spare.

Pakistan 216 (Mushtaq Mohammad 66; G. G. Arnold 5-58) and 255 (Asif Iqbal 146, Intikhab Alam 51; K. Higgs 5-58); England 440 (K. F. Barrington 142, T. W. Graveney 77, F. J. Titmus 65, G. G. Arnold 59; Mushtaq Mohammad 4-80) and 34-2.

ENGLAND V INDIA, THIRD TEST

Geoffrey Wheeler, 1972

August 19, 20, 21, 23, 24, 1971. India won by four wickets.

India's victory in the 1971 Oval Test was their first on English soil, and it also gave them the series. Wisden's report recognises the significance of the occasion – although neglects to mention an elephant which took the field at lunch on the fourth day. Indian supporters had arranged for Bella, as the animal was called, to be borrowed from Chessington Zoo in order to honour a Hindu festival.

India made cricket history by winning a Test match on English soil for the first time. In doing so, they brought to an end England's record run of 26 official Tests without defeat. The Indian match-winner was the wrist-spinner Chandrasekhar who took six for 38 as England were dismissed in their second innings for 101 runs, their lowest score against India and their third-lowest total since the war. For once the all-rounders and bowlers could not redeem the failures of the established batsmen.

The Indians were left 173 to make in the fourth innings and by consistent batting on a slow, turning pitch gained a victory which gave them the series. It was an unexpected win, for until Chandrasekhar's inspired spell on the fourth day England seemed to have the match well in hand…

England played exhilarating cricket on the first day. They totalled 355 after Illingworth had won the toss for the third time in the series. Jameson (82), Knott (90) and Hutton (81) attacked the bowling with relish, Jameson recalling the dash of Colin Milburn, so powerfully did he drive and pull…

England faltered when four wickets went for 46 in an hour after lunch, but Knott and Hutton set a new seventh-wicket record for England against India by adding 103 in 66 minutes. Knott swept and cut so audaciously and profitably that his runs came from only 117 balls in the same number of minutes. Hutton's off-driving recalled his famous father as he played in the classic manner.

Friday was lost to rain and prospects looked bleak on Saturday morning. Yet play was resumed only 15 minutes late and India were soon struggling, losing their openers, Gavaskar and Mankad, for 21 runs. Then Sardesai, for the first time showing the form he had produced in the West Indies, helped Wadekar in a partnership of 93 before Illingworth reduced India to 125 for five by dismissing Sardesai, Viswanath and Wadekar in 23 balls without conceding a run. Engineer and Solkar hit back with a spirited partnership of 97, the left-hander showing much more freedom than in the previous Tests. The outfield was so slow that Engineer, who played with typical enterprise, never reached the boundary in his 59. Both fell in the closing minutes of the day, but the last three wickets brought another 50 runs on Monday morning, limiting England's first-innings advantage to 71.

Everyone expected that England would set India a stiff task in the fourth innings of the match. Wadekar made no attempt to restrict the batsmen and went straight into the attack with his spinners. After Jameson had been run out for the third time in four innings for England – Chandrasekhar deflecting a straight drive from Luckhurst into the stumps – the innings disintegrated and was all over in two and a half hours. Some poor strokes were played, but Chandrasekhar gave his batsmen no relief. He was wonderfully accurate for a bowler of his type and his extra pace made him a formidable proposition even on the sluggish Oval pitch. Luckhurst denied him for an hour and 50 minutes while making 33, but having refused a single, strangely trying to protect Hutton, he was caught at slip next ball.

India finished the fourth day with 76 for two. Gavaskar was lbw to Snow without scoring, but Mankad played his longest innings of the series and then Wadekar and Sardesai denied England a breakthrough. Next morning, Wadekar was run out attempting a quick single to D'Oliveira before a run had been added.

The tension was high and the Indians, avoiding all risks, took three hours to make the last 97 runs. Illingworth, in his own way, again bowled beautifully, but without luck; and his field placings were masterly, as was his handling of the attack. Underwood was dangerous when operating in a slower style, but was not as consistently taxing as his captain. Sardesai and Viswanath batted in dedicated fashion and when they were out Engineer struck some telling blows. Abid Ali cut the winning boundary to bring the jubilant Indian supporters racing on to the field to acclaim their heroes, who had shown that their success in the West Indies was well merited and in no way a fluke. So India won in England for the first time in 39 years.

England 355 (J. A. Jameson 82, A. P. E. Knott 90, R. A. Hutton 81) **and 101** (B. S. Chandrasekhar 6-38); **India 284** (D. N. Sardesai 54, F. M. Engineer 59; R. Illingworth 5-70) **and 174-6.**

ENGLAND V INDIA, FOURTH TEST

Terry Cooper, 1980

August 30, 31, September 1, 3, 4, 1979. Match drawn.

The drawn Oval Test of 1979 was a classic encounter which featured a remarkable innings from Sunil Gavaskar as India fell nine runs short of chasing down 438 with two wickets spare.

The match was drawn after the most gripping closing overs in a home Test since the draw at Lord's against West Indies in 1963, a match it closely resembled as all four results were possible with three balls left. Gavaskar's inspiring and technically flawless 221 earned him the Man of the Match award and brought that rarity in recent Tests in England – a final day charged with interest. Botham played the major part in preventing an Indian victory and confirmed his status as Man of the Series. As the team fought each other to a standstill, there were many Englishmen in the crowd who would not have displayed their customary dejection at a Test defeat.

Gavaskar's innings was the highest by an Indian against England, overtaking the unbeaten 203 by the younger Nawab of Pataudi at Delhi in 1963-64, and his stand of 213 with Chauhan surpassed the previous-best opening partnership for his country against England – 203 by Mushtaq Ali and Vijay Merchant at Manchester in 1936. India's 429 for eight – they were set 438 in 500 minutes – was the fourth-highest score in the fourth innings of a Test. To reach their target they would have needed to set a new mark for a side batting fourth and winning, but this generation of Indian batsmen have some notable performances in that department and the job did not frighten them...

At 76 for no wicket on the fifth morning, India wanted roughly a run a minute. Their rate was never brisk – 48 in the first hour, 45 in the second, and 44 in the third. Hendrick, allowing only 11 runs in six overs, did most to peg India's progress and, in mid-afternoon, Willey conceded only two runs in eight grudging overs. However, Hendrick disappeared for good with shoulder trouble after his spell, and Brearley's capacity for restriction was limited.

England were despairing of wickets when, after five and a quarter hours, Chauhan edged Willis. The despair soon returned as Vengsarkar joined Gavaskar in an accelerating stand which produced 153 at better than a run a minute. Gavaskar masterminded the show, doing all the thinking and playing most of the shots. Tea came at 304 for one and, after a mere six overs between the interval and five o'clock – England ruthlessly slowed down the game – the last 20 overs began at 328 for one with 110 wanted, and India favourites.

At 365 Botham uncharacteristically dropped Vengsarkar on the boundary – an error for which he swiftly compensated by transforming the match with three wickets, a catch and a run-out in the remaining 12 overs. He collected a simple catch off Vengsarkar at 366 and Willey swept aside the promoted Kapil Dev. Yashpal Sharma and Gavaskar rattled the score along to 389, when Botham returned with eight overs left. It was a gamble by Brearley, for Botham had looked innocuous during the day. But he struck with the key wicket, Gavaskar drilling a catch to mid-on shortly after England had taken a drinks break – a rare move, tactically based, with the end so near. Gavaskar's memorable innings lasted eight hours nine minutes, and he hit 21 fours, most of them coming from firm clips past midwicket and his unexpectedly powerful cover-drive. However, his cool control of the developing crisis was missed by India as much as his runs.

Viswanath unerringly found one of the widely spaced fielders, as had Vengsarkar and Gavaskar. Then Botham firmly ended India's hopes by having Yajurvindra Singh and Yashpal Sharma lbw in successive overs and, in between, making a slick stop to run out Venkataraghavan. Botham's final four overs brought him an absolutely crucial three for 17. A target of 15 from the last over was too much, and the climax came with fielders encircling the bat.

England 305 (G. A. Gooch 79, P. Willey 52) **and 334-8 dec** (G. Boycott 125, D. L. Bairstow 59);
India 202 (G. R. Viswanath 62; I. T. Botham 4-65) **and 429-8** (S. M. Gavaskar 221,
C. P. S. Chauhan 80, D. B. Vengsarkar 52).

ENGLAND v INDIA, THIRD TEST

Michael Carey, 1983

July 8, 9, 10, 12, 13, 1982. Match drawn.

By comparison the draw between the same teams at The Oval in 1982 was dull, but it will be remembered for Ian Botham's only Test double-century, which he brought up in fine style on the final day.

Though left drawn after a highly unprepossessing last day, a result which gave England a 1–0 win in the series, the third and final Test had, like its predecessors, its share of excitement and drama. Notable was the batting of Botham, Lamb and Kapil Dev, and a cruel injury to Gavaskar, who took no further part in the match after a stroke by Botham broke a bone in his left shin on the first day.

Despite their captain's absence, and in the face of a huge total, India batted boldly and with a good deal of character, avoiding the follow-on, albeit with seven wickets down. The match then died a lingering death on the fifth day with England delaying their declaration until India were right out of contention...

Botham and Lamb provided entertainment of the highest quality... Lamb was run out after completing his maiden Test century, but Botham went on, with increasing power and majesty, to his highest score at this level and to one of the fastest double-centuries in Test history... The Indians found it virtually impossible to bowl to him as he drove with rare ferocity, one straight six off Doshi leaving its mark for posterity in the shape of a hole in the pavilion roof. When he was caught, off his controversial reverse sweep, he had hit four sixes and 19 fours.

England 594 (G. Cook 50, A. J. Lamb 107, I. T. Botham 208, D. W. Randall 95; D. R. Doshi 4-175) **and 191-3 dec** (C. J. Tavaré 75*); **India 410** (R. J. Shastri 66, G. R. Viswanath 56, S. M. Patil 62, Kapil Dev 97) **and 111-3** (G. R. Viswanath 75*).

ENGLAND v PAKISTAN, FIFTH TEST

David Field, 1988

August 6, 7, 8, 10, 11, 1987. Match drawn.

Pakistan were the visitors to The Oval in 1987, a match which produced a slew of superb innings from the tourists and some outstanding bowling from leg-spinner Abdul Qadir. It required some dramatic last-day resistance from Mike Gatting and Ian Botham to save the draw, but the result was enough to ensure Pakistan their first series victory on English soil.

Gatting and Botham stoically withstood Pakistan's push for victory on the final day to bring England belated solace in a summer of diminishing returns. Their four-and-a-quarter-hours' diligence pegged Pakistan to a 1–0 win in the series, their first series victory in England...

Imran called correctly for the first time in four Tests, and by lunch on the second day his batsmen had ensured England's third successive defeat in a home series. By tea on the third, England were engaged in a formidable rearguard action; by the close of play on the fourth, and already following on, they were still 381 runs behind with seven wickets in hand...

Miandad undermined England's bid to square the series by first completing an overdue maiden Test century against them and then progressing to his fourth double-hundred in Tests...

Imaginative strokeplay sent Malik darting from 64 to the 90s early on the second day as he moved impressively to his sixth Test hundred... Out soon afterwards, in almost four and a half hours he had faced 237 balls, hit only six fours and added 234 with Miandad, a record for Pakistan's fourth wicket against England. Next Imran, who insisted this was to be his last Test, registered his first hundred against England, racing from 57 to three figures while Miandad remained runless. Miandad, by now, had tired, despite his intention of attacking Sobers's Test record of 365 not out, and after ten hours 17 minutes, during which he faced 521 balls and hit a six and 28 fours, he tapped back a return catch to Dilley...

On the third morning, Ijaz and Yousuf continued their partnership to 89, a record for Pakistan's seventh wicket against England, and Dilley picked up late wickets to return six for 154... Because of the worsening light, Imran had had to abandon any notion of declaring and so the innings ran its mammoth course. Pakistan's 708, in 13 hours 40 minutes, was their highest total, surpassing their 674 for six against India in Faisalabad in 1984-85; it was also the sixth largest in any Test match and the second highest conceded by England...

England's position worsened when Broad was caught behind off Imran's fourth ball, and the miserable canvas soon portrayed 78 for four before Gatting, with a sturdy half-century, and Botham saw them to

Saturday's close without further loss. For England to survive, either of these two had to bat throughout the fourth day. But soon Qadir's bouncy leg-spin began to have its effect. Only Emburey withstood to any extent, hitting a six and six fours as Qadir brought England to their knees with his best Test figures of seven for 96, including a spell of three for 13 in 37 balls.

Following on, 476 runs behind, England contemplated the humiliation of losing by a bigger margin than any previous England defeat. And that ignominy took on a realistic look when they lost Moxon, Robinson and Gower. On the final day, however, when Pakistan were without Wasim Akram, in hospital for an appendix operation, the wicket of Broad was their only setback. Gatting reached his ninth Test hundred, the fifth in his last 14 matches and although giving chances of varying degrees of difficulty at 5, 23, 58, 60 and 107 he batted for five and three-quarter hours in all... Botham, batting with immense responsibility, denied the attacking principles on which his game had been founded for ten years by refusing to commit the slightest indiscretion. He joined the fight 45 minutes before lunch and stayed with his captain until the grim, necessary job was completed at 5.25pm.

Pakistan 708 (Mudassar Nazar 73, Javed Miandad 260, Saleem Malik 102, Imran Khan 118, Ijaz Ahmed 69; G. R. Dilley 6-154); England 232 (M. W. Gatting 61, J. E. Emburey 53; Abdul Qadir 7-96) and 315-4 (M. W. Gatting 150*, I. T. Botham 51*).

ENGLAND V INDIA, THIRD TEST   David Field, 1991

August 23, 24, 25, 27, 28, 1990. Match drawn.

England escaped with another draw in 1990 after a match-saving innings from David Gower.

Gower's sublime strokeplay, unwavering determination and considerable stamina throughout the final day erased India's chances of squaring the series, though their hopes were high when they enforced the follow-on after scoring their third-best score of all time... While Gower's innings was conclusive in saving the game, Gooch had also continued his record-breaking summer, unchecked by a lightweight Indian attack never capable of marrying its industry to quality and penetration.

This time when Azharuddin won the toss, he needed no persuasion to take first use of an outstanding batting pitch... Shastri settled in to give England their own headache... playing permanently straight, waiting to punish the wayward delivery, and progressing to his tenth Test hundred...

England had to keep India to a score of 450 or less to retain any hope of victory. But by tea on the second day, their concern was to salvage the match. India had already passed their previous-highest total of 510 in England, made at Leeds in 1967, and they marched on to their biggest score against England in either country.

The target of 407 to avoid the follow-on was ultimately beyond England... Once Russell had been wastefully run out by a direct hit from Wassan on the fourth morning, England were prepared for the worst, although Hemmings, helped in a last-wicket stand of 41 by Malcolm, seized the opportunity to score his second Test fifty before England were dismissed for 340...

India were soon to regret their lack of firepower. Azharuddin limped off with a sore heel and Shastri, taking over the reins, was to spurn the second new ball, instead keeping Hirwani's leg-breaks probing away into the footmarks in a marathon – and largely unrewarded – 59 consecutive overs from the Vauxhall End...

Thanks to Gower's elegant, day-long guidance, [England] finished 211 ahead with six wickets in reserve. His unbeaten 157, from 271 balls and graced with 21 boundaries, provided a satisfying climax to his 109th Test, and convinced spectators that the former captain would, after all, be in the England team to tour Australia.

India 606-9 dec (R. J. Shastri 187, M. Azharuddin 78, Kapil Dev 110, K. S. More 61*);
England 340 (G. A. Gooch 85, R. A. Smith 57, E. E. Hemmings 51; M. Prabhakar 4-74) **and**
477-4 dec (G. A. Gooch 88, M. A. Atherton 86, D. I. Gower 157*, A. J. Lamb 52, Extras 55).

England v Pakistan, Fifth Test
Mark Baldwin, 1993

August 6, 7, 8, 9, 1992. Pakistan won by ten wickets.

Waqar Younis was well acquainted with The Oval when Pakistan visited in 1992, at which point he was in the middle of three seasons spent at

Surrey. Forming a deadly pace duo with Wasim Akram, he inspired Pakistan to a devastating victory that sealed the series.

A game billed as The Showdown Test became instead a perfect showcase for the awesome fast-bowling talents of Wasim Akram and Waqar Younis. Pakistan won 15 minutes before lunch on the fourth day, a more comprehensive victory than even they could have dared hope for – and the crowning triumph of the summer for their captain Javed Miandad...

Gooch won an important toss in conditions near-perfect for batting and for much of the opening day England's battle-plan went smoothly, even through Gooch himself and Stewart fell in the first session, after a flying start against the new ball...

England were 40 minutes into the final session, on 182 for three, when Aqib Javed knocked out the first brick and then left Wasim to push over the whole structure... with a little help from Waqar, [he] then took just 45 minutes more to rout England's lower order with a thrilling spell of five for 18 in 7.1 overs.

Pakistan's top order then set about the business of building a match-winning lead, with five of the first six threatening but ultimately failing to play a major innings...

Latif's vital contribution left England 173 behind and facing a long struggle to save the match, but Waqar, bowling with great pace and spirit, hungrily lapped up the cream of their batting. By tea he had single-handedly reduced them to 55 for three, and it was 59 for four when Gower shouldered arms to one that came back off the seam and took his off stump. The contest was effectively over.

Sunday morning brought just a final exhibition of Wasim and Waqar's ability to brush aside a tail. Smith's brave unbeaten 84... represented a personal triumph against the leg-spin and googlies of Mushtaq which had mystified him all summer. Thanks to Smith, Pakistan were at least required to bat again. But a wide from Ramprakash and a square-cut boundary next ball from Sohail were sufficient to send into raptures the hundreds of Pakistani fans who gathered in front of the pavilion to salute their heroes.

England 207 (M. A. Atherton 60; Wasim Akram 6-67) **and 174** (R. A. Smith 84*; Waqar Younis 5-52); **Pakistan 380** (Shoaib Mohammad 55, Javed Miandad 59, Asif Mujtaba 50, Rashid Latif 50; D. E. Malcolm 5-94) **and 5-0**.

ENGLAND V SRI LANKA, ONLY TEST David Hopps, 1999

August 27, 28, 29, 30, 31, 1998. Sri Lanka won by ten wickets.

Sri Lanka played a one-off Test at The Oval for the first time in 1998. As had been the case with Pakistan in 1954, they won at their first attempt, although this time the result never looked in doubt after the third day. Muttiah Muralitharan, who had been called for throwing in Australia two years earlier, made the headlines for the right reasons.

Only three weeks after a Test series victory against South Africa had encouraged talk that English cricket was embarking upon a more successful era, the unique bowling talents of the Sri Lankan off-spinner, Muralitharan, brought England back down to earth in the final Test of the summer. Muralitharan, the hill-country Tamil and son of a biscuit manufacturer, born with a deformity of the elbow joint and a highly manoeuvrable wrist, produced one of the most phenomenal bowling displays in Test history as Sri Lanka won by ten wickets inside the final hour. Muralitharan's 16 for 220 was the fifth-best match analysis in Test history; his nine for 65 in England's second innings was seventh on the all-time list. On the way, he passed 200 Test wickets in his 42nd Test. Among spinners, only Clarrie Grimmett had reached 200 in fewer Tests; another Australian, Shane Warne, also took 42. Many who observed Muralitharan's prodigious performance wondered whether, given continued fitness, he could become the greatest Test wicket-taker in history.

England had long identified Muralitharan as Sri Lanka's prime bowling threat (indeed, Sri Lanka's captain, Ranatunga, had no compunction in referring to him as his only real asset), and the nature of the Oval surface strengthened that conviction. Slow and largely unresponsive to the seamers, the pitch negated the England trio of Gough, Fraser and Cork that had been central to the defeat of South Africa. Salisbury's leg-spin, seemingly fraught with anxiety, also failed to impress. That left the only battle between Muralitharan, his own exhaustion and the tortuous resistance of the England batsmen. Muralitharan's unorthodox action, angled in from wide of the crease, achieved turn and dip from the outset, and provided an engrossing spectacle, even against batsmen largely committed to survival...

Rarely has a Test innings encouraged more misleading conclusions than England's first. England took not far short of two days to make 445 and were assumed, at the very least, to be safe from defeat: they weren't...

The widespread condemnation of Ranatunga, for putting England in to bat, had to be gradually re-addressed. Ranatunga later crowed that he had wanted Muralitharan to have a rest in between innings, a points-scoring explanation which required us to believe that, had Sri Lanka batted first, they would have automatically made England follow on...

Hick's fifth Test hundred came in the rarefied atmosphere of No. 3. A sound innings against a limited attack proved little as to how he might fare in more pressurised circumstances. By tea on the second day, Hick had been overshadowed: Crawley, on his return, drove expansively, played purposefully off his legs and curbed Muralitharan's growing threat...

None of this could match the entertainment in store on the third day. Sri Lanka, 79 for one overnight, danced to 446 for three. Jayasuriya, who had suffered a lean Test year since taking 340 off India in Colombo, stroked 213 in 346 minutes from 278 balls, with 33 fours and a six. De Silva, habitually pulling good-length balls, collected a hundred, which made him the first Sri Lankan to pass 5,000 Test runs. Together, they added 243, breaking their own record for Sri Lanka's third wicket. Even though England fought back staunchly on Sunday, when six wickets fell for 86, debutant Suresh Perera and Muralitharan put on 59 to extend Sri Lanka's lead to 146.

Muralitharan had two wickets by the close, including Hick for a duck. Next day, Ramprakash's run-out of his captain, Stewart, proved significant. Perhaps it cost England the game; just as possibly, it robbed Muralitharan of the opportunity of joining Jim Laker as only the second bowler to take all ten wickets in a Test innings. Crawley was bowled on the stroke of lunch, attempting an extravagant drive; Hollioake fell first ball immediately afterwards. Only when Gough, who reined himself in for almost two and a half hours, joined Ramprakash did England suggest they might achieve a draw, to match that at Old Trafford earlier in the summer. It was marvellous cat-and-mouse – Ramprakash cleverly protecting Gough from Muralitharan, the bowler regularly switching ends to try to get at him. Finally, Ramprakash's hair-shirt defiance, more than four hours for 42, ended when he pushed to short leg. Gough was bowled behind his legs, sweeping. All that remained was for Sri

Lanka to score 36 to win, and for Muralitharan to retrieve the match ball and assert once again that he was doing no wrong.

England

M. A. Butcher c Jayasuriya b Wickremasinghe......	10	– st Kaluwitharana b Muralitharan................	15
S. P. James c and b Muralitharan.................	36	– c Jayawardene b Muralitharan...................	25
G. A. Hick c Kaluwitharana b Wickremasinghe......	107	– lbw b Muralitharan............................	0
*†A. J. Stewart c Tillekeralne b Perera	2	– run out......................................	32
M. R. Ramprakash c Jayawardene b Muralitharan ...	53	– c Tillekeratne b Muralitharan..................	42
J. P. Crawley not out......................	156	– b Muralitharan..............................	14
B. C. Hollioake c Alapattu b Muralitharan.........	14	– lbw b Muralitharan..........................	0
D. G. Cork b Muralitharan	6	– c Katuwitharana b Muralitharan................	8
I. D. K. Salisbury b Muralitharan	2	– lbw b Muralitharan	0
D. Gough c Kaluwitharana b Muralitharan........	4	– b Muralitharan..............................	15
A. R. C. Fraser b Muralitharan	32	– not out......................................	0
B 1, lb 11, w 2, nb 9	23	B 7, lb 8, w 1, nb 14.....................	30

1/16 (1) 2/78 (2) 3/81 (4) (158.3 overs) 445
4/209 (5) 5/230 (3) 6/277 (7)
7/333 (8) 8/343 (9) 9/356 (10) 10/445(11)

1/25 (1) 2/25 (3) (129.2 overs) 181
3/78 (2) 4/93 (4) 10/445 (11)
5/116 (6) 6/116 (7) 7/127 (8) 8/127 (9) 9/180 (5)
10/181 (10)

Wickremasinghe 30–4–81–2; Perera 40–10–104–1; Dharmasena 18–3–55–0; Muralitharan 59.3–14–155–7; Jayasuriya 11–0–38–0. *Second innings*—Wickremasinghe 4–0–16–0; Perera 11–2–22–0; Muralitharan 54.2–27–65–9; Dharmasena 19.3–13–12–0; Jayasuriya 28–14–30–0; de Silva 10.3–3–16–0; Jayawardene 2–0–5–0.

Sri Lanka

S. T. Jayasuriya c Stewart b Hollioake..............	213	– not out.......................................	24
M. S. Atapattu lbw b Cork......................	15	– not out.......................................	9
D. P. M. D. Jayawardene c Hollioake b Fraser........	9		
P. A. de Silva c Stewart b Hollioake................	152		
*A. Ranatunga lbw b Gough	51		
H. P. Tillekeratne lbw b Gough	0		
†R. S. Kaluwitharana c Crawley b Cork.............	25		
H. D. P. K. Dharmasena lbw b Fraser	13		
A. S. A. Perera not out	43		
G. P. Wickremasinghe b Fraser	0		
M. Muralitharan c Stewart b Salisbury.............	30		
B 15, lb 20, w 1, nb 4	40	Lb 4...................................	4

1/53 (2) 2/85 (3) 3/328 (1) (156.5 overs) 591
4/450 (5) 5/450 (6) 6/488 (7)
7/504 (4) 8/526 (8) 9/532 (10) 10/591(11)

(no wkt, 5 overs) 37

Gough 30–5–102–2; Fraser 23–3–95–3; Hollioake 26–2–105–2; Cork 36–5–128–2; Salisbury 25.5–7–86–1; Ramprakash 5–0–24–0; Butcher 11–2–16–0. *Second innings*—Fraser 2–0–19–0; Cork 2–0–3–0; Hollioake 1–0–11–0.

Umpires: E. A. Nicholls and D. R. Shepherd. Third umpire: J. W. Holder.

Close of play: first day, England 228-4 (Hick 107, Crawley 10); second day, Sri Lanka 79-1 (Jayasuriya 59, Jayawardene 4); third day, Sri Lanka 446-3 (de Silva 125, Ranatunga 50); fourth day, England 54-2 (James 20, Stewart 15).

ENGLAND V PAKISTAN, FOURTH TEST

Hugh Chevallier, 2007

August 17, 18, 19, 20, 21, 2006.
England were awarded the match when the opposition refused to play.

Few greater controversies have taken place at The Oval than in 2006, when umpire Darrell Hair was at the centre of a ball-tampering affair that led to

Pakistan refusing to take the field after tea on the final day. England thus won the match by forfeiture – the first such instance in Test history. This was subsequently changed to an abandonment by the ICC, who later reverted to the original result.

One day before the scheduled end of a Test series previously remarkable for a lack of serious controversy, cricket made up for lost time and plunged into crisis – and the water turned out to be deep, cold and very murky. Outraged at being punished for ball-tampering, the Pakistan team refused to take the field after tea and, in front of a full and voluble house, Darrell Hair, the senior of the two umpires, melodramatically removed the bails. The gesture brought a symbolic and actual end to the game, the first ever forfeited in 1,814 Tests and 129 years. It also unleashed a media frenzy that splashed cricket over the front pages for days.

The first signs of the impending turmoil came shortly after 2.30 on the fourth afternoon, when Trevor Jesty, the fourth umpire, brought out a box of balls. It was assumed that the current ball, 56 overs old, had gone out of shape through wear and tear. However, the choice of its replacement fell not to the umpires, but to the batsmen – an indication that the officials believed the ball had been doctored. Umpire Hair then slowly tapped his left shoulder with his right hand: five penalty runs were awarded to England's total. Without warning, without opportunity to defend themselves and without apparent thought to the ramifications, Pakistan were very publicly found guilty of cheating. Though visibly shocked, the Pakistan captain, Inzamam-ul-Haq, did not seem to dwell on the incident, and play continued until bad light forced the players off at 3.47. Several observers commended Inzamam for his restraint. Matters were about to change.

Almost an hour later, under brighter skies, the umpires took the field for the resumption. The England batsmen, Collingwood and Bell, appeared on the balcony, but the Pakistan players did not. A couple of minutes later, as umpires Hair and Doctrove returned to the pavilion, Inzamam briefly emerged from the dressing-room, shrugged his shoulders and went back in. At 4.55, the umpires, now joined by the batsmen, walked back to the middle. The Pakistan dressing-room door remained resolutely shut, and the umpires decided they had ceded the game.

Behind that closed door fervent diplomatic activity was taking place involving, among others, the ECB chairman David Morgan and Shaharyar Khan, his PCB counterpart. The Pakistan team, livid at what they saw as national humiliation, were eventually persuaded to abandon their protest and, at 5.23, Inzamam led his players on to the field. They spent a minute or two standing around then, in the absence of umpires, traipsed off. These various tableaux were acted out to a soundtrack of boos and jeers from spectators – most of them baffled as to what was actually happening – and a resounding silence from the tannoy. Some in the crowd amused themselves by creating 40ft snakes of stacked plastic beer glasses before, at 6.13, the announcement came that play was called off for the day.

Not until four hours later was it confirmed that the Test really was over, and that England had won. The two boards, both teams and the referee, Mike Procter, had wanted to resume next morning, but the umpires objected. The ECB promised 40% refunds for the 20,000 spectators attending on Sunday, and full refunds for the 11,000 with tickets for Monday.

Hair, who had a track record of embracing controversy, was now accused of a heavy-handed approach on the field – why had he not had a quiet word with Inzamam about the ball? – and intransigence off it. He and Doctrove argued that, by not resuming after tea, the Pakistanis had irrevocably forfeited the match. The cricket may have stopped, but the revelations, recriminations and repercussions were just starting.

One crucial revelation was missing, however: the perpetrator of the crime. Not one of the 26 TV cameras at The Oval had captured any sign of ball-tampering. When charges were brought, they were against Inzamam as captain, rather than any individual, suggesting the umpires, too, had little evidence other than the state of the quarterseam. But Inzamam was also charged with bringing the game into disrepute. Word leaked out that, if their captain were banned from the forthcoming one-day series, Pakistan might abandon the tour...

Given the violence of the storm that blew up that Sunday afternoon, it was easy to forget that an intriguing game of cricket had been lost...

Pakistan deservedly led by 331 as England batted again. And when Asif plucked out the forlorn Trescothick for four, an innings defeat seemed likeliest.

Come the fourth morning, Kaneria, fizzing the ball out of the rough, was posing huge problems for the left-handers. He bowled Cook through the gate from a no-ball, then had Strauss lbw with one that spun in outrageously. Cook rode his luck to make a useful 83 before Gul summoned a majestic inswinging yorker out of nowhere. (And that perhaps was what prompted Hair to scrutinise the ball: four overs later came the penalty runs.)

The right-handed Pietersen, though, was equal to Kaneria's challenge. In other circumstances, his 96 might have been the talk of the Test: a small-scale reprise of his Ashes-clinching epic the previous September. Within one shot of a dazzling hundred, Pietersen – his eyes lighting up at the introduction of the innocuous Shahid Nazir – slashed too hard. It was a shrewd and cool piece of captaincy by Inzamam, who seemed to have yanked the game away from England and put the ball-tampering far from his mind. As it happened, neither was the case.

England 173 (Mohammad Asif 4-56, Umar Gul 4-46) **and 298-4** (A. J. Strauss 54, A. N. Cook 83, K. P. Pietersen 96); **Pakistan 504** (Mohammad Hafeez 95, Imran Farhat 91, Mohammad Yousuf 128, Faisal Iqbal 58*; S. J. Harmison 4-125).

ENGLAND v INDIA, FOURTH TEST   Lawrence Booth, 2012

August 18, 19, 20, 21, 22, 2011. England won by an innings and eight runs.

The Oval was a much happier place five years later, when England celebrated their rise to the top of the Test rankings with victory over India to complete a whitewash. Close to a decade on from his Oval double-hundred, Rahul Dravid carried his bat in India's first innings, but Sachin Tendulkar's solo effort on the final day came agonisingly short of bringing up his 100th international century.

England, already confirmed as Test cricket's No. 1 team, had completed their first whitewash of a supposedly top-class team in a series of four games or more... and they had done it with their eighth innings win in 17 games – a sequence beyond even Clive Lloyd's West Indians and the Australian sides of Steve Waugh and Ricky Ponting...

For a while it seemed as if England's brilliance might be overshadowed by a light at the end of India's tunnel. Fretful for much of the series, Tendulkar looked set to reward the thousands of his compatriots who had secured fifth-day tickets by notching his 100th international hundred. But, nine runs short, he was given out leg-before to Bresnan, a brave but justifiable decision from Rod Tucker which at once drained the life from Tendulkar's features and the Indian innings. Including the nightwatchman, Mishra, who had fallen four balls earlier to end a gutsy partnership of 144 – India's highest of the series – their last seven wickets crashed for 21...

In truth, a Tendulkar century would have been wasted on India, who were spared an even worse hiding by Dravid, the third Indian to carry his bat in Tests after Gavaskar and Sehwag...

On the second morning, India's bowlers briefly remembered their virtues. Cook reverted to his early-series form by nibbling at the fifth delivery, while Strauss managed only two singles in an hour before driving loosely. But Bell and Pietersen were in no mood to give it away. United only in their right-handedness, they were an intriguing study in contrasts: Bell full of back-foot elegance, especially on the late cut; Pietersen a front-foot force of nature. Runs came in flurries – after lunch, Pietersen tucked into Mishra, while Bell took five fours in eight balls from Sreesanth – and India wilted.

Bell was first to three figures, his 16th Test hundred, at a record eighth British venue (oddly, only Edgbaston, his home ground, continued to elude him). Then, from the first ball after tea, Pietersen moved to his 19th century with a pull for four off Sharma...

The partnership eventually reached 350 before Pietersen checked a drive to provide a return catch to Raina. Momentarily shocked, The Oval duly rose. Only Compton and Edrich had added more for England's third wicket, against South Africa at Lord's during their summer of summers in 1947, and no pair had done better for any England wicket against India. It was also England's biggest partnership in Tests since 1985, when Gooch and Gower put on 351 against Australia on another Oval flat one.

Bell pressed on the following morning... by the time he fell on the slog-sweep for a blissful 235 – England's highest score against India at The Oval – he had stroked the bowlers into submission with a velvet glove....

Strauss's declaration meant India's respite was short-lived. Sehwag cracked a couple of fours, then fell in his first over for the third innings in a row, and Laxman feathered Broad. When Swann struck three times in the evening sunshine – his victims including Tendulkar, who swept once too often, and Raina, marginally stumped for a 29-ball duck – England had made up for lost time.

All the while, Dravid stood firm, like a lonely security guard repelling a gang of looters.... [and] steered India to their first total of 300 of the series. It was a pyrrhic victory for, with India still trailing by 291, Strauss invited Dravid to start all over again. Almost cruelly, he reappeared ten minutes later, but was soon walking back – 133 runs worse off – to another round of generous applause, adjudged caught at short leg off Swann by TV umpire Steve Davis after Tucker had ruled not out. Dravid later admitted he got an edge...

Tendulkar was granted a life on 34 when England carelessly failed to appeal for a stumping off Swann, and resumed on the fifth morning in the knowledge that a century would at least line India's cloud with silver.

Initially, luck was with him. Cook missed a sharp chance at short leg when Tendulkar had 70, and on 79 he was fortunate to survive a leg-before shout on the sweep. Prior dropped him on 85, and two balls later he padded up perilously...

Moments later, Bresnan – with the first ball of a new spell – persuaded Tendulkar to aim across the line. For a moment, time seemed to stand still. This was not quite Bradman's Oval duck of 1948, but the impact on India was immediate... When England claimed the second new ball the end came with embarrassing ease.

England 591-6 dec (I. R. Bell 235, K. P. Pietersen 175); **India 300** (R. S. Dravid 146*)
and 283 (S. R. Tendulkar 91, A. Mishra 84; G. P. Swann 6-106).

ENGLAND v PAKISTAN, FOURTH TEST   Osman Samiuddin, 2017
August 11, 12, 13, 14, 2016. Pakistan won by ten wickets.

In 2010 Pakistan had made a victorious return to The Oval, scene of the ball-tampering affair four years earlier, only for the spot-fixing scandal to blow up in the final Test of the series at Lord's. It was another six years before they returned to The Oval, where they levelled the series to reach the top of Test rankings.

Younis Khan has always been a twitchy presence, his odd movements dictated by an unusually long reach and torso. But, officially aged 38 (unofficially, he was probably over 40), he had raised questions by failing in the first three Tests... Here, with Pakistan needing a win to square a series they had led less than a month earlier, Younis stood a little taller and recalibrated his point of impact with the ball, letting it come to him further back in the crease... The result, an incandescent 218 by the third afternoon, was nothing less than his fierce will emerging from a personal swamp. It contained all the qualities for which he is renowned – punches and drives in the arc between the umpire and point, dominance of the spinner – but there were lesser-seen gems too, including some flashing cuts.

Younis also batted wonderfully with the tail. He had 128 when Sarfraz Ahmed fell... at which point Pakistan were 397 for seven in reply to England's 328. Yet with care, authority and trust, he helped add 145 to the team total, and 90 to his own. He was intelligent, too: on the third afternoon, facing a deep-set field, he dinked Moeen Ali to midwicket with exactly the right force to fetch him two. The next ball went into the stands beyond wide long-on to bring up his sixth double-century, equalling Javed Miandad's Pakistan record...

The key partnership, however, had come on the second day with Asad Shafiq... So often it had been Younis guiding a younger player through a partnership. But here the roles were neatly reversed: it was Shafiq's presence that seemed to calm Younis at the start of a 150-run stand...

Having won the toss, and armed with a 2–1 lead... [England's] dismissal inside 77 overs was a waste – not that it necessarily felt that way at the time. Rather, the sense was that Pakistan had let England off the hook, after a mixture of poor shots and energetic bowling from Wahab Riaz... had them 74 for four before lunch...

After Azhar Ali held Ballance at third slip off Wahab to make it 110 for five, he dropped Moeen Ali, on nine, off the unfortunate Amir. Much in the manner of their second-innings partnership at Edgbaston,

Moeen and Bairstow cashed in, adding a bristling 93. Bristling is what Bairstow does best anyway, in attack or defence, and he had done it all summer. But Moeen's was the innings that made England's day.

He had begun inauspiciously, in the middle of a brutal Wahab spell, his helmet pinged so hard that the first ball he faced rebounded to backward point. Three deliveries later he flicked Wahab through square leg almost as cleanly as he had been hit. Thus began not an innings but a demonstration, of a liquid exquisiteness of sporting movement more commonly associated with tennis star Roger Federer – whips here, lashes there, the entire operation orchestrated by soft and powerful wrists…

Once Pakistan had opened up a lead of 214, the only question was how they would exploit it… Amir began with a maiden for the first time all summer, Sohail produced another, and the mood was set. After nine overs, England had only nine runs; in the tenth, Wahab's first, Cook was caught at slip. It was left to Yasir to work a way to victory… taking care of England's top order with balls that did not spin much, but zipped off the pitch.

Pakistan needed only 40, and not long after tea Azhar launched Moeen over long-on, with one stroke winning the Test, levelling the series, and taking his team to the brink of the No. 1 ranking. It was a euphoric moment, arriving on the 69th anniversary of the founding of the country, and lifting spirits back home after a terrorist attack in Quetta. The result also came as a tribute to Hanif Mohammad, who had played a part in their grandest triumph, at The Oval in 1954, and who died during this Test. For Pakistanis everywhere, this game took its place in the pantheon.

England 328 (J. M. Bairstow 55, M. M. Ali 108; Sohail Khan 5-68) **and 253** (J. M. Bairstow 81; Yasir Shah 5-71); **Pakistan 542** (Asad Shafiq 109, Younis Khan 218) **and 42-0.**

SURREY v SUSSEX   1904

September 3, 4, 5, 1903. Match drawn.

Many of Asia's best players have played at The Oval, for or against Surrey. One of the pioneers in the English domestic game was the great

Ranjitsinhji of Sussex. Born and raised in India, Ranji qualified to play for England after arriving at Cambridge University in 1891. He played the last of 15 Tests in 1902, and a year later made 204 at The Oval as Sussex captain.

So heavy was the scoring in the concluding county match of the season that 965 runs were obtained for the loss of only 17 wickets, and thus the game terminated in a draw... Fry and Vine laid the foundation of the big total of Sussex by making 153 for the first wicket. Vine's 104 was his first hundred since the season of 1899. Brann helped Ranjitsinhji to add 122, and Newham assisted his captain to put on 141, both batting in capital style. The big feature of the match was, of course, the cricket of Ranjitsinhji, who gave a truly superb display, hitting all round the wicket with equal skill and facility, and giving no chances in eight hours and a quarter. The Surrey bowling lacked sting, and their fielding was slack...

Sussex 600-7 dec (C. B. Fry 81, J. Vine 104, K. S. Ranjitsinhji 204, G. Brann 54, W. Newham 50); **Surrey 365** (H. S. Bush 78, T. W. Hayward 54, E. G. Hayes 54; A. E. Relf 5-123).

SURREY V OXFORD UNIVERSITY 1932
June 24, 25, 26, 1931. Match drawn.

The senior Nawab of Pataudi, another titan of Indian cricket, represented both England and his country of birth. Playing for Oxford University in 1931, he took the Surrey attack for a century in each innings.

The Nawab of Pataudi invested this match with special interest by his achievement in putting together two separate hundreds. The two displays presented strong contrasts. On Wednesday Pataudi took half an hour to reach double-figures and had other spells of quiet play intermingled with a lot of polished all-round run-getting. Altogether he scored 165 out of 301 in four hours and three-quarters, the only real blemish being a difficult chance at the wicket when 142. On Friday he hit up 100 not out of 158 in just over two hours without a real mistake...

Oxford University 328-8 dec (Nawab of Pataudi 165, E. M. Wellings 55; H. C. Lock 4-57) and 199-5 dec (Nawab of Pataudi 100); Surrey 298 (E. F. Wilson 59, P. G. H. Fender 52, E. W. Whitfield 60; W. H. Bradshaw 4-82) and 134-2 (R. J. Gregory 69*).

SURREY V MIDDLESEX 1971

May 27, 28, 29, 1970. Match drawn.

In 1968 the county game opened its doors to overseas players and Surrey were one of the first counties to take advantage. Intikhab Alam, Pakistan's leg-spinning all-rounder, played for the club from 1969 to 1981 and enjoyed one of his finest matches in this London derby.

Intikhab with the ball and bat gave Surrey a considerable first-innings advantage and the bulk of the bonus points. His eight for 74 was leg-spin bowling at its best, and only Murray, whose driving was the feature of his 71, could judge his flight and spin. Murray reached 50 out of 71 in 19 overs. Intikhab then went in when five Surrey wickets had gone for 94, batted three hours 40 minutes for 106, his highest first-class innings, and hit one six and 17 fours on a pitch taking spin quite freely, but more slowly than the bowler liked. His all-round performance was of no ultimate avail, for Parfitt, scoring his first century of the season, and Featherstone batted beautifully in the Middlesex second innings....

Middlesex 212 (J. T. Murray 71; Intikhab Alam 8-74) and 341-6 dec (P. H. Parfitt 133, N. G. Featherstone 67); Surrey 323 (M. J. Stewart 65, Intikhab Alam 106) and 197-7.

SURREY V GLOUCESTERSHIRE 1977

June 12, 14, 15, 1976. Match drawn.

In 1974 Zaheer Abbas — another great Pakistan cricketer of that era — became the first Asian to score a double-century in an Oval Test, and two years later he put Surrey to the sword when representing Gloucestershire. It was one of a record four occasions when Zaheer scored a double-century and a hundred in a match for Gloucestershire – and he was not out in all eight innings.

Zaheer Abbas batted for eight hours 35 minutes for 216 not out and 156 not out in the cause of Gloucestershire, who for the first time could boast a batsman scoring a double-century and a century in the same match. But it was not enough to produce a victory. Surrey also had a batsman of equal character in Edrich and when they were left all the last day to score 470 to win, or more to the point six hours in which to save the game, he struck the third century and this averted defeat... Zaheer's first hundred came in three hours, and the second in just over two hours. He hit one six and 30 fours and was helped by Stovold in a stand of 156 and Brown in one of 119. Surrey, already without Arnold and Pocock, lost Smith ill, and Jackman toiled from lunch to the close of the innings, and then went in as nightwatchman! Zaheer hit one six and 14 fours in his second knock of 156.

Gloucestershire **390-7** (A. W. Stovold 81, Zaheer Abbas 216*) **and 264-2 dec** (A. W. Stovold 57, Zaheer Abbas 156*); **Surrey 185** (Younis Ahmed 59; B. M. Brain 5-74, M. J. Procter 4-39) **and 325-8** (J. H. Edrich 120; D. A. Graveney 5-77).

SURREY V WARWICKSHIRE 1991

July 7, 9, 10, 1990. Surrey won by 168 runs.

A trio of fine Pakistani players turned out for Surrey from the 1990s to the 2000s. The first of them was young pace bowler Waqar Younis, who enjoyed three summers with Surrey in which he took 232 first-class wickets.

Ward's consistent middle-order batting, mirrored in his fourth first-class hundred in 11 innings, gave Surrey an advantage they never conceded. It was driven home by Waqar Younis, whose seven for 73 was the best return of his brief career. Ultimately he finished with match figures of 11 for 128. Ward arrived with Surrey 13 for two; at 47 for three, Warwickshire's decision to put them in was looking a sound one. However, Lynch shed his natural exuberance and joined Ward in a vital stand of 208. He was out eight runs short of a century after facing 199 balls. Ward's 126 contained three sixes and 11 fours in 220 deliveries. On the second day, Younis scythed through the Warwickshire innings, illustrating his pace by hitting the stumps five times and having an lbw and a caught behind in his impressive tally. Warwickshire were nine wickets down when they avoided the follow-on, Benjamin being dropped in the gully with a single needed, but Surrey purposefully extended their lead to 317 by the close of play. To some extent they were helped by the back strain which prevented Donald from bowling. Next morning Surrey added 45 in 35 minutes and set a target of 363. Apart from Ostler and Benjamin, Warwickshire had no consistent answer to Younis, who was well supported by Feltham.

Surrey 303-6 dec (D. M. Ward 126, M. A. Lynch 92) and 236-8 dec (J. E. Benjamin 5-72); Warwickshire 177 (Waqar Younis 7-73) and 194 (D. P. Ostler 59; Waqar Younis 4-55, M. A. Feltham 4-59).

SURREY V DERBYSHIRE   1999

August 6, 7, 8, 1998. Surrey won by 226 runs.

The Pakistani spinner, Saqlain Mushtaq, took a match-winning 11 for 107 in Surrey's 1998 Championship match against Derbyshire. However the game was particularly notable for the surprise selection of Alan Butcher, six years after his retirement from first-class cricket, to cover for the large number of unavailable players.

Surrey, hit by injuries, Test calls and their decision to suspend Ratcliffe for one match for disciplinary reasons, called on 44-year-old Alan Butcher, now the Second Eleven coach, to play his first game for the club for 12 years. Butcher contributed 22 and 12 to Surrey's victory, and began his first innings while son Mark was on his way to a maiden Test hundred at Headingley. Greeted by a doff of the panama from umpire Kitchen, he drove his first ball through the covers for four. Once again, however, it was Saqlain Mushtaq's match. Making good use of his mystery ball – a leg-break delivered with an off-break action – he took 11 wickets for the third time in the season, including, for the second match running, career-best figures, this time eight for 65. Brown's fourth

Championship hundred of 1998 had been the centrepiece of Surrey's first innings, when left-arm spinner Blackwell also claimed the best figures of his career: five for 115. Hollioake's decision not to enforce the follow-on spared his bowlers from flogging away in draining heat, though Bicknell used the respite to score 81, at No. 9, leaving Derbyshire with a target of 433. They succumbed with a day to spare.

Surrey 333 (A. D. Brown 132; I. D. Blackwell 5-115) **and 238-9 dec** (M. P. Bicknell 81; I. D. Blackwell 4-94); **Derbyshire 139** (B. C. Hollioake 4-36) **and 206** (M. J. Slater 99; Saqlain Mushtaq 8-65).

SURREY V GLOUCESTERSHIRE, NATWEST T20 BLAST   2016

July 1, 2015 (day/night). Surrey won by four wickets.

Azhar Mahmood, the last of the Pakistani trio, played for Surrey from 2002 to 2007 before rejoining in 2013. His contribution to this Twenty20 match with Gloucestershire in 2015 will live long in the memory for those in the ground.

Azhar Mahmood brought the crowd to boiling point on the hottest July day on record by pulling the final ball of the match, from Craig Miles, for six over square leg to end a run of three home defeats. On a slow pitch, Surrey sweated over their chase, and left themselves 45 from the last five overs. They were let off the hook by a fusillade of extras in the final stages, and by Azhar's hitting.

Gloucestershire 154-5 (20 overs); **Surrey 155-6** (20 overs).

SURREY V NOTTINGHAMSHIRE, RL ONE-DAY CUP SEMI-FINAL   2016

September 7, 2015. Surrey won by four runs.

More recently, Surrey have employed one of Sri Lanka's greatest cricketers, Kumar Sangakkara, who played a gem of an innings in Surrey's 50-over semi-final in 2015.

Kumar Sangakkara produced the highest score of the tournament, his innings a model of acceleration as he shot from 100 to 150 in 29 balls. He mixed drives and ramps in a commanding performance that lasted 138 deliveries, and came close to exhaustion because a huge boundary towards the gasometers, plus a slow pitch, limited him to 13 fours and a six. Foakes gave diligent assistance in a second-wicket partnership of 87, and Wilson helped Sangakkara up the pace in a stand of 149 for the fourth; Broad went wicketless in a rare county appearance...

Surrey 300-5 (50 overs) (K. C. Sangakkara 166); **Nottinghamshire 296-7** (50 overs) (G. P. Smith 124, S. R. Patel 51, D. T. Christian 54).

Chapter 13

A Home from Home

O f all the overseas tourists who have played at The Oval, none are more readily identified with the ground than West Indies. Throughout their era of dominance in the late 1970s and 1980s, large partisan crowds would flock out of south London and into the stands at The Oval. They brought with them a carnival atmosphere, and turned the ground into a West Indian fortress.

The team responded wonderfully, with those such as Michael Holding and Viv Richards producing some of the finest performances ever seen at The Oval. Richards eventually bowed out of Test cricket beneath Kennington's gasholders in 1991.

West Indies had been increasingly regular visitors to the ground during the 20th century, famously beating Surrey in 1900. But it wasn't until 1928 that they played a Test at The Oval (see chapter 6), and a further 22 years before they beat England there.

Curiously, the great Garry Sobers had a relatively modest record as a batsman in his four Oval Tests (averaging 35 and failing to reach three figures), but he did show the ground a dash of his genius with twin hundreds for Nottinghamshire in 1970.

In modern times The Oval has been the setting for a brilliant century by Brian Lara, a famous West Indian victory in the Champions Trophy *(see chapter 11), and latterly some explosive T20 hitting from Chris Gayle, with their current status as "secondary tourists" meaning that they have not played a Test at the ground since 2004.*

Surrey v West Indians

1901

July 30, 31, 1900. West Indies won by an innings and 34 runs.

West Indies were victorious on their very first visit to The Oval against a Surrey side that had dominated the County Championship in the past decade.

Though Surrey gave a rest to all their leading players except Brockwell and Richardson, the performance of the West Indians in this match was the best during the tour. They finished off the game in two days, winning in brilliant style by an innings and 34 runs. Ollivierre and Cox gave a splendid display of batting, scoring 208 together for the first wicket. Cox for the first time in England played a three-figure innings, making 142 out of 261. In face of a total of 328 Surrey lost seven wickets before the drawing of stumps on Monday for 86 runs and though they did better after following on they never looked to have any chance of saving the game. Woods had a big share in the victory of his side, taking 12 wickets at a cost of only 116 runs. Still more remarkable, however, was the bowling for Surrey of L. Walker, who went on with the total at 205 and obtained eight wickets for 72 runs. Out of compliment to the West Indians Mr John Shuter, for this one match, reappeared in the Surrey team.

West Indians 328 (C. A. Ollivierre 94, P. I. Cox 142; L. Walker 8-72);
Surrey 117 (J. Woods 7-48) **and 177** (W. T. Burton 4-67, J. Woods 5-68).

England v West Indies, Third Test

Norman Preston, 1940

August 19, 21, 22, 1939. Match drawn.

West Indies played their first Test matches on the tour of England in 1928. On their third visit to The Oval in 1939, the tourists notched up their

highest interwar total away from the Caribbean, with most of their strong
batting line-up – including George Headley and Learie Constantine –
contributing to their score of 498. Second-innings centuries by Len Hutton
and Wally Hammond ensured a draw.

The final Test was notable for the enterprising batting of both teams. In
the course of three days 1,216 runs were scored while only 23 wickets
fell. West Indies had special cause for satisfaction as, after facing a total
of 352, they so severely thrashed the England bowling that they gained
a first-innings lead of 146 runs. The two Stollmeyers, Weekes and
Constantine were in brilliant form and R. S. Grant's men proved that,
given real cricketing weather, West Indies could hold their own in the
best company...

England gained first innings on a perfect pitch. They soon suffered
a setback as, with only two runs on the board, Keeton played the ball on
to his leg stump... West Indies, encouraged by this early success,
bowled and fielded splendidly... but Hardstaff treated the crowd to a
magnificent display. He drove cleanly and vigorously and with Nichols
put on 89 in 65 minutes. This stand was proving very troublesome to
West Indies when Constantine, the bowler, fielded the ball at cover and
threw down the wicket in amazing style. This incident led the way for
West Indies to dismiss the tail cheaply, for the last four wickets went
down for 19...

Not for a long time had England spent such an unsatisfactory day
in the field [as they did on the second day]. In brilliant sunshine the
West Indies batsmen gave an exhibition of the cricket they play in their
own islands. First thing J. B. Stollmeyer and Headley set out on a policy
of wearing down the bowling. During a stay of two hours 20 minutes,
Headley made some delightful square-cuts, strong forcing shots off his
legs and a few excellent drives. His dismissal was, at the time, a severe
mishap for West Indies and, as Gomez failed to settle down, four men
were out for 164.

Any hopes England entertained of bringing about a collapse were
frustrated by the promotion in the batting order of Weekes. The left-
hander... raced to his first century in Test cricket in 110 minutes and
when he fell to a superb right-hand catch by Hammond high at first
slip, he had scored 137 out of 225 in two and a quarter hours. Besides

lifting Hutton for six, he hit 18 fours. Weekes always hit fearlessly though his stance and footwork were somewhat unorthodox...

It was a real joy to watch the carefree cricket of West Indies on the last day. Constantine, in the mood suggesting his work in Saturday afternoon League cricket, brought a welcome air of gaiety to the Test arena. He revolutionised all the recognised features of cricket and, surpassing Bradman in his amazing strokeplay, he was absolutely impudent in his aggressive treatment of bowling shared by Nichols and Perks. While the four remaining wickets fell those two bowlers delivered 92 balls from which Constantine made 78 runs out of 103. Seldom can there have been such a spreadeagled field with no slips, and Hammond did not dare risk further trouble by changing his attack. With an astonishing stroke off the back foot Constantine thumped Perks for six to the Vauxhall End – a very long carry – and helped himself to 11 fours before he was last out to a very fine catch by Wood; running towards the pavilion the wicketkeeper held the ball that had gone high over his head.

England lost Keeton and Oldfield for 77 and then Hutton and Hammond, with a definite result already impossible, set up a new Test world-record third-wicket partnership by adding 264 in three hours. Hutton enjoyed another personal triumph at The Oval for, following his 364 against Australia a year before, he hit 283 for once out in this match. Hutton never looked in trouble and, defying the bowling for five hours and ten minutes, he claimed 17 fours. Towards the end of his innings Hammond hit at everything and, although it was not one of his best efforts, there were 21 fours in his 138.

England 352 (L. Hutton 73, N. Oldfield 80, J. Hardstaff 94; L. N. Constantine 5-75) and 366-3 dec (L. Hutton 165*, W. R. Hammond 138); West Indies 498 (J. B. Stollmeyer 59, G. A. Headley 65, V. H. Stollmeyer 96, K. H. Weekes 137, L. N. Constantine 79; R. T. D. Perks 5-156).

ENGLAND v WEST INDIES, FOURTH TEST   Leslie Smith, 1951

August 12, 14, 15, 16, 1950. West Indies won by an innings and 56 runs.

West Indies finally won an Oval Test at their fourth attempt, thanks mainly to the batting of Frank Worrell – despite being out of sorts – and the iconic spin pair of Sonny Ramadhin and Alf Valentine. Hutton carried his bat for 202 in the first innings, but in vain.

Even a wonderful display by Hutton could not save England, and West Indies won the rubber by three matches to one, confirming their all-round superiority in emphatic style...

Goddard won the toss, and, as events turned out, this became vitally important. It was soon obvious that the new England attack would fare no better than its predecessors, despite the fact that Wright bowled superbly. Rae and Stollmeyer scored slowly, and their opening stand produced 72 in one and three-quarter hours. Worrell was nearly dismissed before scoring, but Simpson's throw from midwicket to McIntyre went too high and the chance was lost. This proved very costly, for the second wicket put on 172. Rae remained as solid as ever and took five hours to score 109...

Worrell did not show anything like the same skill as at Nottingham in the previous Test, and, indeed, batted like a man out of form... When Rae left at half-past five, England faced the prospect of the last hour bowling to Worrell and Weekes, but Weekes, too, did not show his best form, and he hit a long-hop into the hands of mid-off, giving Wright his only success off one of the extremely rare bad balls he sent down that day.

On Monday, Worrell took three-quarters of an hour over six runs, but his slowness was explained when he retired through an attack of giddiness due to stomach trouble... The sight of Worrell resuming his innings at 446 for six must have been a heart-breaking moment for the England team, but he added only 22 runs. Worrell batted five hours five minutes for 138 and hit 17 fours.

Hutton and Simpson, making little effort to score during the last 70 minutes, obtained 29 runs... Next day the grim fight for runs continued... and at 120 for two Compton joined Hutton.

Compton took some time to fathom the wiles of Ramadhin and Valentine, but Hutton never looked in trouble and he completed his first 100 of the Tests in four and a quarter hours. Then he opened out and brought off many scorching cover-drives. Compton showed increasing confidence and all looked to be going well when tragedy occurred. Their stand of 109 ended when Compton was run out.

Hutton turned a ball to leg and Compton ran. Hutton started, but checked himself and refused the call. Compton, instead of turning back, ran on and was out by half the length of the pitch...

Hutton remained all day and was 160 not out at the close. Heavy overnight and morning rain followed by warm sunshine made the pitch treacherous on Wednesday and the early play was packed with drama. Everything hinged on whether England's last six wickets could score 72 more runs to make West Indies bat on the difficult surface. England failed by ten.

Hutton again rose magnificently to the occasion, but he lost partners rapidly against balls which lifted and turned nastily after the first few overs. Wright, the last man, joined Hutton with 28 still wanted to save the follow-on. Hutton took most of the bowling and excitement became intense as the runs slowly came, but at length Wright was lbw and England were made to bat again 159 behind. Hutton carried his bat for 202 and did not give a single chance during his stay... Nobody who saw his effort of concentration and perfect strokeplay will forget the great attempt he made to save his country.

Hutton immediately went in again and, not unnaturally, this time he failed. The England innings was almost a procession. At teatime the score stood at 70 for four, and the match was over three-quarters of an hour later... West Indies fielded splendidly, notably Weekes at slip and short leg. In the match Weekes held five catches and Trestrail, who acted as deputy for Worrell, made two catches.

West Indies 503 (A. F. Rae 109, F. M. M. Worrell 138, G. E. Gomez 74, J. D. C. Goddard 58*; D. V. P. Wright 5-141); **England 344** (L. Hutton 202*; A. L. Valentine 4-121, J. D. C. Goddard 4-25) **and 103** (A. L. Valentine 6-39).

ENGLAND V WEST INDIES, FIFTH TEST   Norman Preston, 1967

August 18, 19, 20, 22, 1966. England won by an innings and 34 runs.

West Indies clinched the inaugural Wisden Trophy series of 1963 at The Oval, but they lost on their return three years later courtesy of an extraordinary performance by England's tail.

[This] was a great triumph after so many humiliations during the summer and proved that England was not so poverty-stricken in talent as previous performances suggested. Personal honours went to Brian Close, captain of his country for the first time and one of the six changes the selectors made after the rubber was lost in the fourth Test at Headingley.

Close set his men a splendid example at short leg and silly mid-off and he used his bowlers shrewdly, not being afraid to introduce Barber with his wrist-spin early in the proceedings. Moreover, Barber took five wickets.

Sharing the honours with Close were Graveney, Murray, Higgs and Snow, all of whom batted magnificently after England, facing a total of 268, lost their first seven wickets for 166. At that stage everything pointed to another runaway win for West Indies, but once again the glorious uncertainty of cricket was demonstrated by these heroes, who caused 361 runs to be added for the last three wickets so that West Indies, batting a second time, faced a deficit of 259.

Never before in Test cricket had the last three wickets produced 361 runs, nor had the last three men scored one hundred and two fifties…

The match was favoured with fine weather, the first three days' cricket being played in a heat wave with the ground crowded to capacity. In spite of Sobers winning the toss for the fifth time, England took the initiative by dismissing Hunte, McMorris, Butcher and Nurse before lunch for 83. There followed a fine stand for West Indies with Kanhai hitting his first Test century in England. He batted for three and three-quarter hours and many of his 14 fours came from drives past cover and mid-off. Sobers, never in difficulty, drove, cut and pulled freely until he mis-hit a short ball, giving mid-off an easy catch…

Sobers, bowling his unorthodox left-handed spin, caused England trouble first thing on Friday. His third ball, a googly, accounted for Barber, and though Edrich and Amiss batted stubbornly, by the lunch interval five wickets had fallen and worse followed before Graveney at last found a reliable partner in Murray, whose neat and efficient wicketkeeping earlier had done so much towards bringing the fielding up to Test standard.

Graveney shouldered the early burden of keeping his end intact amid numerous failures. He showed the determination to build a long innings and when Murray settled down both men drove gracefully and hit to leg with power. When stumps were drawn on Friday, this pair had seen England take the lead; the total reached 330 with Graveney 132 and Murray 81. The form of Murray, who incidentally hit a century in May against the West Indies for MCC, was a revelation. He looked every bit as good as Graveney.

On Saturday the same batsmen continued serenely until Gibbs smartly ran out Graveney, who had spent six hours hitting his 165, which included 19 fours. Murray went on to 112, more than double his previous best Test score, before he was leg-before to Sobers at 399. He batted four and a half hours and hit 13 fours.

The West Indies bowlers must have looked forward to an early rest, but the England opening bowlers, Higgs and Snow, displayed their talent for batting in a highly diverting partnership of 128 in two hours, defying all the pace and spin the West Indies could offer and the new ball...

England were in sight of victory provided they could contain Sobers on the two remaining days. This they did. In fact, England captured the remaining six wickets on Monday in two and a quarter hours... West Indies being all out for 225, their lowest total of the series.

West Indies 268 (R. B. Kanhai 104, G. S. Sobers 81) **and 225** (B. F. Butcher 60, S. M. Nurse 70); **England 527** (T. W. Graveney 165, J. T. Murray 112, K. Higgs 63, J. A. Snow 59*).

ENGLAND V WEST INDIES, FIRST TEST

Norman Preston, 1974

July 26, 27, 28, 30, 31, 1973. West Indies won by 158 runs.

The 1973 Test, played in front of a rambunctious crowd that got behind the tourists, presaged an era of West Indian dominance that would stretch out over the next two decades.

This was the first Test win for West Indies since 1969 and their first over England since 1966. There was no question that it was fully deserved...

Among the many splendid individual performances, that of Keith Boyce on his first appearance against England in taking 11 wickets for

147 as well as making 72 was an exceptionally fine effort... Kallicharran excelled with 80 in each innings and Clive Lloyd made his 132 at a critical time in the early stages of the match.

In the main England were let down yet again by their batsmen, for only Boycott and Hayes could be satisfied with their achievements...

Hayes gave a most impressive display for a young man with rather limited experience of first-class cricket. He was never afraid to play his shots. Indeed, going in late on the second day he made 14 runs – 4, 6, 4, and those last ten runs were struck from Inshan Ali off the last two balls of the day...

Large crowds were present on the first four days and the local West Indian population kept up their customary noisy good humour the whole time. Frequent invasions of the playing area were very annoying, notably when Clive Lloyd was 99 and again when he completed his hundred. The players were mobbed and the pitch trampled on, but fortunately with the weather dry the pitch stood up well...

In the early stages of the match, the West Indies batsmen struggled for survival... West Indies had six left-handed batsmen and two of them, Lloyd and Kallicharran, came to the rescue in a brilliant stand of 208 which was only broken late in the day...

For the most part Boycott played splendidly for his 97 until just before lunch on Saturday when he glanced a ball from Julien to the wicketkeeper. There was some fine sustained pace bowling by Sobers, who gave so little away that his three wickets cost only 27 runs from 22 overs, but the main damage came from the hostile Boyce, who had never bowled better, with a long rhythmic run and not too many no-balls.

On this day the West Indies held their catches and after a sensible stand of 62 by Greig and Illingworth they captured the last five England wickets for ten runs to earn a valuable lead of 158 runs. Going in again, they lost three men for 52, but once more England were troubled by two left-handers and before nightfall Headley and Kallicharran raised the score to 95 for three.

On Monday a full house of 26,000 saw West Indies assert their superiority. This time Kallicharran stayed nearly three hours and hit 11 fours... Sobers, ninth out, served his side admirably for two and a half hours, there being eight boundaries in his 51, and so England faced the gigantic task of making 414 to win.

While Boyce was again the spearhead of the attack and rounded off the tail, Gibbs put in some telling work with his accurate off-spin and when he lured Boycott... into coming forward and presenting a return catch, the only real resistance came from Hayes and Illingworth. Six wickets had fallen for 136, but with plenty of time in hand West Indies were surely marching to victory although they saw this pair put on 93 in two hours before Illingworth was bowled round his legs. So Hayes was left to take out his bat after a stay of nearly four hours. His clean hitting produced 12 fours. Apart from a difficult chance to Kanhai at square leg when 56, the young Lancastrian gave a faultless display, notable for his neat footwork when dealing with the spinners and for the power of his strokes, particularly off the back foot.

West Indies 415 (C. H. Lloyd 132, A. I. Kallicharran 80, K. D. Boyce 72; G. G. Arnold 5-113) and 255 (A. I. Kallicharran 80, G. S. Sobers 51); England 257 (G. Boycott 97; K. D. Boyce 5-70) and 255 (F. C. Hayes 106*; K. D. Boyce 6-77).

Note: a report of the 1973 one-day international between England and West Indies at The Oval appears in chapter 11.

ENGLAND V WEST INDIES, FIFTH TEST   Norman Preston, 1977

August 12, 13, 14, 16, 17, 1976. West Indies won by 231 runs.

The 1976 Test is one of the most famous in The Oval's history, with Viv Richards and Michael Holding slaughtering England in sweltering conditions.

The previous time England went down by a similar margin in a home series was in 1948 against Bradman's Australia side. West Indies, moreover, recorded their fifth victory in the last eight Tests in England, and many by wide margins.

This contest produced many splendid personal performances. Holding achieved two bowling records for West Indies by taking eight first-innings wickets for 92 and with six for 57 on the fifth day his full analysis was 14 for 149 – a great triumph for one of the world's fastest bowlers of all time.

After Lloyd had won the toss for the fourth time in the five Tests, Richards gave yet another glorious display with the bat. Making 291 out of 519, he hit 38 fours in a stay of eight minutes short of eight hours.

For England, Amiss made a memorable return to the Test match scene. He looked the only class batsman in the side as he held the England first innings together by scoring 203 out of 342 before being seventh to leave, bowled behind his legs...

Willis struck early for England when he removed Greenidge leg-before, but Richards soon took charge and with Fredericks and Rowe providing sound assistance West Indies reached 373 for three by the end of the first day. Greig caused a surprise when, after Willis had dismissed Greenidge with the last ball of his second over, he put on Underwood.

A superb right-hand catch by Balderstone, who dived to his right at cover, dismissed Fredericks and at six o'clock Knott stumped Rowe for his 220th victim in Tests against other countries and beat Godfrey Evans's record.

Richards, 200 overnight, continued his majestic exhibition and he and Lloyd put on 141 in the 32 overs England sent down on the second day before lunch, Richards getting 83 to Lloyd's 48... One imagined that he would challenge Sir Garry Sobers's 365, the highest for all Tests, but having driven Greig high towards the Vauxhall End he went to repeat the stroke next ball only to touch it into his stumps.

During this period Greig bowled his off-spin with much skill and he accounted for Lloyd at 547, but the runs still flowed until, shortly before half-past five, Lloyd declared, setting England the task of making 488 to prevent the follow-on...

With the pitch slow and dusty, West Indies' decision to rely on the pacemen to the exclusion of any recognised spinner caused a good deal of comment, but Holding's speed through the air provided the answer, particularly as his side had so many runs on the board.

Amiss and Woolmer safely negotiated the 12 overs they faced at the end of the second day when some classic strokes by Amiss (22) helped the score to 34 without loss. Next morning, Holding began his devastating work by getting Woolmer leg-before to a ball that kept low.

Then Steele defended steadily while putting on 100 with Amiss before also being plainly leg-before. As Holding promptly removed Balderstone, England were in sore straits, but Willey resolutely kept up his end in a stand of 128 and all the while Amiss imbued confidence by the way he faced the bouncers, taking two quick steps back with a very open stance.

Greig raised hopes of a long stay with two grand cover-drives off Holding, but trying again he was bowled off his pads. A disgraceful scene followed. A huge section of the crowd, mainly West Indians, swept over the ground and trampled on the pitch with the departure of the England captain. The umpires led the players off the field at about 6.10pm. When peace was restored Amiss and Underwood played out the last seven minutes, England's total at the weekend being 304 for five with Amiss 176.

Amiss again played well on Monday morning, but Underwood soon became another Holding victim. There was spirited late resistance by Knott and Miller, but West Indies finished the halfway stage with a lead of 252.

With Daniel injured and Holding needing a rest, Lloyd preferred to bat again and leave England to face the last innings. This time, the two West Indies openers enjoyed themselves at the England bowlers' expense and in two hours 20 minutes took their unbroken partnership to 182, Greenidge hitting 12 fours and Fredericks nine.

So Lloyd left England six hours 20 minutes to get the runs or save the match and although Woolmer and Amiss hit freely on the fourth evening for 43, the first hour of the fifth day left England without a ghost of a chance. Half the wickets crashed for 78 and although Knott made his second fifty and Miller was again in form the West Indies sailed home with 80 minutes to spare.

West Indies

R. C. Fredericks c Balderstone b Miller	71	– not out	86
C. G. Greenidge lbw b Willis	0	– not out	85
I. V. A. Richards b Greig	291		
L. G. Rowe st Knott b Underwood	70		
*C. H. Lloyd c Knott b Greig	84		
C. L. King c Selvey b Balderstone	63		
†D. L. Murray c and b Underwood	36		
V. A. Holder not out	13		
M. A. Holding b Underwood	32		
B 1, lb 17, nb 9	27	B 4, lb 1, w 1, nb 5	11

1/5 (2) 2/159 (1) (8 wkts dec, 182.5 overs) 687   182
3/350 (4) 4/524 (3)
5/547 (5) 6/640 (7) 7/642 (6) 8/687 (9)

A. M. E. Roberts and W. W. Daniel did not bat.

Willis 15–3–73–1; Selvey 15–0–67–0; Underwood 60.5–15–165–3; Woolmer 9–0–44–0; Miller 27–4–106–1; Balderstone 16–0–80–1; Greig 34–5–96–2; Willey 3–0–11–0; Steele 3–0–18–0. *Second innings*—Willis 7–0–48–0; Selvey 9–1–44–0; Underwood 9–2–38–0; Woolmer 5–0–30–0; Greig 2–0–11–0.

England

R. A. Woolmer lbw b Holding	8	– c Murray b Holding	30
D. L. Amiss b Holding	203	– c Greenidge b Holding	16
D. S. Steele lbw b Holding	44	– c Murray b Holder	42
J. C. Balderstone b Holding	0	– b Holding	0
P. Willey c Fredericks b King	33	– c Greenidge b Holder	1
*A. W. Greig b Holding	12	– b Holding	1
D. L. Underwood b Holding	4	– (9) c Lloyd b Roberts	2
†A. P. E. Knott b Holding	50	– (7) b Holding	57
G. Miller c sub (B. D. Julien) b Holder	36	– (8) b Richards	24
M. W. W. Selvey b Holding	0	– not out	4
R. G. D. Willis not out	5	– lbw b Holding	0
B 8, lb 11, nb 21	40	B 15, lb 3, w 8	26

1/47 (1) 2/147 (3) 3/151 (4) (129.5 overs) 435   1/49 (2) 2/54 (1) (78.4 overs) 203
4/279 (5) 5/303 (6) 6/323 (7)   3/64 (4) 4/77 (5)
7/342 (2) 8/411 (8) 9/411 (10) 10/435 (9)   5/78 (6) 6/148 (3) 7/196 (8)
   8/196 (7) 9/202 (9) 10/203 (11)

Roberts 27–4–102–0; Holding 33–9–92–8; Holder 27.5–7–75–1; Daniel 10–1–30–0; Fredericks 11–2–36–0; Richards 14–4–30–0; King 7–3–30–1. *Second innings*—Roberts 13–4–37–1; Holding 20.4–6–57–6; Holder 14–5–29–2; Fredericks 12–5–33–0; Richards 11–6–11–1; King 6–2–9–0; Lloyd 2–1–1–0.

Umpires: W. E. Alley and H. D. Bird.

Close of play: first day, West Indies 373-3 (Richards 200, Lloyd 15); second day, England 34-0 (Woolmer 6, Amiss 22); third day, England 304-5 (Amiss 176, Underwood 1); fourth day, England 43-0 (Woolmer 21. Amiss 14).

ENGLAND V WEST INDIES, FIFTH TEST   Pat Gibson, 1985

August 9, 10, 11, 13, 14, 1984. West Indies won by 172 runs.

Another victory over England in 1984 allowed West Indies to complete a 5–0 series victory, dubbed a 'Blackwash' by a banner in the Oval crowd – and subsequently by the English press.

England responded as best they could to a call from their captain, Gower, for one last, big effort, but they were powerless to prevent West Indies from completing a 5–0 victory in the series. It was the first whitewash – or, as one prominent Kennington banner proclaimed, blackwash – in a five-Test series in England and the fifth in the history of the game…

After Lloyd, having shaken off a virus infection to play his last Test in England, had won the toss and elected to bat, it looked as though the England selectors might just have stumbled on a winning formula. Agnew's line and length were affected by first-match nerves, but, with the ball moving about, Allott and Ellison bowled well in support of the mercurial Botham, who took five wickets in a Test innings for the 23rd time.

There were those who had felt that Botham should be left out of the England side in view of the fact that he had declared himself unavailable for the forthcoming tour of India, but the selectors were not ready to contemplate picking a team without him and he responded to his detractors in characteristic manner. He captured the crucial wickets of Greenidge, Richards and Dujon, thereby becoming only the third Englishman, after Willis and Trueman, to have taken 300 wickets in Tests, as West Indies subsided to 70 for six. But then Lloyd, showing that he had lost none of the character that had sustained his side so often over the years, batted with great resolution for three hours 20 minutes, scoring an undefeated 60 and conjuring 120 runs from the last four wickets.

A total of 190 was still West Indies' lowest of the series, but any English euphoria was short-lived. By the end of the first day they had already lost Broad, and next morning they were devastated by Marshall, who took five for 35 in an almost brutal display of fast bowling that many considered to have been barely within the bounds of the law relating to short-pitched deliveries.

Fowler was soon forced to retire hurt with a bruised forearm, and although he returned later, to make the highest score of 31, the innings was damaged beyond repair. Pocock, who had gone in as nightwatchman and was not spared the short-pitched bowling, held on gallantly for 46 minutes; but Gower and Tavaré, playing his first match of the series, perished in quick succession to Holding. Any hope England had of taking a first-innings lead disappeared when Marshall removed Lamb and Botham in the space of five balls.

England were all out for 162, 28 runs behind, yet they were still in with a chance when Agnew, claiming Greenidge and Richards as his first illustrious victims in Test cricket, and Ellison reduced West Indies to 69 for three. Throughout the summer, however, Lloyd's side had dug into their reserves of talent whenever their supremacy had been threatened, and this time it was Haynes who mocked England's efforts. He had scored only 100 runs in the four previous Tests, but he batted now for more than seven hours to put his side in an impregnable position. Lloyd himself played another captain's innings in a stabilising fourth-wicket partnership of 63, and, with Haynes, Dujon made a dashing 49 out of 82 in 18 overs for the fifth wicket.

So England were left needing to score 375 to win or to bat for more than ten hours to save the match – neither of which seemed remotely within their capabilities. Broad, resisting for almost three hours, and Tavaré, who was his old, obdurate self for three hours 20 minutes, put a brave face on their predicament, but England's moment of truth arrived when Holding, having been somewhat overshadowed by Marshall and Garner, suddenly felt the urge to bowl off his full run for the first time in more than a year. In 17 balls, he dismissed Broad, Gower and Lamb at a personal cost of five runs and that was virtually that.

There was still Botham to preserve a flicker of optimism for the final day, which England began at 151 for five, but although he struck four defiant boundaries to reach 54, the last five wickets went down for 51 runs in an hour.

West Indies 190 (C. H. Lloyd 60*; I. T. Botham 5-72) **and 346** (D. L. Haynes 125);
England 162 (M. D. Marshall 5-35) **and 202** (I. T. Botham 54; J. Garner 4-51, M. A. Holding 5-43).

ENGLAND v WEST INDIES, FIFTH TEST   David Field, 1989

August 4, 5, 6, 8, 1988. West Indies won by eight wickets.

England were outclassed again in 1988, when a West Indian team containing Haynes, Greenidge, Richards, Marshall, Ambrose and Walsh put the seal on a 4–0 series victory.

As Logie on-drove DeFreitas for the winning boundary 19 minutes after tea on the fourth day, the flag of St George fluttered at half-mast on the pavilion roof, a sad symbol of England's failure to compete on the same plane as a formidable team re-emerging as the world's best. It was England's 18th successive Test without a victory. Nevertheless, Gooch, captaining England for the first time, could derive comfort from his own staunch batting and from England's commitment until lunch on the third day, when it was conceivable that they could have forced a winning position. From there, however, West Indies stepped firmly on the throttle and were uncatchable.

Gooch was named as the fourth England captain of the series in his 67th Test; only four men had played more matches before leading England for the first time.

Gooch, winning the toss, decided to bat first on a pitch containing bounce and reasonable pace. It did not, initially, disclose the movement it was to provide for the quicker bowlers. But in the eighth over, Gooch received an unplayable ball from Ambrose and immediately the inexperienced middle order was exposed. Maynard apart, they acquitted themselves commendably without threatening to usurp the authority of the West Indian bowlers... Smith announced himself with a pull off Benjamin which almost carried for six, then settled down to bat for almost three and a half hours. But a rash stroke from Maynard broke the heart of the resistance and England ended the first day 203 for nine, dejected and vulnerable.

Next morning, Foster lifted their morale with a spectacular piece of fast bowling which removed West Indies' first five batsmen. On the hottest day of the series, he went to work from the Vauxhall End and the ultimate result was a small but significant first-innings lead of 22, England's first over West Indies in 13 matches...

As their openers put on 50, England had cause to hope that an overdue victory in a summer of disillusion was within their compass. Alas, they lost Curtis, Bailey and Smith inside half an hour, Smith being lbw without offering a stroke...

Gooch held centre stage on the Saturday, allying grim determination to his solid technique without ever finding his best touch or timing. Having entered the arena at five o'clock on Friday afternoon, he left it some 24 hours later, having batted through the innings and spent seven hours eight minutes over his 84. It was the longest he had batted without making a hundred; with the ball moving about disconcertingly, it was also an immense feat of concentration. Only Foster, as nightwatchman, supported him with any vigour, striking a fearless 34 in 106 minutes.

When Gooch led England out on Saturday evening with a disappointing lead of 224 to defend, it was amid an atmosphere of inevitability. Within seven balls, he was back in the pavilion having badly dislocated the third finger of his left hand in attempting to catch Haynes at first slip, ironically from a no-ball by DeFreitas. He took no further part and Pringle, in his 18th Test, took over. He was to discover the difficulty of setting a field for Greenidge at his attacking best. The West Indian vice-captain moved quickly and ruthlessly to his fifty before the close, to all intents and purposes closing the door on England. West Indies resumed on Monday needing another 154 with all their wickets in hand. Greenidge fell first ball after lunch, but by then Haynes was firmly entrenched and their 12th century opening partnership had smoothed the path to victory in the only Test of the series not interrupted by the weather.

England 205 (R. A. Smith 57) **and 202** (G. A. Gooch 84; W. K. M. Benjamin 4-52);
West Indies 183 (P. J. L. Dujon 64; N. A. Foster 5-64) **and 226-2** (C. G. Greenidge 77, D. L. Haynes 77*).

England v West Indies, Fifth Test   David Field, 1992
August 8, 9, 10, 11, 12, 1991. England won by five wickets.

Many see the Oval Test of 1991 as marking the end of the West Indian era of dominance. England's unlikely victory earned them a share of the series and also brought the curtain down on Viv Richards's Test career.

As if by calculation, Botham struck his only delivery of England's second innings to Compton's corner to complete the victory which secured a drawn series against West Indies for the first time since 1973-74. Compton's famous sweep for the Ashes triumph of 1953 had finished in the same spot, and in many ways this match was just as memorable in Oval Test history. Certainly it could hardly have had a more popular final scene to gladden English hearts, Botham, with his Comptonesque flair for the big occasion, sealing the win in his first Test appearance for two years. It was, moreover, his first taste of victory in 20 Tests against West Indies.

This was the *coup de grâce*, but notwithstanding Smith's hundred, it was the left-arm spinner, Tufnell, who played the key role in a result many thought beyond England... His six for 25 on a hot Saturday afternoon obliged West Indies to follow on for the first time against England in 22 years and 48 Tests, and presented his captain, Gooch, with a priceless equation of runs and time.

Richards, in his 121st Test and his 50th as captain, was leading West Indies for the last time...

Gooch, winning the toss, decided to have first use of a pitch containing its usual generous bounce. This was exploited fully by West Indies' fast bowlers on the first afternoon, after Gooch and Morris had fought their way to 82 by lunch. No law was broken by Ambrose, Patterson and Walsh, but as the bouncer became a regular weapon, the spirit of the game was sorely tested at times... Smith's valiant sixth Test hundred, his second of the series, enabled England to reach 400 against West Indies for the first time in 15 years. His square-cut was again profitable, and he hit 13 fours in almost six hours (257 balls) at the wicket...

The third day belonged to Tufnell, when Richards might have been expected to take command on his farewell stage. From 158 for three, West Indies declined rapidly to 176 all out as Tufnell spun the ball generously in a devastating spell of six for four in 33 deliveries either side of lunch... Haynes, who carried his bat for the second time in Test cricket, faced 198 balls in four and three-quarter hours, and he batted eight minutes under three hours (114 balls) when West Indies followed on 243 behind. England collected three more wickets by the close.

There were no easy pickings for Tufnell on the fourth day, however. Twice Hooper struck him for six during a magnificent display of stroke-making which illuminated the first hour. Then Richards, given a standing ovation to the wicket, put on 97 for the fifth wicket with Richardson to put his side ahead for the first time in the game. Richards began needing 20 runs to guarantee an average of 50 in Tests, and he had gone well past that when he drove Lawrence to mid-on. He left the Test arena to rapturous applause, stopping on the way to raise his bat and maroon cap to both sides of the ground in gracious acknowledgment. Richardson finally reached his hundred, a dedicated effort, after six and a half hours…

> **England 419** (G. A. Gooch 60, R. A. Smith 109, Extras 54) **and 146-5;**
> **West Indies 176** (D. L. Haynes 75*; P. C. R. Tufnell 6-25) **and 385**
> (R. B. Richardson 121, C. L. Hooper 54, I. V. A. Richards 60; D. V. Lawrence 5-106).

England v West Indies, Sixth Test
Alan Lee, 1996

August 24, 25, 26, 27, 28, 1995. Match drawn.

The teams arrived for the final Test of a riveting series locked at 2–2. The ensuing draw might have not have lived up to its billing, but the Oval crowd were treated to a superb century by Brian Lara.

Not for many years had a Test in England received such advance attention; in the circumstances, the draw was a deflating anti-climax… It left the series drawn, justly and honourably…

Only 22 wickets fell in five full days of cricket and the body language of many a bowler told of the bias of the conditions… It was only the speed with which West Indies, in particular Lara, scored runs that imposed pressure on England to bat out time on the last day…

Atherton won the toss for the fourth time in five Tests and might have been revising his views on the pitch when Ambrose's second ball struck him in the ribcage… England were uneasy at the end of the first day, having lost the assertive Thorpe and Wells in successive balls from Ambrose…

After more than 11 hours in the field, West Indies' out-cricket bore signs of fatigue and resentment. But patriotic belief that their batting would disintegrate proved fanciful in the extreme: for the ensuing two days, they dwarfed England's once-imposing 454 to lead by 238.

England paid dearly for some missed opportunities on the third morning… Lara, habitually a chancer in his early overs, could have been run out just before lunch. He did not err again, his majestic 179 coming from only 206 balls and containing 110 in boundaries: 26 fours and a six...

West Indies' total of 692 for eight was their biggest against England and the tenth-highest in Test cricket; five of the ten have been achieved at The Oval...

When Walsh removed Thorpe just after lunch, England were still 106 behind and defeat remained possible. Atherton stood firm with Hick, however, and when finally he fell after six hours, the fourth man in the match to be out in the nineties, Wells had time to register three Test runs...

It was an occasion to savour, at the end of a compelling series, but it was not a good cricket match, because neither side ever really looked likely to win it.

England 454 (J. P. Crawley 50, G. P. Thorpe 74, G. A. Hick 96, R. C. Russell 91;
C. E. L. Ambrose 5-96) and 223-4 (M. A. Atherton 95, G. A. Hick 51*);
West Indies 692-8 dec (S. L. Campbell 89, B. C. Lara 179, R. B. Richardson 93,
C. L. Hooper 127, S. Chanderpaul 80).

ENGLAND V WEST INDIES, FIFTH TEST

Richard Hobson, 2001

August 31, September 1, 2, 3, 4, 2000. England won by 158 runs.

In 2000 England regained the Wisden Trophy for the first time in 31 years after a euphoric Oval Test match in front of a sell-out and raucous fifth-day crowd – this time supporting the home team.

Earlier in the season, a critic of the sport had described cricket as "a grey game played by grey people". The misguided journalist should have been at The Oval on the final day to see the conclusion of a momentous contest, itself the culmination of a memorable series. This was sport at its vibrant, colourful best, and it rekindled the public's love affair with cricket. Some 18,500 spectators crammed into the ground; thousands more were turned away, left to wander the Harleyford Road, hearing the roar that urged England on to triumph. In a show of admirable common sense, the Surrey club – who also admitted children at no cost – gave several hundred luckier fans access to the executive boxes.

Consensus suggested it was the first sell-out on a final day in England since Hutton, Compton, et al. recovered the Ashes here in 1953. Now, as then, England needed merely to hold their nerve. A victory would complete a summer that had already seen Zimbabwe beaten in a Test series, and both West Indies and Zimbabwe overcome in the one-day NatWest Series.

When Cork trapped Walsh 12 minutes after tea to complete the 3–1 win, the jubilant crowd packed in front of the pavilion and stretched back as far as the square to witness the presentation ceremony. Some of them, a year previously, had booed Hussain, the England captain, after a miserable defeat by New Zealand, but such churlishness was long forgotten as England celebrated a first series win against West Indies in 31 years. There could be no doubting the choice of Man of the Match. Atherton, who hinted during the game at retirement after the 2001 Ashes series, top-scored in both innings, in all batting for more than 12 hours on a pitch that showed enough life to keep the bowlers interested throughout.

Even so, Adams's decision to bowl was surprising, and once Atherton and Trescothick had put on 159 in 62 overs for the first wicket, England never ceded the initiative... Atherton remained ever vigilant but, next day, after Thorpe had succumbed to Walsh's slower ball for the second time in three Tests, the lower order offered only flimsy resistance between showers. For almost an hour on a gloomy evening, Campbell and Griffith remained resolute under a searching examination of bounce and swing from Gough and Caddick. However, the frailties of the tourists' top order, which had become increasingly evident through the summer, resurfaced spectacularly on Saturday morning. Eight wickets fell for 73 runs before lunch, including five batsmen for seven runs in 22 balls, the collapse begun when Campbell dragged one that kept low on to his stumps.

For a moment, it looked as if they might not get past the follow-on target of 82, but some lusty hitting by McLean saw them over that hurdle. White, who had shared the first six wickets with Cork, was rewarded for bowling fast and straight with the last two wickets, giving him figures of five for 32... His victims included Lara, bowled leg stump going too far across the crease, for his first golden duck at Test level. Trescothick's stunning catch at gully to remove Sarwan typified the general improvement in England's fielding.

Not even the dismissal of Hussain for a pair, completing his woeful series with the bat, could dampen home optimism. Atherton, largely eschewing the drive, again dug in courageously against the pace attack, as though roused by the challenge of the indefatigable Walsh, who on the fourth morning conceded just four runs in a magnificent 11-over spell. Regularly he would narrowly miss the edge. But Atherton, beaten three times in one perfect over, would smile ruefully, and then concentrate on the next ball rather than worry about the last.

Stewart, White and Cork all chipped in, but Atherton's 108, chiselled out in 444 minutes from 331 balls, was more than four times greater than the second-highest contribution. His century, modestly acknowledged, prompted a standing ovation to match that given Stewart at Old Trafford. It seemed he would carry his bat until he gave a thin edge to Jacobs, and became Walsh's 34th victim of the series. West Indies needed 374, their highest-ever winning fourth-innings total, to level the series, but wickets fell steadily once Hick held Campbell at second slip. Gough and Caddick managed to pin down Lara, as well as making further inroads, and an underarm throw by Thorpe accounted for Sarwan. Then as Lara began to expand his range, he was unfortunate to be given lbw to Gough. England formed guards of honour for Ambrose, playing his final Test, and Walsh, his last in England, as they strode to the crease, but there was nothing either man could do to reverse the result.

England 281 (M. A. Atherton 83, M. E. Trescothick 78) **and 217** (M. A. Atherton 108; C. A. Walsh 4-73); **West Indies 125** (C. White 5-32) **and 215** (A. R. Caddick 4-54).

Note: a report of the 2004 Champions Trophy final between England and West Indies appears in chapter 11.

SURREY V NOTTINGHAMSHIRE 1971

May 20, 21, 22, 1970. Surrey won by seven wickets.

Several West Indian stars have also put in some great performances at The Oval in English domestic cricket. In 1970 Garry Sobers did for Nottinghamshire what he never managed for West Indies: score a hundred at The Oval. In fact he made two of them in the Championship match against Surrey – and still finished on the losing side.

The spoils belonged to Surrey, the honours to Sobers, who saved his side with dazzling centuries in both innings. Arnold and Jackman, who bowled purposefully throughout to earn six wickets, had four wickets down for 28 when Sobers began an innings of 160 which contained two straight-driven sixes and 28 fours in four and three-quarter hours. In the second innings he played resolutely for two hours, being particularly tested by Pocock, but hit his final 61 in 47 minutes. Sobers had indifferent support both from the other batsmen and bowlers, and Surrey made light of the loss of Edrich, who was struck down by influenza. They batted consistently to gain four bonus points, Edwards and Younis in the van again. Finally they were left two hours 35 minutes in which to score 222, and Edwards launched them truly by hitting 79 out of an opening stand of 129. Storey and Intikhab then brought victory in dashing style by hitting the final 91 in 12 overs.

Nottinghamshire 281 (G. S. Sobers 160; R. D. Jackman 6-55) **and 218-8 dec** (G. S. Sobers 103*);
Surrey 278-4 dec (M. J. Edwards 71, Younis Ahmed 52, S. J. Storey 56*)
and 225-3 (M. J. Edwards 79, S. J. Storey 50*).

SURREY V NORTHAMPTONSHIRE 1988

September 2, 3, 4, 1987. Surrey won by ten wickets.

The finest West Indian to play for Surrey was Sylvester Clarke, the fast bowler who terrified batsmen up and down the country throughout the 1980s including, on this occasion, Northamptonshire.

Clarke's pace and penetration claimed six wickets on the last day, taking his total for the match to 12 and Surrey into third place on the Championship table with their third successive victory. Surrey were put on a sound footing when Lynch and Jesty stylishly stabilised the middle of their first innings with 136 in 26 overs. And a solid score of 304 took on an imposing air as Clarke and Martin Bicknell worked their way through the Northamptonshire order on the second day. Only Geoff Cook, and for a while Lamb, remained for any length of time. The last six wickets went for seven runs in five overs, and when Northamptonshire followed on, the same bowlers had three more wickets in the bag by close. Next day, only Lamb stood firm as Clarke moved unrelentingly towards career-best innings and match figures, leaving Darren Bicknell and Smith to complete the formalities for a maximum-points win.

Surrey 304 (M. A. Lynch 69, T. E. Jesty 72; N. G. B. Cook 4-33) **and 64-0; Northamptonshire 137** (G. Cook 51; S. T. Clarke 4-43, M. P. Bicknell 5-28) **and 230** (A. J. Lamb 70; S. T. Clarke 8-62).

Chapter 14

The Ashes since Bradman

Between the wars, the contests between England and Australia had been enlivened by the brilliance of Hobbs and Bradman, who retired from Test cricket in 1930 and 1948 respectively. In the decades that followed, Ashes cricket continued to be hard-fought, fascinating and dramatic, retaining its place at the heart of English sporting culture. Among many highlights at The Oval were Fred Trueman's 300th Test wicket in 1964 and England's nail-biting triumph four years later.

The latter decades of the 20th century were characterised by West Indian dominance and the rise of India, but matches between England and Australia at The Oval were still imbued with a special charisma that is reserved for the most historic rivalries. In the 1990s, just as Australia were supplanting West Indies as the team to beat, England produced a couple of face-saving performances. It had become an English habit to gloss over a poor summer with a morale-boosting victory in the final Test at The Oval.

The 2005 Ashes series will never be repeated; lightning doesn't strike twice in the same spot. But England's triumph was no flash in the plan. In the decade since 'The Greatest Match' (see chapter 1), England have lifted the urn three more times at The Oval despite mixed results in the Tests themselves: winning in 2009, losing in 2013 and drawing in 2015.

Note: a report of the 1953 Ashes Test at The Oval appears in chapter 8.

ENGLAND V AUSTRALIA, FIFTH TEST   Leslie Smith, 1965

August 13, 14, 15, 17, 18, 1964. Match drawn.

Two Yorkshiremen at opposite ends of their careers were at the centre of the 1964 Oval Test. The first was Fred Trueman, who after a summer of 'will he or won't he' became the first Test bowler to take 300 Test wickets. The second was Geoffrey Boycott, who was making his first appearance in an Oval Test.

Rain prevented a ball being bowled on the last day and ruined the faint chance England possessed of sharing the rubber, but once more the cricket only rarely rose above moderate.

The batting of Boycott and Cowdrey, the bowling of Hawke and the slip fielding of Simpson stood out in an otherwise ordinary match...

Dexter won the toss, but England failed to make the best use of the success. They found the pitch far from easy, but it was never difficult enough to justify their dismissal in four and a half hours for 182...

Hawke deserved credit for a splendid bowling effort, his six for 47 being his best Test performance. Dexter had the unusual experience of seeing his bat break in halves over its full length when attempting a drive. Half the bat flew to cover, farther than the ball reached.

Bad light delayed the Australian reply and they made three without loss before the close. Next day they batted slowly, being happy enough to build a good position without worrying about time.

Lawry stayed five and a quarter hours for 94 which included ten fours... Cartwright and Titmus bowled with commendable steadiness and they kept the batsmen tied down completely.

Australia forged ahead with seven wickets in hand and finished the second day with five men out for 245. They went on to a lead of 197 but the drama of the third day came right on lunch time. Trueman, previously ineffective, suddenly bowled Redpath middle stump and had McKenzie caught at slip off successive balls.

There was no time for another delivery before the interval and the crowd hurried back to their places to see whether Trueman could complete his hat-trick. He also needed one more wicket to become the only bowler to take 300 wickets in Test matches. Hawke survived the first ball, but eventually provided Trueman with his 300th victim. Trueman followed by dismissing Corling and finished with four for 87. He could not disturb Veivers, who hit aggressively for 67 which included a six off Titmus.

England, as they have often done in the past, made a good recovery after a poor first effort. They scored 132 for two before the close... Dexter did his best to score quickly in an effort to gain time, but was well caught at slip. Titmus went in as nightwatchman and next day gave further stubborn resistance, although more enterprise would have been valuable. His 56, made in three and a half hours, included a straight drive for six off Veivers.

Boycott proved that he had arrived as an England opening batsman with a fine innings lasting five hours. His maiden Test century was full of splendid strokes, particularly drives and square-cuts.

When the fourth wicket fell at 255 England were only 58 on but Cowdrey and Barrington put them on top. They proceeded carefully for a time, opening up after tea, and their unbroken stand of 126 took two and a half hours...

England finished the fourth day 184 ahead and fast scoring with an early declaration was expected. Unfortunately any chance of a good finish was ruined by the weather which prevented a ball being bowled on the last day.

England 182 (N. J. N. Hawke 6-47) and 381-4 (G. Boycott 113, F. J. Titmus 56, M. C. Cowdrey 93*, K. F. Barrington 54*); Australia 379 (W. M. Lawry 94, B. C. Booth 74, T. R. Veivers 67*; F. S. Trueman 4-87).

ENGLAND V AUSTRALIA, FIFTH TEST   Norman Preston, 1969

August 22, 23, 24, 26, 27, 1968. England won by 226 runs.

The final Ashes Test of 1968 was the spark that lit the D'Oliveira Affair. After scoring a hundred in this game, Basil D'Oliveira, a South African-born cricketer of mixed race, was not selected for the winter tour to apartheid

South Africa. But he was later called up as a replacement, a move that irked the South African officials to such an extent that the tour was cancelled; by 1971 South Africa had been frozen out of international cricket. Quite separately, this Test is also remembered for the events of the final day, when spectators helped the groundstaff with a major mopping-up operation following a torrential storm.

England won by 226 runs with six minutes to spare and squared the rubber with one victory to each country… but the Ashes stayed with Australia.

Down the years Kennington has generally proved a good place for England and now, after rain had robbed Cowdrey's men at Lord's and Edgbaston, even a storm that flooded the ground at lunch time on the last day could not save Australia.

Just before the interval England's final task appeared to be a mere formality with Australia toiling at 85 for five. In half an hour the ground was under water, but the sun reappeared at 2.15pm and the groundsman, Ted Warn, ably assisted by volunteers from the crowd, armed with brooms and blankets, mopped up to such purpose that by 4.45pm the struggle was resumed.

Only 75 minutes remained and even then the deadened pitch gave the England bowlers no encouragement. Inverarity and Jarman stood up nobly to Brown, Snow, Illingworth and Underwood, no matter how Cowdrey switched his attack with a cordon of ten men close to the bat.

Finally, Cowdrey turned to D'Oliveira, who did the trick with the last ball of his second over; it moved from the off and hit the top of the off stump as Jarman reached forward.

Now 35 minutes were left for England to capture the four remaining wickets. Cowdrey promptly whisked D'Oliveira from the Pavilion End and recalled Underwood, who finished the contest by taking those four wickets in 27 deliveries for six runs.

The Kent left-arm bowler found the drying pitch ideal for this purpose. He received just enough help to be well-nigh unplayable. The ball almost stopped on pitching and lifted to the consternation of the helpless Australians.

Underwood had Mallett and McKenzie held by Brown in the leg trap in the first over of his new spell; Gleeson stayed 12 minutes until his off stump was disturbed and to everyone's surprise Inverarity, having defied England for four hours with rare skill, offered no stroke at a straight ball and was leg-before.

So Underwood, with seven wickets for 50 runs, achieved his best bowling analysis in Test cricket and headed the England averages for the series with 20 wickets at 15.10 runs apiece. No praise could be too high for the way he seized his opportunity on this unforgettable day.

In fact the match produced many heroes. Cowdrey, the winning captain, led his team splendidly. Edrich, D'Oliveira, Graveney, Lawry, Redpath, Inverarity and Mallett stood out for their determined batting, and besides Underwood, there was much excellent bowling by Brown, Snow and Illingworth for England and by Connolly, Mallett and Gleeson for Australia...

Cowdrey won the toss and on the first day England scored 272 for four, Edrich holding the innings together by contributing 130. The pitch was firmer than expected after heavy rain the previous weekend. It was the fourth hundred by Edrich in 13 Tests against Australia and altogether he batted seven and three-quarter hours for his 164.

England had an anxious time on that first day until Graveney settled down and in his own graceful style put on 125 with Edrich. In the last hour D'Oliveira began his fine effort. He hooked the short ball superbly and next day drove magnificently... until he was last out for 158. Apart from Knott, the later England batsmen were singularly lacking in enterprise.

There remained 75 minutes on the second day for Australia to begin their reply and they lost Inverarity to a fine short-leg catch by Milburn while making 43.

On Saturday, Lawry stood between England and a complete breakthrough. The tall left-handed Australian captain stayed at his crease all day. At first Redpath with his free strokes batted well with him and before lunch they put on 77 to the overnight 43...

For two and a half hours England toiled in vain and then Redpath was held in the slips by Cowdrey. Four more wickets suddenly fell and

Australia were faced with the possibility of having to follow on. McKenzie defended stoutly after tea and Australia at the close were 264 for seven, having lost only McKenzie to the second new ball. Lawry was 135 not out at the weekend.

The struggle went mostly England's way on Monday. Lawry fell without adding to his score, being taken on the off side by Knott from an inside edge off a rising ball...

For all his youth, Mallett defended with the skill of an experienced Test campaigner for just over three hours, but England held a valuable lead of 170 runs.

Some of the best cricket came when England sought to score quickly in their second innings. Cowdrey alone stayed longer than an hour. The Australians fielded magnificently. Milburn set his side on the venturesome path. He hooked the first ball from McKenzie for four and pulled Connolly from outside the off stump for six. In an hour England reached 67 for three and in three hours they mustered 181, setting Australia 352 to win.

Again Milburn began Australia's downfall with a fine low catch in the first over at short leg from Lawry who thus was dismissed twice in the day. Then, facing the last ball before the close, Redpath padded away from Underwood and was leg-before. To remove these two stalwarts in 35 minutes at the end of a momentous day was a great feat by England and put them in sight of victory.

Next morning, with the sun shining as it had done throughout the proceedings so far, England drove home their advantage, mainly through Underwood and Illingworth. Inverarity, who defied England for four hours, alone gave any cause for anxiety, and except for the thunderstorm, England would surely never have had to battle against the clock.

To Australia's credit must be set their sportsmanship. They averaged 20 overs an hour when England were pressing for runs and their batsmen passed each other on the way to the wicket even in that hectic final period, nor did they fritter time away by gardening...

England 494 (J. H. Edrich 164, T. W. Graveney 63, B. L. D'Oliveira 158) and 181 (A. N. Connolly 4-65); Australia 324 (W. M. Lawry 135, I. R. Redpath 67) and 125 (R. J. Inverarity 56; D. L. Underwood 7-50).

ENGLAND V AUSTRALIA, FOURTH TEST   Geoffrey Wheeler, 1976

August 28, 29, 30, September 1, 2, 3, 1975. Match drawn.

The six-day Test of 1975 was an epic draw which was enough for Australia to retain the Ashes. But it was a victory of sorts for England, who had been asked to follow on and then blunted the Australian attack for the best part of three days.

By the end of the first day of this six-day match, England had lost nearly all hope of winning the game to square the series. The Australian score then stood at 280 for one and subsequently England faced an uphill struggle to save the match.

That they did so was due to a fine second-innings recovery to which all the batsmen contributed, Woolmer justifying his promotion to No. 5 with a marathon effort which brought him his maiden Test century as he stayed eight hours 19 minutes for 149, his highest first-class innings.

Another factor in England's favour was the slowness of the pitch, which even at the end of the six days showed little signs of wear, confounding both captains' predictions that it would help the slow bowlers before the end.

Ian Chappell, playing his 30th and last match as Australia's captain, won the toss for the first time in the series… Turner was soon dismissed, but thereafter England did not take a wicket until Friday morning… From 66 for one at lunch Australia accelerated to 185 for one at tea and consolidated in the final session…

England had a relatively successful second day, taking eight wickets for 252 before Ian Chappell declared… Old was the pick of the England bowlers…

Edrich and Wood, who played out time on Friday, found that weather conditions had changed ominously on Saturday morning. Whereas Australia had batted in two days of unbroken sunshine, England had to contend with bad light and an atmosphere particularly helpful to Walker's brand of swing bowling. The light and drizzle delayed the start until 12.45 and the England openers were still together at lunch.

Wood's dismissal soon afterwards was the prelude to a collapse… Only Steele stayed for long and England finished the day perilously placed at 169 for eight.

Thomson soon took the last two wickets on Monday before England followed on 341 behind and began to fight back...

Wood scored only 22, but he stayed nearly three hours while he and Edrich made 77, which provided a sound foundation for the big total England had to make. Edrich and Steele took the score to 179 for one by the close of the fourth day, and rarely looked in trouble.

The rearguard action carried on throughout the next day and when bad light stopped play 65 minutes early the score had climbed slowly to 333 for four, only eight being needed to make Australia bat again.

England were still in peril when Greig went early on the last day for they then led by no more than 30 with five hours and only five wickets remaining. Woolmer was equal to the challenge.

Three times edged strokes off Lillee flew through the slips but he survived and gradually wore down the fast bowler, who made a great last effort to win the match for his country.

Knott was a perfect foil for his county colleague and by lunch, after a two-and-a-half-hour morning session, England at 427 for five were nearly safe.

With the game drifting towards a draw Walters took four wickets in the afternoon. Knott was caught behind after making 64 of a partnership of 151 and Woolmer was last out on the stroke of tea when Australia needed 198 in roughly 85 minutes.

They lost two wickets before the end, the extra half hour not being claimed. One of these was Edwards, warmly received by the England players and the spectators on his farewell to Test cricket.

Australia 532-9 dec (R. B. McCosker 127, I. M. Chappell 192, K. D. Walters 65) **and 40-2**; **England 191** (J. R. Thomson 4-50, M. H. N. Walker 4-63) **and 538** (J. H. Edrich 96, D. S. Steele 66, G. R. J. Roope 77, R. A. Woolmer 149, A. P. E. Knott 64; D. K. Lillee 4-91, K. D. Walters 4-34).

ENGLAND V AUSTRALIA, SIXTH TEST

John Thicknesse, 1986

August 29, 30, 31, September 2, 1985. England won by an innings and 94 runs.

England required only a draw at The Oval in 1985 to claim back the Ashes. In the event, first-innings hundreds from Graham Gooch and David

*Gower put England in a winning position, leading to joyous celebrations
on the Oval balcony.*

Australia's modest chance of salvaging the Ashes effectively vanished
on the opening morning when Gower won an exceptionally good
toss and was then blessed by a good deal of luck in the first hour of
what blossomed into a match-winning second-wicket stand of 351
with Gooch.

The Essex opener made a chanceless 196; but though Gower, too,
went on to play brilliantly in scoring 157, he had started loosely,
lobbing the slips at two whilst attempting to kill a rising ball from
McDermott.

Australia's one moment of supremacy came after 37 minutes
when McDermott yorked Robinson with a late inswinger. Had
Gower's mis-hit gone to hand in the young Queenslander's next
over, England would have been 29 for two… Because of their sluggish
over-rate of 13 an hour, Australia were already on "overtime", in the
hottest weather for weeks, when Gower lashed a cut to deep gully
after a partnership with Gooch in which the runs had come at 4.6 an
over. Twenty-five minutes later Gatting was caught at the wicket off
Bennett from a ball that turned – an ominous portent for Australia –
but when England reached close of play on the first day at 376 for
three, with Gooch 179, it seemed certain they were heading for a total
of at least 600.

Against long odds, the innings ended two hours later, improved
fast bowling and overconfident batting accounting for most of the six
wickets which fell for 61. But the early loss of Wood to a possibly
unlucky decision, and the mortifying sight of vice-captain Hilditch
falling into Botham's hooking trap for the third time in the series,
combined with their drubbing on the first day, knocked the fight out of
Australia…

They batted with little resolve or basic technique, even Border
taking too little account of the extra pace in the pitch as he played on to
Edmonds, attempting a forcing stroke against the spin. A brilliant
overhead catch at second slip by Botham to remove Lawson hastened
the end, and 15 minutes after lunch on the third day, Australia followed
on 223 behind.

After a lengthy stoppage through rain at 12 for no wicket, Hilditch and Wood picked up the second innings. But the faults of the first innings were soon in evidence. With only one run added, Botham bowled Wood, and three overs later Hilditch, having resisted several temptations to hook Botham, drove a widish ball from Taylor to cover point. When Wessels chased an even wider one from Botham, Australia were 37 for three, Downton taking a fine catch at full length to his left... At close of play Australia were 62 for four, still 161 behind, with Border 26.

As on the previous three, every seat had been sold in advance for the fourth day's play, a crowd of 15,000 assembling to see if Australia's captain had one more heroic saving innings in him... The day began ominously for England when in overcast conditions Downton missed Border in the first over before he had added to his score... However, the captain's resolution struck no chord among his team-mates... at eight past noon Australia's last vestige of resistance disappeared when Border edged Ellison to second slip. There was time for Botham, leaping to his left to drag down a fast edge by McDermott, to add another to his galaxy of slip catches before Taylor caught and bowled Bennett to end the match and the series. In 96 minutes Australia had lost six for 67, Ellison finishing with five for 46.

As in 1926 and 1953, when the Ashes were also regained at The Oval, several thousand spectators massed in front of the pavilion when the match was over, to hail the England captain and his team and to give Allan Border a heartfelt cheer.

England 464 (G. A. Gooch 196, D. I. Gower 157, Extras 50; G. F. Lawson 4-101, C. J. McDermott 4-108); **Australia 241** (G. M. Ritchie 64*) and **129** (A. R. Border 58; R. M. Ellison 5-46).

ENGLAND v AUSTRALIA, SIXTH TEST   Matthew Engel, 1994

August 19, 20, 21, 22, 23, 1993. England won by 161 runs.

Eight years later came an example of the 1990s phenomenon by which England pulled off fantastic performances at The Oval when the series was already dead.

To general astonishment, England reversed the form of the summer, outplayed Australia and won the final Test deservedly and decisively... It brought about a halt, at least temporarily, in the mood of national teeth-gnashing that had accompanied England's previous failures. For Australia, who had enjoyed a triumphal progress round the British Isles with only trivial setbacks, the defeat came hours before they flew home; it was like having the perfect holiday and then being nabbed by customs.

The win was a particular triumph for the England captain Mike Atherton, in his second game in charge...

The combination of Fraser, Malcolm and Watkin... on a pacy wicket transformed England. None had played a game before in the series; they shared the 20 wickets between them...

England made their familiar good start, racing to 143 for one. Australia were again unchanged... The batsmen were right on top all day but, in familiar English fashion, they got themselves out, often for no good reason – Hick, in particular, was blazing away and hit a regal six to reach 80 two balls before being caught at third man off a thoroughly ill-judged cut...

Next morning, England were all out for 380 and the consensus was that they had scored a hundred too few. But that assumed England's attack would live up to past form. Instead, Malcolm's speed, Watkin's resilience and Fraser's relentlessness completely transformed their prospects. The wicket was hard enough to favour strokeplay and to ensure that class bowlers could always make a batsman uncomfortable. England fielded tightly, with the young men darting everywhere and Gooch loyally putting on the short-leg helmet. Australia crumpled to 196 for eight. But then England could not finish them off and the last two wickets took the score past 300.

Australia could have got back in the game but, once again, the top three England batsmen tore into some jaded bowling and by the middle of Saturday afternoon England, at 157 for one, already looked fireproof...

The innings meandered later and England's prospects were hindered on the fourth day by the loss of two hours' play to the weather... But the presence of the seventh specialist batsman, Ramprakash, enabled England to take the lead to 390 before they were bowled out to save Atherton having to decide whether to risk a declaration.

The rain effectively ruled out the remote chance of an Australian win. Could England do it? Again the luck was with them... Umpire Meyer gave them two successive decisions that might have gone the other way... Then Taylor played on and it was 30 for three. There was a stand between Mark Waugh and Border, who was caught behind straight after lunch and left an English cricket field for what was presumed to be the last time without once looking up...

At 5.18pm England won. The heroes of the hour were English but the heroes of the summer were Australian: it was Border who was presented with a replica of the Ashes. What England had won, at the very last minute, was some self-respect.

England 380 (G. A. Gooch 56, M. A. Atherton 50, G. A. Hick 80, A. J. Stewart 76)
and 313 (G. A. Gooch 79, M. R. Ramprakash 64); **Australia 303** (M. A. Taylor 70,
I. A. Healy 83*; A. R. C. Fraser 5-87) **and 229** (S. L. Watkin 4-65).

ENGLAND V AUSTRALIA, SIXTH TEST
Matthew Engel, 1998

August 21, 22, 23, 1997. England won by 19 runs.

The 1997 Oval Test was a repeat dose. The match produced one of Phil Tufnell's finest moments and a brilliant second-innings bowling display from England.

Too late to rescue the Ashes, but not too late to rescue their self-respect, England won a sensational victory after a contest fit to rank with the great games of Ashes history. The match was over at 5.24pm on the third day, but the cricket that did take place was amazing, and the climax utterly riveting. Australia, needing only 124 to win, were bowled out for just 104...

Australia's collapse maintained their reputation for vulnerability in a run-chase, and for flunking the Tests that matter least. It was the third time in 1997 they had lost the last match of a series they had already won. It did not much dent their reputation as one of the great Ashes teams. The result meant far more to England...

Like so many great matches, this came about thanks to what is conventionally known as a bad pitch. It was too dry, and by the second day it was crumbling. This came as a surprise to just about everyone. When England were all out on the first day, it was assumed to be yet another pathetic batting failure... The assumption was correct, because the pitch was still mild and there was no excuse at all for their collapse from 128 for three to 132 for seven.

But for once the luck favoured England in this contest... England were able to bat first and hoped to give Australia the runaround in steamy, Brisbane-like heat. They must have fancied 500; even afterwards, Atherton thought 350 was par; they made 180, a useful total only at darts...

Stewart, Hussain and Thorpe gave England hope of a decent score. But McGrath once again was both insistent and persistent, and the middle order suddenly crumpled in a sort of cataleptic fit... Caddick and Martin each hit a six, which was something, but England were all out before tea. McGrath finished with seven for 76, including England's top six; he did little more than bowl fast and straight.

Tufnell removed Australia's openers in the evening session, but even so England's position looked dire, and direr still when Australia were 94 for two. But then the game changed. Over the years, Tufnell had displayed more than his share of the slow left-armer's traditional eccentricity; now he displayed the breed's quieter virtues. He kept his line and his patience and, in the afternoon, as the pitch began to wear visibly, he reaped his reward. Bowling unchanged for 35 overs, he worked his way through the Australian batting. He, too, finished with seven and, until Warne began slogging him, he conceded hardly more than a run an over.

And so, after tea, England were in again, their hopes renewed. But the first three batsmen were gone before they had even wiped off their narrow deficit. And Saturday began with a blow: to the third ball of the morning, Hussain toe-ended a cut straight to Elliott. England were effectively 12 for four.

But the luck had turned. England supporters had long since assumed that injuries happened only to their side. However, Warne had been struggling on the second night, and now it was obvious he had a nasty groin strain. He was only able to lope in off three paces, and it seemed to curb his variety. That did not stop him turning the ball viciously out of the rough, and could not save the likes of Hussain, bent on doing something daft. But the next pair avoided the daft, and put on 79.

Thorpe, not for the first time, failed to convert a fifty into a century but, since he scored the only fifty of the match, that was wholly forgivable. It was an innings of exceptional quality and tenacity. Ramprakash made 48, which was worth at least double, and began at long last to bat for England with the certainty he showed for Middlesex...

The England tail was useless yet again – the last four wickets fell for three – and Kasprowicz followed McGrath and Tufnell in taking seven in an innings; three bowlers had never done this in the same Test. Australia needed just 124 to win. But there was a sense that the situation was not hopeless. The crowd roared Malcolm in as he took the new ball, and he responded by straightening his fourth delivery to dismiss Elliott...

Caddick removed Taylor and Blewett, given out caught behind... the Waughs soon followed. Australia were 54 for five and suddenly all England was agog...

Ponting and Healy battled back, with a stand of 34. But Tufnell finally trapped Ponting on the back pad, and Caddick took a return catch from Healy, juggled with it one-handed twice, and then clung on. Warne, batting with a runner, tried to lash out again. This time Martin got underneath his first big hit... England were confident now. The last act was Thorpe catching McGrath at mid-off – Tufnell's 11th victim...

This was the first three-day Test at The Oval since 1957. On the Saturday evening Mark Taylor received a replica Ashes urn from the master of ceremonies David Gower, who had waved around a similar copy 12 years earlier. But this was greeted with only casual applause. It was a moment for England, and not just for the team...

England 180 (G. D. McGrath 7-76) and 163 (G. P. Thorpe 62; M. S. Kasprowicz 7-36); Australia 220 (P. C. R. Tufnell 7-66) and 104 (P. C. R. Tufnell 4-27, A. R. Caddick 5-42).

Note: a report of the 2005 Ashes Test at The Oval appears in chapter 1.

ENGLAND V AUSTRALIA, FIFTH TEST   Matthew Engel, 2010

August 20, 21, 22, 23, 2009. England won by 197 runs.

Despite winning every home Ashes series since 2005, England's only Oval victory against Australia this century was in the final Test of the 2009 series. It was a match they needed to win to regain the urn and avenge the 5–0 drubbing suffered in the previous series down under.

At 5.49pm on a warm and mellow summer's evening, Alastair Cook snapped up a bat-pad catch off Graeme Swann, and England recaptured the urn that had been confiscated from them in disgrace at Perth seven Tests, two years and 248 days earlier...

Australia were set 546 to win on a pitch variously condemned by commentators – not all of them Australian – as "dodgy", "an abuse", "overbaked" and "crumbling". This figure was 128 beyond the existing Test record for a winning total in the fourth innings, and even 33 beyond the record in all first-class cricket. Yet even so, the stands and press box (and perhaps, for all we know, the dressing-room) were full of English defeatists, convinced that it was not the ball that was liable to kick spitefully and unpredictably, but fate.

Indeed, at 217 for two and 327 for five, even the stoutest English heart began to quiver a little. But when the end came, it came quickly, with a day to spare...

The surface was certainly unusually dry, with the ball going through the top on the first day and clouds of dust appearing from the first minute. It offered bounce, as The Oval usually does, but not predictably so. This bounce got slower as the game progressed, giving the batsmen time to adjust. It was one of those pitches that was not, theoretically, ideal but actually produces heroic cricket. What irked the Aussies was the persistent rumour that it had been prepared to the precise specifications of the ECB.

The ECB did not tell Ponting to guess wrong at the toss (for the fourth time out of five). Nor did they tell the Australian selectors to stick with their Headingley team and omit their sole specialist spinner, Nathan Hauritz. It was the Oval Test precisely a hundred years earlier that moved *Wisden*'s editor Sydney Pardon (in his 1910 Notes) to his most famous phrase – that the England selectors had "touched the confines of lunacy". Now the press, seated in the Sydney Pardon gallery, saw Australia's selectors not merely touch those confines but burst through them. Even if you presumed the pitch to be more Ovalish, you could not possibly justify playing without a front-line spinner...

Strauss had no doubt about batting first... and once again batted serenely himself before playing a rare false stroke... on 55. Even with this lapse, England still reached 176 for two, although the evidence was piling up that this was not a straightforward pitch. Bell received a physical pummelling from Johnson but came through, so that shortly before tea Ponting was forced to confront the reality of Australia's selection error by bringing on North's clubby off-breaks, which would be better reserved for charity matches.

Curiously, that heralded the collapse, though North did not take a wicket... All out for 332 early on the second morning... [England] seemed to have wasted a chance to seize control. As Watson and Katich put on 73 for the first wicket, English gloom was intense, even though Swann was already getting turn and bounce.

Just before lunch, it started to rain, and nearly an hour was lost. On the restart, Strauss rejected Swann and turned... to his fifth-choice bowler, Broad. And suddenly, the 2009 Ashes turned head-over-heels again – for one final time. Bowling from the Vauxhall End, Broad took four wickets in his first five overs: Watson and Hussey were plumb lbw; Ponting played on; and the burst culminated in Australia's most dangerous batsman of the summer, Clarke, being brilliantly snaffled by Trott at short extra cover. He later bowled Haddin with an away-swinging yorker and completed his single 12-over spell just before tea with five for 37. The crowd forgot Flintoff and hailed Broad as their new hero... Success made him strong and reduced the Australians to gibberers. Lunch: 61 for nought. Tea: 133 for eight.

Australia had just avoided the follow-on (not that Strauss would have dreamed of enforcing it) and the eventual lead was 172. England themselves lost three wickets before the close to make it a 15-wicket day.

The two teams' selection decisions now came home to roost. The Australian attack was in such a pickle that North – to general embarrassment – became the mainstay of their attack. In Trott, however, England had found a player of sound technique, considerable self-confidence and a big-match temperament. It was Strauss who went, to North for 75, and Trott who went on to a remarkable century. Swann kept him cheery company, making 63 inside an hour.

Strauss felt confident enough to declare with 21 overs plus two days remaining... This time, there was no collapse. The crowd grew anxious. But then The Man intervened.

Flintoff had hardly been at the races at all: word had leaked before the game about his impending knee operation and he was obviously not match-fit – he had been bowled sparingly, taken a solitary wicket (Hilfenhaus), twice been clapped to the crease and quickly clapped back in again. Now his moment came.

Hussey played the ball to mid-on; Flintoff threw to the far end, and hit, with Ponting short of his ground. Flintoff marked the occasion with another of his Christ-like poses destined to adorn countless adverts. Five balls later, Clarke was even more narrowly run out by Strauss from backward short leg, after the ball was deflected by forward short leg's boot. Then Prior, neatly, made North the only stumping victim of the series... Hussey and Haddin regrouped... but when the dam burst... the last five went down for 21...

The England players did all the regulation cavorting. The vanquished Australians were appropriately gracious. But this was not 2005 or even 1953. There was a sense of restraint in the crowd, partly because a four-year gap is not the same as a 20-year gap and partly because – for the first time all series – this was a real crickety kind of crowd... The ECB and the players remembered, too, so the late-night celebrations were discreet and open-top buses forgotten...

England 332 (A. J. Strauss 55, I. R. Bell 72; P. M. Siddle 4-75) **and 373-9 dec** (A. J. Strauss 75, I. J. L. Trott 119, G. P. Swann 63; M. J. North 4-98); **Australia 160** (S. M. Katich 50; G. P. Swann 4-38, S. C. J. Broad 5-37) **and 348** (R. T. Ponting 66, M. E. K. Hussey 121; G. P. Swann 4-120).

Chapter 15

From Micky to Alec (with a couple of trophies in between)

Surrey's greatest triumphs have almost always come in clusters. The
1890s, 1950s and the period at the turn of the 21st century will forever
be seen as great eras in the history of the club. The last four decades
of the 20th century are less fondly remembered by the Surrey faithful, with
the exception of a standalone Championship title in 1971 and two sporadic
one-day successes in 1974 and 1982.

However, this was a period which featured many of the club's finest
and most popular players. In the 1960s, Ken Barrington and John Edrich
starred under the leadership of Micky Stewart (who also became Surrey's
first manager between 1979 and 1986), and later there were favourites
such as Pat Pocock, Graham Roope, Alan Butcher, Robin Jackman, Geoff
Arnold and Jack Richards – not to mention the club's first overseas stars,
including Intikhab Alam, Younis Ahmed and Sylvester Clarke.

These charismatic players inspired some brilliant games of cricket at
The Oval and brought fans to the edge of their (somewhat decrepit) seats.
But the Surrey trophy cabinet began to mirror the condition of the ground:
historic and revered but in need of some new shine.

By the mid-1990s, Alec Stewart (Micky's son) and Graham Thorpe
had established themselves as the backbone of the batting order – for club

and country – offering hope that another Surrey era was imminent. In 1996, under Stewart's captaincy, they won their first silverware in 14 years and set the stage for Adam Hollioake to lead them to seven trophies over the next seven seasons.

Surrey v Middlesex   1965

July 25, 27, 28, 1964. Match drawn.

Micky Stewart, an understated figure among high-profile team-mates in the 1950s, took over the Surrey captaincy from Peter May in 1963. A year later he hit his highest score in a pulsating draw with Middlesex.

This was an extraordinary match. Apart from Willett, Surrey failed miserably with the bat on the opening day against two strange Middlesex opening bowlers, Waite and Clark. Later, when Surrey needed 246 to avoid an innings defeat, Stewart made 227 not out in seven hours, the highest innings of his career, and Willett hit the fastest hundred (19 fours) at that stage of the summer in 80 minutes. Stewart excelled with the drive, cut, hook and pull in hitting 32 fours. The stylish left-handed Smith helped Stewart to score 219 in Surrey's best opening stand of the season and while they were batting Barrington at Old Trafford was getting 256 for England. On the last day, when 119 overs were bowled, Waite and Clark sent down only 14 between them, Drybrough persisting with his slow bowlers on a pitch from which the ball turned only slowly. Except for some brisk hitting by Smith and Clark, the Middlesex batting generally lacked inspiration.

Surrey 119 (M. D. Willett 73*; A. C. Waite 4-25, E. A. Clark 5-61) **and 462-4** (M. J. Stewart 227*, W. A. Smith 91, M. D. Willett 102); **Middlesex 365** (W. E. Russell 75, E. A. Clark 56, J. T. Murray 67; R. Harman 4-109).

Surrey v Middlesex   1968

July 8, 9, 10, 1967. Match drawn.

John Edrich, one of the club's greatest batsmen, hit his highest score for Surrey against the same opponents three years later.

Edrich made his highest score for Surrey, 226 unfinished with only one six and 29 fours in five and a half hours, and his partnership with Barrington, who spent nearly four hours reaching 100, produced 297 in four and a half hours. Edrich's weighty strokeplay dominated the Middlesex attack in the afternoon, when he advanced from 54 to 226 in three and a half hours. Jackman took two Middlesex wickets on the first evening, and Arnold two early the next day, but a stand of 87 by Russell and Titmus, who played aggressively for his 80, and excellent tail-end batting by Herman put Middlesex past the follow-on mark. As was often the case The Oval pitch favoured spin in the later stages, and Titmus, Latchman and Parfitt skittled Surrey for 133, the last eight wickets falling for 55. Without Pocock, Surrey lacked the spin to retaliate, and the match was quietly left drawn.

Surrey 372-3 dec (J. H. Edrich 226*, K. F. Barrington 113) **and 133** (A. H. Latchman 4-29); **Middlesex 277** (W. E. Russell 66, F. J. Titmus 80) **and 138-5** (M. J. Harris 57).

GEOFF ARNOLD – CRICKETER OF THE YEAR   Norman Preston, 1972

Micky Stewart's crowning glory as captain was the County Championship won by Surrey in 1971, a season in which seamer Geoff Arnold was at the height of his powers. Wisden *recognised his contribution in its 1972 edition.*

One of the cricketers who played a vital part in Surrey winning the County Championship after an interval of 11 years was Geoff Arnold, who in the process headed the national bowling figures with 83 wickets at 17.12 runs each. He was one of the excellent attack Micky Stewart, the captain, had at his command. It was well balanced with Arnold, Willis and Jackman to use the new ball, Storey medium-paced and three fine slow bowlers with varied spin in Intikhab Alam, Pocock and Waller.

Geoffrey Graham Arnold… was 18 when in 1963 he made his debut in first-class cricket, against Derbyshire at The Oval, claiming W. F. Oates, Derbyshire's top scorer in the match, as his first victim. *Wisden* remarked that he made a promising start, but he was young and with

Loader, Sydenham and Gibson in the side, Arnold figured in only six Championship matches that season.

Two years later Arnold really came to the fore. He headed the Surrey bowling with 77 wickets for all first-class matches at 17.21 runs each, and he was top again in 1966. Not until 1967 when he took 109 wickets, average 18.22, did Arnold receive his county cap and that same year… he was chosen for England for the last two Tests against Pakistan. He distinguished himself at The Oval by taking five wickets for 58 when, in heavy misty atmosphere, Brian Close sent Pakistan in to bat…

These days there is not much pleasure for fast bowlers toiling at The Oval on the slow pitches which now prevail, affording little bounce, and it is significant that of the 83 wickets credited to Arnold in 1971, only 24 were obtained at Surrey's headquarters.

SURREY V GLAMORGAN   1972

September 8, 9, 10, 1971. Match drawn.

Had Surrey taken one more wicket against Glamorgan in 1971, they would have won the County Championship in front of their home fans. Instead they had to make do with a thrilling climax which postponed the celebrations until later in the month on the south coast.

Glamorgan's last pair held out at the finish, depriving Surrey of the win which would have made sure of the Championship, eventually gained at Southampton in the final game. To force victory on a sluggish pitch was difficult, and for much of the final day Glamorgan had a good chance of success themselves. Stewart led Surrey's bid on the first day with a chanceless three-figure innings of three and three-quarter hours, though the pitch frustrated many of his stroke-making attempts. Owen-Thomas drove well, but Surrey doubtless hoped for more than three batting points. They added five for bowling on the second day, when Glamorgan found the spinning skill of Pocock and Intikhab hard to combat. A second-wicket stand of 107 between Edrich and Roope enabled Stewart to give his bowlers five hours to bowl out their opponents on the last day, but forceful batting by Fredericks and Majid made Glamorgan's target of 287 look distinctly feasible. More good bowling by Pocock and Intikhab swung the scale, as Surrey came desperately close to their ambition.

Surrey 304 (M. J. Stewart 108) **and 204-7 dec** (J. H. Edrich 62, G. R. J. Roope 58; P. M. Walker 4-28); **Glamorgan 222** (P. I. Pocock 5-73) **and 262-9** (Majid Khan 78).

SURREY V YORKSHIRE, B&H CUP QUARTER-FINAL 1975

June 12, 1974. Surrey won by 24 runs.

The next trophy to be added to the Oval cabinet was the Benson and Hedges Cup of 1974, during which Surrey overcame a strong Yorkshire side in the quarter-finals.

It was an interesting and well-fought match with the result in doubt until late in the day. Howarth provided the backbone of the Surrey innings with a splendid 80, which won him the Gold Award. Owen-Thomas batted pleasantly and Storey and Intikhab attacked aggressively. Yorkshire received a setback in only the fourth over of their innings when Jackman bowled Boycott with a beautiful ball. Sharpe and Leadbeater kept Yorkshire with a chance of victory, but the visitors were finally foiled by Jackman and Arnold. Old briefly raised their hopes with 26 off 19 balls, including two massive sixes.

Surrey 225-7 (55 overs) (G. P. Howarth 80); **Yorkshire 201** (52.5 overs) (B. Leadbeater 62, P. J. Sharpe 50; R. D. Jackman 4-35).

SURREY IN 1977 Harold Abel, 1978

A disgruntled Oval spectator was a sign of hard times during the 1977 season.

[One] suffering Surrey member… having watched the side disintegrate from 60 for one to 71 for nine against Leicestershire at The Oval, entered the office, put his pass on the counter and asked for his money back. A humorous gesture it was thought at the time. It was only the end of

May. But by the end of August others felt like joining him in his protest and it seemed that a new drive from the management reflected in a better standard in the middle would be necessary before support picked up again.

Robin Jackman – Cricketer of the Year   John Thicknesse, 1981

Robin Jackman opened the bowling for Surrey for 17 seasons. He retired before the start of the 1983 season when he was at the top of the game, having been a member of England's Ashes squad the previous winter. Wisden commemorated Jackman in 1981, the year in which he made his Test debut at the age of 35.

For Robin David Jackman, Surrey's lion-hearted opening bowler, there was nothing much wrong with 1980... With 121 wickets in the first-class game, 17 in five Gillette Cup ties and 19 more in other limited-overs matches, he was far and away the country's leading wicket-taker...

From mid-season there had never been much doubt that, short of a broken bowling arm, he would be among *Wisden*'s Five Cricketers. But pleased as he was to be chosen, an even more satisfying honour was in store when he was voted the Cricketers' Cricketer for 1980, an annual award given by the 250 or so county professionals to the player they considered made the greatest contribution to his team's success – in hard work and dedication as much as, or more than, statistically...

He took nine Hampshire wickets in Surrey's opening Championship match and never looked back. Compensating by accuracy, consistency and willingness for the extra yard of pace that would have made him a certain choice for England, he played an indispensable part in Surrey's season, keeping them snapping away at Middlesex's heels till the penultimate Schweppes [County Championship] match and steering them to the final of the last Gillette Cup, in which their batting let them down and, much to their disgust, they were again beaten by their London rivals.

Obviously Jackman didn't do it on his own. Sylvester Clarke, his West Indian opening partner, Alan Butcher and Roger Knight were

239

other key members of the side. But an analysis of his figures shows just how much Surrey owed to him: of his 114 Championship wickets, 67 were in the top five of the order. In cricket parlance, he kept knocking over the best players, often before they reached 20. Of his 34 wickets in July (15 of them, for 80 runs, in three Gillette Cup ties) no fewer than 27 were specialist batsmen – and 17 of those were out in single figures…

He is the sort of bowler any captain would like to have on hand – fit, strong, aggressive and as full of guts and bounce at the end of a day as at the start of it… His best two seasons, strangely on the surface, have been the last two (93 wickets and 121). But not to Jackman.

"Put it down to Sylvester Clarke," he said. "It would be over-modest if I didn't say I'd bowled well; but it's made a tremendous difference to a bowler of my type – fast-medium length-and-line – to have a genuine quick one at the other end."

SURREY V LEICESTERSHIRE, B&H CUP SEMI-FINAL   1982

July 8, 1981. Surrey won by three runs.

Surrey may have lost to a powerful Somerset team in the 1981 Benson and Hedges Cup final, but their semi-final victory over Leicestershire was a classic.

Surrey won by three runs when Higgs, needing four off the last two balls, attempted a single and was thwarted by Pocock's throw. Parsons had already hit a six off the third ball of his final over, bowled by Jackman, to restore the balance in a fluctuating game. Electing to bat, Surrey opened at a rate of nearly four an over before steady bowling restricted them, and it needed a late flourish from Roope to take them to their modest total. After a promising start, Leicestershire lost the wickets of Steele, Gower and Davison at 84 but Roberts and Garnham revived the innings with 39 in five overs before Roberts was brilliantly caught by Roope. The Gold Award went to Payne who, playing in the absence of Clarke, accounted for Balderstone, Gower and Davison.

Surrey 191-9 (55 overs) (G. R. J. Roope 55*); **Leicestershire 188** (54.5 overs).

SURREY V MIDDLESEX, NATWEST TROPHY SEMI-FINAL   1983

August 18, 19, 1982. Surrey won by 125 runs.

Under Roger Knight's captaincy, Surrey played four consecutive Lord's one-day finals from 1979 to 1982. The first three were lost before the hoodoo was broken in the 1982 NatWest Trophy. Surrey's semi-final victory over Middlesex was achieved largely thanks to the fearsome bowling of Sylvester Clarke.

Clarke, with four for eight in his first six overs, initiated a Middlesex collapse from which there was no escape. The medium-pacers finished off the job and there was no need for Clarke to bowl a second spell, although he took two catches in hastening the end. Earlier Butcher and Smith laid the foundation for a reasonable Surrey total with a second-wicket stand of 88 after Howarth had been caught behind off the tenth ball of a first day limited to just under an hour by the weather.

Surrey 205-9 (60 overs) (A. R. Butcher 53; W. W. Daniel 4-24);
Middlesex 80 (41.5 overs) (S. T. Clarke 4-10).

SURREY V LANCASHIRE   1991

May 3, 4, 5, 7, 1990. Match drawn.

The 1990 Championship match against Lancashire was a batsman's paradise. Surrey captain Ian Greig made 291 but was outshone by Neil Fairbrother's triple-century as the record books were rewritten.

This record-breaking match will long be remembered and chronicled for its quite phenomenal feats of scoring on a pitch exemplifying the tougher standards laid down by the Test and County Cricket Board. Greig, the Surrey captain, drove an extremely hard tactical bargain by amassing 707 for nine declared in the hope that his bowlers could take 20 wickets for an innings victory. However, it presented Lancashire with a *fait accompli*. Needing 558 to avoid the follow-on, and realising that victory for them was out of the question, they settled down to revel in the sumptuous batting conditions. The home bowling was savaged for a colossal 863, the highest Championship total of the century and second only to Yorkshire's 887 against Warwickshire at Birmingham in 1896.

Lancashire's dapper left-hander, Fairbrother, was unstoppable in the run-glut, thrashing 366 to pass by two runs the previous best score at The Oval – 364 by Sir Leonard Hutton in the 1938 Test match against Australia. Greig, who, coming in at No. 7, had made the highest Championship innings by a Surrey player since 1926 and by anyone on the ground since 1921, could hardly have envisaged his career-best 291 off 251 balls being bettered the next day...

Surrey enjoyed a bountiful first day, reaching 396 for six, with Lynch falling just short of three figures... Greig's stand of 205 with Bicknell the next day was a Surrey best for the eighth wicket, surpassing their oldest record partnership which had stood since 1898... Surrey powered on to the highest total conceded by Lancashire...

Lancashire, having responded with 179 for one from 55 overs by the close, took over inexorably on day three. Mendis, 97 overnight, was out soon after reaching his hundred, but Atherton eased to a personal top score of 191 and Fairbrother strode on to 311. By lunch Fairbrother had reached 100 from 102 balls (125 minutes), and in the next two sessions he scored 108 from 109 balls (135 minutes) and 103 from 110 balls (120 minutes), leaving the statisticians with Sunday to wonder if he might beat the English record of 424, set by another famous Lancastrian, A. C. MacLaren. Already the Atherton-Fairbrother alliance of 364 had eclipsed the county's third-wicket record of 306 by E. Paynter and N. Oldfield against Hampshire at Southampton in 1938. Lancashire's captain, Hughes, gave Fairbrother the chance of batting throughout the final day to pass MacLaren, but fatigue had its way. He eventually departed to his 407th ball, having batted for 500 minutes and struck five sixes and 47 fours, the eighth-highest number in the list of boundary hits. His 366 was the third-highest in the Championship after MacLaren's 424 and G. A. Hick's 405 not out. Surrey reached 80 for one in the remaining time, with Stewart passing 50 for the second time and the aggregate for the match soaring to 1,650 runs, a new mark in Championship cricket and the second-highest for a match in England.

Surrey

R. I. Alikhan st Hegg b Fitton	55		
G. S. Clinton c Patterson b DeFreitas	8	– c Watkinson b Atherton	15
A. J. Stewart c Fowler b Patterson	70	– (1) not out	54
M. A. Lynch c and b Watkinson	95	– (3) not out	6
G. P. Thorpe c Atherton b Fitton	27		
†D. M. Ward c Hughes b Fitton	36		
˙I. A. Greig c Jesty b Hughes	291		
K. T. Medlycott c Fairbrother b Patterson	33		
M. P. Bicknell c Hegg b Hughes	42		
N. M. Kendrick not out	18		
B 6, lb 16, nb 10	32	B 2, lb 1, nb 2	5
1/10 2/118 3/187 (9 wkts dec, 165.1 overs)	707	1/57 (1 wkt, 33 overs)	80
4/261 5/275 6/316			
7/401 8/606 9/707 100 overs: 335-6			

A. J. Murphy did not bat.

Patterson 27–4–108–2; DeFreitas 26–4–99–1; Watkinson 23–2–113–1; Fitton 45–6–185–3; Atherton 22–5–75–0; Hughes 22.1–0–105–2. *Second innings*—DeFreitas 4–0–10–0; Fitton 16–4–42–0; Atherton 13–5–25–1.

Lancashire

G. D. Mendis run out	102	˙D. P. Hughes not out	8
G. Fowler run out	20	J. D. Fitton c Stewart b Murphy	3
M. A. Atherton c Greig b Kendrick	191	B. P. Patterson c Greig b Medlycott	0
N. H. Fairbrother c Kendrick b Greig	366	B 8, lb 15, w 1, nb 9	33
T. E. Jesty retired hurt	18		
M. Watkinson b Greig	46	1/45 2/184 3/548 (224.5 overs)	863
†W. K. Hegg c Ward b Bicknell	45	4/745 5/774 6/844	
P. A. J. DeFreitas b Murphy	31	7/848 8/862 9/863 100 overs: 401-2	

Jesty retired hurt at 665-3.

Murphy 44–6–160–2; Bicknell 43–2–175–1; Kendrick 56–10–192–1; Medlycott 50.5–4–177–1; Lynch 5–2–17–0; Greig 19–3–73–2; Thorpe 7–1–46–0.

Umpires: B. Dudleston and A. A. Jones.

Close of play: first day, Surrey 396-6 (Greig 56, Medlycott 33); second day, Lancashire 179-1 (Mendis 97, Atherton 56); third day, Lancashire 665-3 (Fairbrother 311, Jesty 18).

SURREY V LANCASHIRE, B&H CUP   1994

May 11, 1993. Lancashire won by six runs.

The same teams played a very different match three years later in the Benson and Hedges Cup first round. It ended in narrow defeat for Surrey, and also marked the first instance of a third umpire in the English game.

Lancashire achieved one of the most dramatic one-day victories of all time after the Surrey innings went from the sublime to the farcical.

They were only 25 runs short of victory thanks to a 212-run partnership between Stewart and Thorpe; they then contrived to lose nine wickets for just 18 runs – and the match. Only Lynch, who walked for a leg-side catch by Hegg, could claim not to have thrown his wicket away. The remainder had no excuses... The TCCB used the game for the first experiment in Britain with a third umpire replaying difficult line decisions on television and communicating with his colleagues on the field by two-way radio. But Allan Jones's only involvement proved that the camera could be as uncertain as the human eye. He was unable to judge whether Wasim should be given run out, and ruled that he should stay. A photograph taken from another angle suggested that Wasim had been lucky.

Lancashire 236 (54.1 overs) (N. H. Fairbrother 87);
Surrey 230 (55 overs) (A. J. Stewart 95, G. P. Thorpe 103).

SURREY V DERBYSHIRE   1995

May 12, 13, 14, 16, 1994. Surrey won by an innings and 138 runs.

An immensely popular player with Oval crowds, David Ward enjoyed his finest hour for Surrey in 1994, when poor weather cruelly denied him the chance to score 300.

At lunch on the second day, Ward was half a dozen paltry runs short of a triple-century and a guaranteed place in cricket history – but the next two sessions were washed out. Had Stewart known how easily Derbyshire would succumb, he might have let him bat on. Ward, however, was happy to put the team first, shared Stewart's preference for a third successive Championship victory and contented himself with 294, including five sixes and 32 fours. His partnership with Thorpe produced 301, after Stewart had been trapped by Andrew Harris's second ball in first-class cricket. Surrey took full advantage of a weak attack – DeFreitas, Cork and Mortensen were injured and flu prevented Malcolm bowling. Benjamin and Martin Bicknell were the pick of the home bowlers, though Cuffy looked good in the second innings. Only

Adams showed any fight for Derbyshire; batting No. 7 because of injury, he followed his century in the Sunday match with another blistering unbeaten hundred. Of his 109, 92 came in boundaries – 17 fours and four sixes.

Derbyshire 208 (M. P. Bicknell 4-56, J. E. Benjamin 4-56) and 224 (C. J. Adams 109*);
Surrey 570-6 dec (G. P. Thorpe 114, D. M. Ward 294*, A. D. Brown 92).

SURREY V GLOUCESTERSHIRE   1996

April 27, 28, 29, 30, 1995. Surrey won by 93 runs.

On four occasions Surrey have won after following on – all of them at The Oval. The first three took place in the span of a decade (1858, 1866 and 1868). It was another 127 years before the fourth came along.

Surrey pulled off a rare feat by winning after following on from 175 behind. But the opening stages were dominated by Andrew Symonds, Gloucestershire's Birmingham-born, Queensland-bred 19-year-old. His clinical dismantling of the Surrey attack – which lost Martin Bicknell early on – prompted calls for him to be named in England's one-day international squad to prevent Australia laying claim to the prodigy. Having spent 21 deliveries on his first nine circumspect runs, Symonds launched a withering attack, taking a further 73 balls to reach an unbeaten century on his Championship debut (despite a chance on 98). Gloucestershire's official overseas player, Srinath, then helped to bowl Surrey out for 217. But Brown then played a mature, career-best innings, uncharacteristically taking 156 balls to reach three figures. His four sixes were his only boundaries in a period of 40 overs, the first bringing up his hundred, the third his 150. Chasing 301, Gloucestershire were bowled out by the ever-dangerous Benjamin with seven overs to spare.

Gloucestershire 392 (R. I. Dawson 51, A. Symonds 161*; J. E. Benjamin 4-77) and 207
(M. W. Alleyne 60, R. C. Russell 56; J. E. Benjamin 4-68); Surrey 217 (M. A. Butcher 71)
and 475 (M. A. Butcher 51, A. J. Stewart 65, A. D. Brown 187; J. Srinath 4-137).

June 16, 1996. Surrey won by ten wickets.

Surrey won their third limited-overs title in 1996 when they topped the Sunday League. This mid-season demolition of Leicestershire served notice of their intentions and did wonders for their net run-rate – which proved crucial at the end of the season.

The shortest Sunday League match on record was completed in 26.3 overs and one hour 53 minutes, 20 minutes quicker than Essex v Northamptonshire at Ilford in 1971. Leicestershire were all out for 48, having scored 311 (and still lost) in 40 overs the previous week. The innings plunged to disaster after Wells was brilliantly caught by Brown at third man in the second over. There was just one boundary and only Extras reached double-figures. Darren Bicknell and Brown then blazed to victory in just 27 balls.

Leicestershire 48 (22 overs); **Surrey 50-0** (4.3 overs).

Note: reports of some other Surrey matches played at The Oval between 1964 and 1994 appear in chapters 11, 12 and 13.

Chapter 16

South Africa at The Oval

As with the whole of their sporting history, South Africa's appearances at The Oval can be squarely divided either side of the international cricketing boycott imposed on the country (1970–1991) on account of its apartheid regime.

Their debut match there was in 1894 and, following a number of games against Surrey, they were granted a fixture against England at the ground in 1907, becoming the first country other than Australia to play an Oval Test. South Africa's next visit was in the 1912 triangular series, when Sydney Barnes took 13 wickets to help England to an easy victory (see chapter 3). From here on they were more regular visitors to Kennington, although their first Oval Test victory didn't arrive until 2012 – their 14th Test at the ground.

The one game to split the pre- and post-isolation phases was the 1970 Oval "Test", the last of a five-match series between England and a Rest of the World XI which included five South Africans. The games had been hastily arranged to replace the scheduled series against South Africa, which had been called off on the request of Her Majesty's Government. These were given Test status at the time, but that was soon rescinded.

Ironically, the consequence of that decision is that South Africa will be England's opponents for The Oval's 100th Test in July 2017.

SURREY V SOUTH AFRICANS   1895

June 1, 2, 1894. Surrey won by an innings and six runs.

South Africa first appeared at The Oval to take on a Surrey side that was dominating the nascent County Championship.

The Africans' failure in this match, their first appearance in London, no doubt told heavily against the financial success of the trip. Rain on the opening day delayed the start till late in the afternoon, and the South Africans, on a wicket that was too wet to be difficult, simply collapsed before Jephson's lobs. Surrey won by an innings and six runs, some excellent play at the finish by Castens and Glover redeeming the credit of the Cape team.

South Africans 52 (D. L. A. Jephson 5-18) **and 146** (H. H. Castens 58; A. E. Street 7-40); **Surrey 204** (C. Baldwin 68; J. Middleton 7-45).

ENGLAND V SOUTH AFRICA, THIRD TEST   1908

August 19, 20, 21, 1907. Match drawn.

Just over a decade later, South Africa's first Oval Test was a pulsating contest that could have gone either way. The match featured a Test century from the polymath C. B. Fry, who among other things played football for England, equalled the long jump world record, stood for Parliament and (allegedly) rejected an offer to become King of Albania.

England, winning the toss, scored 226 for seven wickets. As the pitch was never easy this was a very good performance. The batting, however, was curiously uneven, the side owing nearly everything to Fry and Foster...

Foster at the opening of his innings was much at fault in running between the wickets, sometimes hesitating, sometimes dashing for dangerously short runs, but when once he had settled down he played very finely, making a number of beautiful hits...

With seven wickets down for 181, England did not seem likely to profit much by getting first innings, but Lilley kept up his end, and without further loss 45 runs were added before the drawing of stumps. Fry was not out 108, and it would be impossible to praise him beyond his deserts. He played with consummate judgment and… scarcely made a mistake. He set himself to master the breaking bowling by defensive means and was rarely tempted to hit unless he could score with perfect safety. As an example of self-control under rather trying conditions his innings has perhaps never been surpassed in Test matches…

On the following morning, after the long delay in resuming the game, Fry changed his methods. It was essential that runs should be put on as quickly as possible and he did his best to force the pace. In this endeavour, however, he was not very successful, and at 271 his great innings – the highest against the South Africans – came to an end… He and Lilley added 90 for the eighth wicket in less than an hour and a half… England's innings, which lasted five hours, came to an end for 295…

The third day's play was from first to last full of incident and excitement. The weather proved fine, and from 11 o'clock till bad light caused stumps to be pulled up the game went on without interruption. In the morning the pitch was very difficult and Blythe bowled so well that in 50 minutes the South African innings was finished off for 178 – five wickets going down for 29 runs. Of these five wickets Blythe took four, and only 14 runs were hit from him.

Leading by 117, England seemed in quite a safe position, but the match underwent a sudden change, Hayward, Fry and Tyldesley being so quickly got rid of that three wickets were down for 20. After such a start no one could tell what would happen, but Foster and Braund, playing with great judgment, saved their side. When lunchtime came they were still together and the score had reached 65. Thus with seven wickets in hand England held a lead of 182…

Acting on instructions, the batsmen who followed tried to force the pace, but the result was disastrous. Schwarz and Vogler, who took up the bowling, made the ball do so much that unguarded methods were almost doomed to failure, and by half-past three the innings, which at lunch had promised so well, was all over for 138 – the last six wickets going down in three-quarters of an hour for 49 runs.

The South Africans were then left to get 256 to win, the time remaining for play amounting to two hours and 40 minutes… The

task seemed impossible but, with everything to gain and nothing to
lose, Sherwell decided that it should be attempted... and in such
brilliant style did Faulkner and Sinclair start the innings, that for a time
it seemed just possible that the runs would be obtained... Runs came at
such a rate that at the end of 35 minutes' play the score stood at 61.
Then to the relief of the England eleven and the spectators Hirst clean
bowled Sinclair. Faulkner, who hit with great brilliancy, was also bowled
by Hirst at 72, and at 76 the Yorkshireman followed up his successes by
shattering White's wicket. After this the South Africans had nothing to
hope for but a draw...

The players left the field just before six o'clock, and a little later
stumps were pulled up, the South Africans with five wickets to fall
wanting 97 runs to win. Apart from the failure in batting in the
morning, the third day's play reflected immense credit on the South
African team.

England 295 (C. B. Fry 129, R. E. Foster 51) **and 138** (A. E. E. Vogler 4-49);
South Africa 178 (S. J. Snooke 63; C. Blythe 5-61) **and 159-5.**

*Note: a report of the 1912 Oval Test between England and South Africa
appears in chapter 3.*

ENGLAND V SOUTH AFRICA, FIFTH TEST   Hubert Preston, 1930
August 17, 19, 20, 1929. Match drawn.

---

*Len Hutton wasn't the only Yorkshire opening batsman to shine at The
Oval. Herbert Sutcliffe, Hutton's senior county colleague, averaged 91.60
in seven Tests at the ground, scoring five centuries. Two of them came in
one match against South Africa in 1929.*

South Africa... had every reason to be proud of their performance for,
after dismissing England in four hours and 20 minutes for 258, they
obtained such a mastery over the English attack that they actually scored
492 before declaring at lunchtime on the third day with eight wickets
down. England thus had to face an adverse balance of 234 but any idea

that they might be beaten was soon dispelled for, after Hobbs and Sutcliffe had hit up 77 in 75 minutes, Sutcliffe and Hammond, as at Birmingham, engaged in a great partnership, staying together until stumps were drawn just before five minutes to six and adding 187 in a little over two hours. As before, each made a hundred, Sutcliffe enjoying, for the second time in his career, the distinction of playing two separate three-figure innings in a Test match. This was a feat no other cricketer had ever accomplished...

Apart from that of Sutcliffe and Woolley, the England batting in the first innings left a good deal to be desired. These two men added 71 for the third partnership, but the honours were carried off by Sutcliffe, who, when rain stopped play for the second time and for the day at ten minutes to five, had obtained 84 out of a total of 166 for four wickets. On Monday the England batting broke down badly, the last six wickets falling in 95 minutes for another 92 runs. Sixth out at 217, Sutcliffe occupied three hours and a half over his 104, his batting, as was almost inevitable, being very restrained...

England 258 (H. Sutcliffe 104; C. L. Vincent 5-105) and 264-1 (J. B. Hobbs 52, H. Sutcliffe 109*, W. R. Hammond 101*); South Africa 492-8 dec (H. W. Taylor 121, H. G. Deane 93, H. B. Cameron 62, D. P. B. Morkel 81, Q. McMillan 50*).

England v South Africa, Fifth Test

Hubert Preston, 1948

August 16, 18, 19, 20, 1947. Match drawn.

In the second Test at The Oval since the end of the war, England and South Africa played out a thrilling game to match their first meeting on the ground 40 years earlier.

After four days of fluctuating play in extreme heat South Africa finished 28 runs short of victory with three wickets in hand...

England occupied seven hours and three-quarters over their first innings... Mann excelled; his first 35 overs, of which 16 were maidens, yielded only 33 runs, with Washbrook and Hutton victims of his slow left-handed guile.

Mitchell, after seven hours and three-quarters in the field, became the central figure of the match... Eighth out at 293 after batting six hours and a quarter... he received little help until Melville saw 86 added, and Dawson showed most freedom with 55 out of 79...

By far the most attractive cricket of the match came when England batted a second time, leading by 125. Hutton and Washbrook fell when forcing the pace, and half the side were out for 180, but Compton, then 53 after an hour of his best and most versatile strokeplay, went on with such freedom that, when caught from an on-drive, he claimed 113 out of 178 put on during an hour and three-quarters... His 14th century of the season was brilliant in every way... Yardley was able to declare 450 ahead, England having scored 325 in three hours and a half...

The final stage belonged to Mitchell. At times dreariness itself, he scored only 36 in two hours and a half before lunch and occupied four hours 50 minutes reaching 102 out of 275. Nourse... showed his usual aggression in hitting a dozen fours while 184 runs came in two hours 25 minutes... This stand suggested the possibility that South Africa might win, but three wickets fell for 34 more runs before Mitchell... completed his hundred... With 111 wanted in the last hour, runs came very fast... Mitchell got 25 and Tuckett 21 in the final 30 minutes, figures indicating what might have been brought about with a little more enterprise at different periods earlier in the day...

The largest crowd, 26,980, assembled on Monday, and the terraces presented a dazzling scene with the sun blazing down on the compact mass of people in the lightest permissible summer attire.

England 427 (L. Hutton 83, D. C. S. Compton 53, N. W. D. Yardley 59, C. Gladwin 51*;
N. B. F. Mann 4-93) and 325-6 dec (D. C. S. Compton 113); South Africa 302
(B. Mitchell 120, O. C. Dawson 55) and 423-7 (B. Mitchell 189*, A. D. Nourse 97).

ENGLAND v SOUTH AFRICA, FIFTH TEST
Norman Preston, 1956

August 13, 15, 16, 17, 1955. England won by 92 runs.

In 1955 England repeated their success of four years earlier (see chapter 8)
by winning the fifth and final Test at The Oval, thus taking a remarkable

series which South Africa had squared after losing the first two matches. A trio of Surrey players were the key to England's victory.

For the first time in the history of cricket in England all five Tests were brought to a definite conclusion, England winning the rubber in this deciding contest. The victory was a triumph for three Surrey players. Peter May, the captain, besides leading his side skilfully, made the highest score, 89 not out, and the two spin bowlers, Laker and Lock, took 15 of the 18 wickets that fell to bowlers in the two South African innings...

The match was memorable for some grand off-spin bowling by Tayfield. On the third day he bowled from half-past 12 until the close, five hours of cricket time, without relief, his figures during this spell being: 52 overs, 29 maidens, 54 runs, four wickets. This sustained effort was considered to be without parallel in Test cricket...

As no team had up to that stage of the summer made 200 runs in the fourth innings at The Oval, it was realised before the start that winning the toss might play an important part and May, by succeeding in this respect for the fourth time in the series, gained England an important advantage...

On Monday... the bowlers held the mastery, 17 wickets falling for 193 runs, and England gained a valuable lead of 39.

The third day found the pitch reasonably docile... May began his important innings which enabled his side to make the highest total of this low-scoring struggle. Graveney, owing to Compton being lame, had been promoted to No. 3 and he and May proceeded to make the best stand of the match, the pair adding 65 in 75 minutes...

Despite severe pain from his swollen knee and his inability to move freely, Compton, by staying two and a quarter hours while the fourth wicket added 62, gave his captain valuable assistance. This was appreciated later, for after Compton left England lost four wickets in the last hour for only 38 more runs... May took out his bat for 89, having defied the opposition for five hours...

The whole outlook changed when in the course of 18 balls England gained four wickets. South Africa's collapse began in Lock's third over when Goddard was caught at first slip and May at forward short leg held a hot catch from Keith at the third attempt...

So Laker and Lock repeated their success of 1953 when they wrested the Ashes from Australia on this familiar Oval pitch. As on that occasion the turf never crumbled, nor did the ball lift. Laker turned the ball only slightly, much the same as Tayfield, but Lock moved it sharply from leg.

England 151 (T. L. Goddard 5-31) and 204 (P. B. H. May 89*; H. J. Tayfield 5-60);
South Africa 112 (G. A. R. Lock 4-39) and 151 (J. H. B. Waite 60; J. C. Laker 5-56,
G. A. R. Lock 4-62).

ENGLAND v SOUTH AFRICA, THIRD TEST   Ted Corbett, 1995
August 18, 19, 20, 21, 1994. England won by eight wickets.

Having resumed international cricket three years earlier, South Africa played their first match at The Oval in 29 years on their 1994 tour. Devon Malcolm, achieving the best Test bowling figures in the ground's history, stole the headlines of a match which enthralled the nation.

It will always be Malcolm's Match, but there was so much more to this astonishing Test than Devon Malcolm's nine for 57 in South Africa's second innings... Runs came at nearly four an over; a wicket fell every 48 balls; Jonty Rhodes went to hospital after being struck on the helmet by Malcolm; Atherton and De Villiers were fined for dissent and both teams for their slow over-rates; and Malcolm delivered himself of a threat so graphic when he was hit in his turn that it has already become part of cricket folklore. The content, excitement and drama were at the level of a Superman film; value for money, even at TCCB ticket prices.

Winning the toss meant batting, but this true, fast pitch offered help to the bowlers too... Soon after Rhodes was escorted off the field, four overs beyond lunch, [England's] attack had effectively reduced South Africa to 136 for six. The half-brothers Gary and Peter Kirsten – opening in a Test at The Oval 114 years after the Grace brothers W. G. and E. M. went out there together for England – Cronje, Wessels and Cullinan... had all been swept aside. The ball from Malcolm that struck Rhodes was fast and nasty. Rhodes ducked so low that Malcolm considered an lbw appeal...

McMillan, who was also hit by Malcolm but survived to make 93 in four and a half hours, and Richardson revived South Africa with a sixth-wicket stand of 124 in 30 overs. But Benjamin, a Surrey favourite in his first Test, and DeFreitas picked up four wickets each. Once it was clear that Rhodes would not be returning yet, South Africa were all out for 332 early on the second day.

England made a traumatic start... [but the] men of Surrey again held sway, as Thorpe made his third successive 70 and Stewart a dashing 62... DeFreitas and Gough added 59 exhilarating runs in the final half-hour and England were only 28 behind when the innings finished next morning... Malcolm was hit on the helmet, straight between the eyes, first ball by De Villiers. He was not hurt, only angry. He stared back at the fielders who gathered round. "You guys are going to pay for this," he was reported to have said. "You guys are history."

Malcolm turned his words into action in 99 balls, the most devastating spell by an England bowler since Jim Laker wiped out the Australians in 1956. It was the sixth-best Test analysis ever and, until Cullinan was caught off Gough, it looked as if Malcolm might join Laker by taking all ten. The Kirstens and Cronje had gone for one run and the last six wickets fell for 38, with only Cullinan, who made 94, standing firm for long. Malcolm produced a series of classic deliveries: five catches to slip and wicketkeeper from lifting balls, a bouncer hooked to long leg, a desperately determined caught and bowled and two sets of stumps sent clattering by yorkers. He answered every question save one. Why did the selectors make him wait so long to bowl against a team who appeared alarmed by fast bowling?

England were left to make 204 and... Gooch showed the value of his experience... His bold strokes inspired Atherton so that 56 came in five overs – when Gooch was bowled – 79 off ten and 107 in 16 by the close. This incisive batting settled the match and the new, mature Hick sealed England's success. He strode towards an undefeated run-a-ball 81 in the style he had so often displayed for Worcestershire...

South Africa

G. Kirsten c Rhodes b DeFreitas	2	–	(2) c and b Malcolm	0
P. N. Kirsten b Malcolm	16	–	(1) c DeFreitas b Malcolm	1
W. J. Cronje lbw b Benjamin	38	–	b Malcolm	0
*K. C. Wessels lbw b Benjamin	45	–	c Rhodes b Malcolm	28
D. J. Cullinan c Rhodes b DeFreitas	7	–	c Thorpe b Gough	94
J. N. Rhodes retired hurt	8	–	(9) c Rhodes b Malcolm	10
B. M. McMillan c Hick b DeFreitas	93	–	(6) c Thorpe b Malcolm	25
†D. J. Richardson c Rhodes b Benjamin	58	–	(7) lbw b Malcolm	3
C. R. Matthews c Hick b Benjamin	0	–	(8) c Rhodes b Malcolm	0
P. S. de Villiers c Stewart b DeFreitas	14	–	not out	0
A. A. Donald not out	14	–	b Malcolm	0
B 8, lb 10, w 1, nb 18	37		Lb 5, nb 9	14

1/2 (1) 2/43 (2) 3/73 (3)   (92.2 overs) 332   1/0 (2) 2/1 (1)   (50.3 overs) 175
4/85 (5) 5/136 (4) 6/260 (8)   3/1 (3) 4/73 (4) 5/137 (6) 6/143 (7)
7/266 (9) 8/301 (10) 9/332 (7)   7/143 (8) 8/175 (5) 9/175 (9) 10/175 (11)

In the first innings Rhodes retired hurt at 106–4.

DeFreitas 26.2–5–93–4; Malcolm 25–5–81–1; Gough 19–1–85–0; Benjamin 17–2–42–4; Hick 5–1–13–0. *Second innings—*
DeFreitas 12–3–25–0; Malcolm 16.3–2–57–9; Gough 9–1–39–1; Benjamin 11–1–38–0; Hick 2–0–11–0.

England

G. A. Gooch c Richardson b Donald	8	–	b Matthews	33
*M. A. Atherton lbw b de Villiers	0	–	c Richardson b Donald	63
G. A. Hick b Donald	39	–	not out	81
G. P. Thorpe b Matthews	79	–	not out	15
A. J. Stewart b de Villiers	62			
J. P. Crawley c Richardson b Donald	5			
†S. J. Rhodes lbw b de Villiers	11			
P. A. J. DeFreitas run out	37			
D. Gough not out	42			
J. E. Benjamin lbw b de Villiers	0			
D. E. Malcolm c sub (T. G. Shaw) b Matthews	4			
B 1, w 1, nb 15	17		Lb 6, nb 7	13

1/1 (2) 2/33 (1) 3/93 (3)   (77 overs) 304   1/56 (1)   (2 wkts, 35.3 overs) 205
4/145 (4) 5/165 (6) 6/219 (5)   2/180 (2)
7/222 (7) 8/292 (8) 9/293 (10) 10/304 (11)

Donald 17–2–76–3; de Villiers 19–3–62–4; Matthews 21–4–82–2; McMillan 12–1–67–0; Cronje 8–3–16–0. *Second innings—*Donald 12–1–96–1; de Villiers 12–0–66–0; Matthews 11.3–4–37–1.

Umpires: R. S. Dunne and K. E. Palmer. Third umpire: A. G. T. Whitehead. Referee: P. J. P. Burge.

Close of play: first day, South Africa 326–8 (McMillan 91, Donald 11); second day, England 281–7 (DeFreitas 37, Gough 25); third day, England 107–1 (Atherton 42, Hick 27).

ENGLAND v SOUTH AFRICA, FIFTH TEST   Hugh Chevallier, 2004

September 4, 5, 6, 7, 8, 2003. England won by nine wickets.

Alec Stewart's final match as a professional cricketer was at his home ground in 2003 – and he went out on a high with England winning a stunning Test to draw the series.

At the start of the second day, bookies were offering 40 to one against an England win – not quite the 500 to one that tempted Rod Marsh and Dennis Lillee at Headingley in 1981, but an indication of the mountain England climbed to claim this epic. South Africa had lost a wicket to the last ball of the first day but, even at 362 for four, a huge score beckoned, and with it victory in the series. That wicket turned out to be the fulcrum on which the match pivoted. From then on, England produced far the sharper cricket. They were especially ruthless in the morning sessions, plundering five wickets for 70 on the second day, hitting 106 without loss on the third and 102 for two on the fourth before scattering the tail to the four winds on the last. On this sublime pitch, South Africa's 484 simply wasn't enough. Only once before in a Test in England, when Arthur Morris and Don Bradman triumphed at Headingley in 1948, had a first-innings total of 450 or more led to defeat.

It was not just the delicious reversal of fortune that made this a classic: there were myriad subplots to intrigue and absorb a packed house for five days. Alec Stewart, at the age of 40 and in his record 133rd and avowedly final Test appearance for England, wrapped himself in the cross of St George for the last time, at least on a cricket pitch. Thorpe, back from the wilderness only because another of Nasser Hussain's brittle bones was broken, achieved redemption with a beautiful hundred. And Bicknell, strutting his stuff on the big stage, hinted at what he might have done as a regular Test cricketer. Huge roars from the crowd regularly filled the air at the exploits of these three, Surrey stalwarts all...

On a pitch aching to give up its runs, Gibbs was first to make hay in the September sunshine, crafting a big, full-blooded hundred bursting with drives and cuts... Gibbs had reason to spurn ones and twos: in the morning, he had run out his captain, though Smith later had the grace to say he did not back up far enough. It hardly mattered, as Gibbs and Kirsten revelled in the conditions, adding 227 untroubled runs for the second wicket...

On the second morning... England bowled with heart, fielded with zest, and South Africa floundered. Gloom-mongers pointed out that England needed 285 to avoid the follow-on, and had adopted an I-told-you-so air when Thorpe, whose last three Test innings against South Africa were ducks, joined Trescothick at 78 for two. But the next five hours left the pessimists squirming. Neither batsman gave a genuine chance as runs came thick, fast and handsome. Thorpe, who likened the occasion to a second debut after dropping out of international cricket 14 months earlier, did what he had done first time round and hit a hundred...

A deafening cheer greeted Stewart, collar up, as he strode through the South Africans' generous guard of honour. Several bat twiddles and knee squats later, he was slotting the ball between the fielders – though not for as long as the crowd wanted. On 38, he played across a straight ball, and a career totalling 8,463 runs at a shade under 40 was almost over. Cue more rapturous applause. Trescothick, meanwhile, was in consummate touch. Recently upbraided for a susceptibility outside off... he silenced his critics with a glorious hundred later converted into a maiden double... Yet despite these riches, there was a danger the innings would peter out as the South Africans' had. Early on the fourth morning, England, eight down, led by a gossamer 18. With the forecast predicting that the tail-end of Hurricane Fabian would drown The Oval – and with the pitch as immaculate as Stewart's whites – the sensible money was on a draw.

Flintoff treated that logic with utter disdain. Beefy shots flashed from his bat as if it had been Ian Botham's; he hit cleanly, he hit hard and he hit often; 85 came from his last 72 balls. If there was an occasional slog-sweep, it disappeared for six, and the only thing agricultural about his innings was the assured way he farmed the strike: Harmison's contribution to a stand of 99 was a level-headed three. For South Africa, the psychological damage of watching ball after ball sail over the rope was as telling as the runs themselves...

Shortly before lunch, Vaughan declared 120 ahead. England had bowled decently on the first day, but without fire. Now the South Africans wilted in the heat... By the close – and still no rain to speak of – South Africa, effectively 65 for six, had nowhere to hide.

The noisy fifth-day crowd craved victory, yet hankered for drama. They had to make do with the win. The South African lower order keeled over feebly against more lionhearted bowling, and England, finding it all very easy, tore to their target at nearly five an over. The massive victory allowed Stewart to end his Test career – which also numbered 54 defeats – as he began it, on the winning side.

South Africa 484 (H. H. Gibbs 183, G. Kirsten 90, J. H. Kallis 66, S. M. Pollock 66*) and 229 (M. P. Bicknell 4-84, S. J. Harmison 4-33); England 604-9 dec (M. E. Trescothick 219, G. P. Thorpe 124, A. Flintoff 95) and 110-1 (M. E. Trescothick 69*).

ENGLAND V SOUTH AFRICA, FIRST TEST   Hugh Chevallier, 2013

July 19, 20, 21, 22, 23, 2012. South Africa won by an innings and 12 runs.

Inspired by the brilliance of Hashim Amla, South Africa's first Oval Test win finally arrived in 2012.

On a warm Sunday evening... news arrived from Paris that... Bradley Wiggins... had been officially crowned as the first Briton to win the Tour de France. Spectators were in the mood for applause, since they had seen a tour de force themselves. There are few clearer proofs of a batsman's mental strength or physical adaptability than a Test triple-century, and minutes earlier Hashim Amla had become the first South African to breathe such rarefied air. For at least four reasons it was a genuinely great achievement: with Petersen gone for nought, it was born in adversity; it came away from home against the team rated best in the world; it was an innings of real beauty, with shots played all round the wicket, off front foot and back; and, like only nine of the previous 25 Test triples, it would lead to victory.

In fact it led to more than that: it led to annihilation. No one was sure when England had been so utterly outflanked, though Hastings in 1066 was a possibility. In losing by an innings, Strauss's team scraped just two wickets, and one of those – Smith bowled via bat and pad – was a touch fluky. Between the dismissal of Ravi Rampaul, West Indies' No. 10, at Edgbaston in June and the end of this Test, England had taken three wickets, once every 260 runs. As the marauding South Africans raced towards their first victory at The Oval, their pack downed batsmen at an average cost of only 31...

A change in the weather meant England, after sailing serenely through the first day, were suddenly blown on to the rocks. Clouds loured over Kennington, making the ball as skittish as a kitten... [and England] nosedived from their overnight 267 for three to 284 for six. Prior counterpunched, but the truth was that six of the top eight fell to soft dismissals, and their total of 385 was more a statement of what might have been than of intent...

The left-handed Smith was initially unsettled by Swann, so he eschewed all risk by lunging defensively forward or playing from the crease – a viable option against such sluggish turn. The result was a fifty high on determination and low on aesthetics; at 160 balls, it was his slowest in Tests. (His next fifty, though, came from just 41, as he became the seventh player to mark his 100th Test with a century.) Session merged into session as milestone after milestone slipped by under increasingly blue skies: 200 stand, 100 for Amla, 250 stand…

On the third afternoon, Smith finally made way for Kallis. Not that it made a ha'p'orth of difference. Still, Strauss did manage a laugh when his throw smashed the sunglasses that had just slipped from his sunhat, a mishap oddly emblematic of England's plight. More century landmarks peppered play on the fourth day, with the bowlers joining in: 100 for Anderson, 200 for Amla, 100s for Bresnan, Swann and Kallis (his 43rd in Tests), 200 stand…

Amla, who had chosen to defer his Ramadan fast, had an insatiable appetite for runs: on the attack, he was strong, elegant and wristy, while his defence, forward or back, was neat, fluent and commanding. No single shot stood out, but that was testament to his all-round dominance… 500 up, 250 for Amla, 250 stand, 300 stand, Amla to 281 (beating de Villiers's national record), 150 for Kallis, 600 up…

Four balls later, in the 184th over, Amla lofted a drive over extra cover. It took him past 300, and from the most exuberant beard in Test cricket there flashed a mile-wide smile. By the time Smith declared at tea, earlier than many expected, Amla had faced 529 balls.

It wasn't quite chanceless – no marathon stretching to 13 hours and ten minutes, the longest undefeated innings in Test history, could possibly be. It was the first triple in England since Graham Gooch's 333 at Lord's in 1990, the first by a visiting batsman since Bobby Simpson's 311 for Australia at Old Trafford in 1964, and unforgettable for its calmness, placement and concentration.

England, trailing by 252, had four sessions in which to save the game. On a pitch that for almost 48 hours had refused bowlers so much as the time of day, it should have been within their compass… When Pietersen, unsettled by Morkel's aggression, lost his middle stump playing inside a straight one, England were 57 for three… Once

Steyn removed Bell with the new ball to leave them 210 for seven, the end was near...

England 385 (A. N. Cook 115, I. J. L. Trott 71, M. J. Prior 60; M. Morkel 4-72)
and 240 (I. R. Bell 55; D. W. Steyn 5-56); **South Africa 637-2 dec** (G. C. Smith 131, H. M. Amla 311*, J. H. Kallis 182*).

SURREY v SOMERSET   2014

April 17, 18, 19, 20, 2013. Match drawn.

In recent years there has been a heavy influx of South African cricketers into English domestic cricket, but none so revered as Surrey's Graeme Smith. In 2013 he made his debut against a Somerset side who had their own South African also making his first county appearance.

South Africa's Test openers made their first appearances for their new counties, and it was the less-heralded Alviro Petersen who grabbed the limelight from Surrey's high-profile captain Graeme Smith. Petersen's 258 runs in the match broke the record for a Somerset debutant of 208 set by another overseas player, the Australian Cameron White, in 2006. Petersen made the most of a slow early-season pitch with some forceful strokeplay during his first-innings 167, although Dernbach kept Surrey in touch with his first five-for in almost two years, including wickets from the first two deliveries with the second new ball. Their reply owed much to left-handers Burns, who confirmed the fine impression of his first full season with some deft placement off his legs, and Davies, who demonstrated a return to form after the sorrows of the previous summer. Somerset wobbled briefly when Meaker – rusty in the first innings – blasted out Trescothick and Compton, but three dropped catches on the final morning and a lack of seam back-up cost Surrey any chance of forcing victory. Petersen came close to a second century, then Buttler just missed one when he holed out at long-on in the dying moments.

Somerset 384 (A. N. Petersen 167; J. W. Dernbach 5-57) **and 251-9 dec** (A. N. Petersen 91, J. C. Buttler 94; S. C. Meaker 5-60); **Surrey 366-9 dec** (R. J. Burns 115, S. M. Davies 147).

Chapter 17

The Hollioake Years

S urrey's third era of dominance coincided with the arrival of a slightly garrulous Anglo-Australian all-rounder who as captain showed an unconventional mien in everything he did: Adam Hollioake.

Forming a tight partnership with head coach and ex-Surrey all-rounder Keith Medlycott, Hollioake's teams oozed talent, spirit, and a competitive team ethic – even if they might not have followed traditional rules regarding conditioning, nutrition and preparation.

In 1996 Surrey won the Sunday League under Alec Stewart – their first trophy since 1982. Hollioake became captain the following season and led the club to seven trophies in the next seven years, including the inaugural Twenty20 Cup in 2003, after which he took early retirement from the game.

Particularly impressive was the way he coped with the gaping holes left regularly in the side by the absence of his middle-order England trio of Mark Butcher, Stewart and Graham Thorpe. It was a testament to Hollioake's leadership that he was able to hold the squad together and maintain the motivation and loyalty of the high-quality replacements who filled in for the England players when necessary.

This period was also marked by tragedy. Wicketkeeper Graham Kersey, aged 25, died on New Year's Day in 1997 following a car crash. Then, in March 2002, 24 year-old all-rounder Ben Hollioake, Adam's younger brother, was killed in the same way. Given these horrors, that the squad went on to win the 2002 County Championship and then do the Twenty20 and Sunday League double of 2003 was, perhaps, their greatest achievement.

SURREY v YORKSHIRE   1996

August 10, 11, 12, 14, 1995. Surrey won by one run.

Adam Hollioake cites the Championship match against Yorkshire in 1995 as the moment when the team began to build the foundations of success. Captaining the side in the absence of Alec Stewart, Hollioake led Surrey to one of their most dramatic victories.

This was Surrey's second one-run win in their history (the other being against Lancashire in 1948). The conclusion was bizarre as well as desperate. Adam Hollioake rapped last man Robinson on the pad and appealed for lbw, while the ball carried on to be well taken by Butcher at slip. Robinson indicated he had got some bat on it and the bowler was turned down, only for Butcher to appeal successfully for the catch. Hollioake had dismissed Yorkshire's last three for one run in 12 balls, for his best-ever figures. Yorkshire, needing a modest 219, began the final morning just 145 from victory, with nine wickets in hand. But they obligingly folded after lunch, losing their last seven in 20 overs for just 32 runs. On the first day, Shahid and Kersey made career-best scores, which lifted Surrey past 400. For Yorkshire, Bevan made his fifth and biggest century of the summer, and Silverwood took five wickets for the first time in a feeble Surrey second innings.

Surrey 409 (M. A. Butcher 57, N. Shahid 139, G. J. Kersey 83; M. A. Robinson 4-64) and 175 (M. A. Butcher 62; C. E. W. Silverwood 5-62); Yorkshire 366 (M. D. Moxon 63, M. G. Bevan 153*; C. G. Rackemann 4-64) and 217 (M. D. Moxon 90; A. J. Hollioake 4-22).

GRAHAM KERSEY – OBITUARY

At the start of the year in which Adam Hollioake took over the Surrey captaincy, the club were rocked by tragedy.

Kersey, Graham James, died in hospital in Australia on January 1, 1997, aged 25, after being injured in a car crash on Christmas Eve. Kersey was a wicketkeeper who played occasionally for Kent in 1991 and 1992 before moving to Surrey the following year. He quickly established himself at The Oval as the first-choice keeper, except on the big one-day occasions when the captain, Alec Stewart, did the job. Kersey was not an especially stylish keeper – apart from anything else, his cap regularly fell off – but he rarely dropped catches, and was a battling batsman who could irritate opposing bowlers with effective use of the sweep. Above all, he was a dedicated team man whose cheerful attitude and combative approach were an important part of Surrey's revival in 1996. Stewart described him as the most popular member of the staff – a true player's player. The Surrey vice-captain Adam Hollioake said: "You could rely on him totally. You could get the best wicketkeeper in the world, but he couldn't possibly fill the gap."

SURREY V LEICESTERSHIRE, B&H CUP SEMI-FINAL

June 10, 1997. Surrey won by 130 runs.

On their way to the Benson and Hedges Cup triumph of 1997, Surrey despatched Leicestershire in some style in the semi-final.

First, Surrey's England batsmen, Stewart, Thorpe and Adam Hollioake, made batting look easy; then their former Test bowler Bicknell made it look next to impossible. He bowled his ten overs straight through for his best figures in the competition, leaving Leicestershire 68 for six as they edged their way towards one of the heaviest semi-final defeats. Surrey had begun badly themselves at 15 for two. Stewart and Thorpe were in commanding form, however, adding 158, a Surrey record for the third wicket in this competition.

Adam Hollioake sped them on their way to 300 as he spanked the wayward bowling for 63 in 40 balls.

Surrey 308-8 (50 overs) (A. J. Stewart 87, G. P. Thorpe 79, A. J. Hollioake 63);
Leicestershire 178 (45.3 overs) (P. A. Nixon 53; M. P. Bicknell 4-41).

Note: a report of Surrey's Championship match against Derbyshire at The Oval in 1998 appears in chapter 12.

SURREY V GLAMORGAN   2000
August 4, 5, 1999. Surrey won by an innings and 124 runs.

The first of three Championship victories came in 1999. This confident win over Glamorgan – completed in just over five sessions – epitomised the growing reputation of Adam Hollioake's team and, in particular, of his brother Ben.

Two abject displays by Glamorgan's batsmen made things easy for Surrey, who won inside two days. Tudor, recovering from a knee injury, and his three England colleagues were scarcely missed. Ben Hollioake, bowling faster and with greater control than usual, took his maiden five-wicket haul in first-class cricket and, with Martin Bicknell, destroyed Glamorgan on the first morning. Brown surpassed Glamorgan on his own with a responsible century that helped his side to a 208-run lead. He then took over behind the stumps after Batty's cheekbone had been broken by a ball from Jones that squeezed through his visor. Seam claimed the first four Glamorgan wickets second time around, whereupon Surrey turned to spin. Yet again, the batsmen failed to read Saqlain Mushtaq, and he ended with five for 18, the final three in one over. Brown made three dismissals, including a stumping, which he greeted with a jig of delight. It was all over 15 minutes after tea on the second afternoon.

Glamorgan 101 (B. C. Hollioake 5-51) **and 84** (Saqlain Mushtaq 5-18);
Surrey 309 (A. D. Brown 124, M. P. Bicknell 57).

SURREY IN 1999 David Llewellyn, 2000

Surrey ended nearly three decades of hurt by winning the Championship in 1999 – without registering a single defeat along the way.

Surrey left the 20th century as they entered it – as champions. One hundred years after winning the 1899 County Championship, Surrey did it again. But the more significant date in everyone's minds was 1971, Surrey's last Championship. It took 28 years for the sequence of failure to be broken. But when success finally happened, it arrived in spectacular fashion.

The triumph erased the memories of 1998, when Surrey led the table nearly all season only to go to pieces in the last match. They emulated the feat of their 1998 conquerors, Leicestershire, by finishing unbeaten... even the legendary Surrey sides of the 1950s, who lifted the title seven years running, never managed this.

MARTIN BICKNELL – CRICKETER OF THE YEAR Tanya Aldred, 2001

Martin Bicknell took 1,026 first-class wickets for Surrey between 1986 and 2006. That he was too often overlooked by England – Bicknell played just four Tests – was to his county's advantage. His experience and skill with the new ball was a critical factor in the team's success under Hollioake.

He's tall, 6ft 4in in his cricket boots, and with more physical presence than possibly he imagines. That floppy chocolate fringe is cropped now, and he wears spectacles off the pitch – a hint of the businessman he will become when he retires. But today, aged 32, Martin Bicknell is one of the finest English bowlers of his generation...

It's been hard work over the years, but it has reaped its rewards. Even by his standards, though, 2000 was remarkable. He took 60 first-division wickets and won his second Championship medal in a row, as well as promotion for Surrey in the National League. He also made 500 vital runs for the first time, at an average of 31. Not bad for a man who doesn't enjoy batting that much...

Bicknell is both a stalwart and a stylist. A classic English new-ball bowler: all short run, high arms and high knees, a natural outswinger with the knack of cutting the ball back into the right-hander. And, like Alec Bedser in the 1950s, he is the rhythmic heart of Surrey. The metronome to Alex Tudor's scattergun and the Saqlain-Salisbury trickery...

Bicknell has warm respect for his captain, Adam Hollioake, with whom he shares a sixth sense about when he should come on. He enjoys bowling with Alex Tudor more than any of his previous partners. He relishes the mateship of playing with a successful, close-knit side, even if he is different from the young pups who have known nothing but success.

SURREY V DERBYSHIRE 2001

August 16, 17, 2000. Surrey won by an innings and 45 runs.

On their way to a second consecutive Championship title in 2000 – the first time the competition was split into two divisions – Surrey's home victory against Derbyshire featured one of the lesser-known achievements of the era (but one happily remembered in Surrey circles): a hat-trick by Gary Butcher.

This was Surrey's seventh consecutive Championship victory since their last defeat – by Derbyshire. Completed by tea on the second day, it was determined 24 hours earlier when Gary Butcher's swing bowling claimed four wickets in four balls, starting with the last delivery of the 52nd over. The first three went to slip catches. Butcher, making his first appearance of the season after Ben Hollioake was dropped, was the first to achieve the feat in the Championship since Surrey's Pat Pocock in 1972. Five for 18 was his best return since joining Surrey from Glamorgan in 1999, and only his second five-wicket haul ever. Then it was brother Mark's turn, putting on 137 with Ward. Despite losing eight for 99 next morning, as Dean took six for 14 in 9.3 overs, Surrey led by 142. Stubbings and Sutton had almost halved that before Salisbury, in his first over, had Stubbings and Di Venuto caught at forward short leg off consecutive balls. That stung Saqlain Mushtaq into action: with seven wickets for just five runs, on a pitch providing pace and bounce, it took him less than an hour to wrap up another abysmal Derbyshire batting effort.

> **Derbyshire 118** (G. P. Butcher 5-18) **and 97** (Saqlain Mushtaq 7-11);
> **Surrey 260** (M. A. Butcher 78, I. J. Ward 57; K. J. Dean 6-51).

SURREY V NOTTINGHAMSHIRE, B&H CUP SEMI-FINAL · 2002

June 25, 2001. Surrey won by 174 runs.

The trophies continued to arrive. In 2001 Surrey won the Benson and Hedges Cup, reaching the final with this Oval annihilation of Nottinghamshire.

Nottinghamshire began their first semi-final in either knockout competition for 11 years in better one-day form than their opponents, who were contesting their sixth in six years. They ended it chastened and demoralised, having conceded more runs than any other first-class county in the history of the competition – admittedly on a strip made for batting – before crumpling in the face of Surrey's international seam attack. Had the last pair not put up some spirited resistance, Nottinghamshire would also have suffered the heaviest defeat inflicted on a first-class county in the Benson and Hedges Cup. Butcher, brought in because Ramprakash was unfit, epitomised the ebullient Surrey strokeplay, hitting a magnificent 84 from 86 balls. Such was Surrey's untrammelled progress against ill-disciplined bowling, however, that he was the sole member of the top six to score at less than a run a ball as they romped to 361, the county's highest total in knockout cricket. Stewart's 67 made him the third batsman after Gooch and Barnett to pass 3,000 runs in the competition. Afzaal and Pietersen did their best to save face.

> **Surrey 361-8** (50 overs) (M. A. Butcher 84, I. J. Ward 58, A. J. Stewart 67);
> **Nottinghamshire 187** (31.5 overs) (K. P. Pietersen 78*).

Just over five years after Graham Kersey's death, another car accident shook English cricket to its core and left Surrey CCC in deep mourning.

Hollioake, Benjamin Caine, died in Perth, Western Australia, on March 23, 2002 when his Porsche 924 left a freeway exit road, made slippery by light rain, and crashed into a brick wall. He had been driving home from the customary family dinner that preceded his and his brother Adam's return to Surrey for the English season, having spent much of the winter with England's one-day squad in Zimbabwe, India and New Zealand. Ben was just 24 years and 132 days old: no England Test cricketer had died so young.

The England captain, Nasser Hussain, flew from the Test series in New Zealand for his funeral, which was attended also by Surrey colleagues and Australian players, testimony to his immense popularity. "Ben was the most naturally gifted cricketer that I have ever played alongside," said Alec Stewart, who captained him for Surrey and England. Everyone recalled his easy-going approach to life and the friendships he fostered with his gentle nature and whimsical sense of humour; Adam, in his funeral address, described him as "a beautiful work of art, a classic sculpture". And in the game's collective memory, the picture of Ben Hollioake remained fixed on a spring afternoon in 1997 when, making his England debut at 19, this tall, loose-limbed all-rounder set Lord's alight with 63 in 48 balls against Australia to take the Man of the Match award...

A cry went up for the Hollioakes' Australian-bred brio to spark an English resurgence... The brothers helped Surrey win the Benson and Hedges Cup. Once more, Ben's batting at Lord's was sublime. Again coming in first wicket down, he struck 98 from 112 balls, using all of his 6ft 2in to drive the ball on the up off the front foot. Again he won the match award. Adam dedicated the victory to Graham Kersey, the young Surrey wicketkeeper, who also died following a car crash in Australia, just as he would dedicate the 2002 Championship title to Ben.

Once England went behind in the [1997] Ashes series, the Hollioakes' selection for the Fifth Test at Trent Bridge was the obvious last throw of the dice. They became the fifth set of brothers to play a Test for England, following the three Graces and the Hearnes in making simultaneous debuts, while Ben, at 19 years 269 days, became England's youngest Test player since Brian Close (18 years 149 days) in 1949...

When accepting the Cricket Writers' Club Young Cricketer of the Year award with a gracious eloquence few of his peers could have emulated, [Ben] brought the house down by remarking that this would be one trophy with only one Hollioake name on it. The years of playing catch-up with a sibling six years older had fuelled an affectionate rivalry...

There was... another Lord's match award [in 2001], as Surrey dethroned the one-day kings, Gloucestershire, in the Benson and Hedges Cup final, and Ben, down the order this time, helped Adam rebuild their innings with a mature 73.

Would he have gone on to greater things? A record of 2,794 runs at 25.87 and 126 wickets at 33.45 from 75 first-class games, alongside 2,481 runs (24.98) and 142 wickets (28.22) in 136 one-day games, is no true indicator. His 309 runs and eight wickets in 20 one-day internationals, his obvious métier, give few clues. Simply seeing him play was the real measure: he gave genuine pleasure to all who watched, whether from the dressing-room or the stand.

SURREY V LEICESTERSHIRE   2003

September 18, 19, 20, 21, 2002. Surrey won by 483 runs.

Surrey made it three Championship titles in four years when they returned to the top of the pile in 2002, capping an emotional summer with this enormous win over Leicestershire.

It was fitting that Surrey should wind up a stunning season with a huge victory. Hollioake's apparently strange decision to bat well into the last day left Leicestershire needing to survive less than two sessions, but Murtagh skittled them within 39 overs. It had been a landmark-strewn match. As Surrey roared to 494 in the first innings, Ward became the third batsman, after Jack Hobbs (twice) and Tom Hayward, to hit four consecutive Championship hundreds for the county, but was upstaged by Newman's muscular maiden century. Srinath then removed Hollioake and Philip Sampson in consecutive balls to grab an unwitting hat-trick; he had forgotten that Ormond had fallen to the final ball of his previous over. And, after Maddy, batting with a runner, and Sutcliffe had provided the backbone of Leicestershire's 361, Hollioake crowned his remarkable season with an incendiary maiden double-century, his first hundred coming between lunch and tea. In all, he batted five hours, struck 21 fours and three sixes in 252 balls and shared a 282-run stand with Brown. At the close of the first day, Hollioake was presented with the Championship trophy in front of 2,000 fans.

Surrey 494 (I. J. Ward 118, S. A. Newman 183, J. N. Batty 74; J. Srinath 5-114) and 492-9 dec
(A. D. Brown 107, A. J. Hollioake 208); Leicestershire 361 (I. J. Sutcliffe 72, D. L. Maddy 127*,
D. I. Stevens 53) and 142 (N. D. Burns 68; T. J. Murtagh 5-39).

Note: a report of the Cheltenham and Gloucester Trophy match between Surrey and Gloucestershire in 2002 appears in chapter 11.

SURREY V KENT, SUNDAY LEAGUE   2004
May 18, 2003. Surrey won by six runs.

Surrey's glut of trophies had begun with the Sunday League in 1996, and winning the same competition seven years later would bring the run to an end. The match against Kent was one of the most exciting of the season.

The match aggregate of 638 was the highest in the competition's history, beating 631 by Nottinghamshire and Surrey at The Oval in 1993. Azhar's 70 in 41 balls made Ramprakash (107 not out in 99) look pedestrian, and four of Surrey's ten sixes sailed out of the ground. But Kent's batsmen were equally savage. Smith (99 from 86 balls) and Walker (80 not out from 62) kept up with the rate, and Hollioake (5–0–52–1) was despatched at will. Kent needed 35 off five overs with six wickets remaining – a breeze given the previous scoring-rates – but they could not feed Walker enough of the strike.

Surrey 322-7 (45 overs) (M. R. Ramprakash 107*, Azhar Mahmood 70; P. D. Trego 4-66);
Kent 316-7 (45 overs) (E. T. Smith 99, M. J. Walker 80*).

SURREY V MIDDLESEX, TWENTY20 CUP   2004

June 13, 2003. Surrey won by four wickets.

For many years the 'after-work' 20-over format had been familiar to club players all round the world. In 2003 English domestic cricket brought it into the professional game for the first time with the Twenty20 Cup. A crowd of 8,500 for the opening night at The Oval was an indication of Twenty20's appeal to fans. Surrey took to it immediately, remaining unbeaten on their way to winning the inaugural competition. In fact their first Twenty20 defeat wasn't until the following year's final. Despite the rapturous welcome it received in England, even the far-sighted observer would have struggled to see how successful 'T20' would be in the coming years. Indeed, Wisden gave only one sentence to that historical match against Middlesex on June 13, 2003:

"Ormond became the first bowler to take five wickets in a Twenty20 game."

Middlesex 155 (20 overs) (A. J. Strauss 52; J. Ormond 5-26); **Surrey 158-6** (19.2 overs).

SURREY IN 2003   David Llewellyn, 2004

Despite Surrey winning two of the four domestic trophies in 2003, Wisden's prescient summary of their season detected signs that their era of dominance was drawing to a close.

Winning is an exhausting business. Surrey made that plain, losing the last three Championship matches very wearily, as they staggered to the finish. In the wake of winning the inaugural Twenty20 Cup, and plodding on to win the National League, they lost their way in the one competition they really wanted – the County Championship – and finished third, below the prize money. Surrey's ultimately unsuccessful defence of their title became the focus of their whole season.

There were plenty prepared to label the summer a failure, despite an operating profit in excess of £400,000 and two of the four main trophies, which would have delighted any other county. Excuses included the usual suspects: injuries, the odd toss, the weather, loss of form, the occasional dodgy decision. But lurking among them were some less obvious ones. Since he first took charge of Surrey, standing in for Alec Stewart in 1995, Adam Hollioake perhaps proved himself the county's best captain since Stuart Surridge more than 40 years earlier. His innovative, imaginative approach often produced seemingly impossible victories, when all others would have surrendered to the percentage result, the draw. But in 2003, his seventh season in sole charge, he looked a tired man, merely going through the motions during the last weeks. On his own admission, Hollioake found it hard to motivate himself, let alone his team. That led to a secondary cause of their downfall – a lack of the famous team spirit which had helped them lift the Championship crown in three of the previous four seasons...

The most prominent absentee in 2004 will be Stewart, who announced his retirement in September. He had wanted one more year, but Surrey had been granted planning permission to develop the Vauxhall End, at a cost of £22m, and claimed there was no spare cash – or sentiment. Stewart was therefore denied a chance to add to the 14,440 Championship runs he had scored since 1981. He was, however, appointed the club's director of new business. There was one other significant departure, that of head groundsman Paul Brind. He was reluctantly allowed to leave after a decade in charge, thus ending a Brind dynasty that started with the appointment of his father Harry in 1975. The job is hardly going to an outsider, though: Brind's deputy, Bill Gordon, took over, and he has been at The Oval for 38 years.

ADAM HOLLIOAKE – CRICKETER OF THE YEAR   Simon Wilde, 2003

Wisden *had paid a fulsome tribute to Hollioake after Surrey won the Championship in 2002, identifying many of his leadership qualities. The article ends with the prediction that "the Hollioake story is not yet run". Yet while the 2003 season did bring him two more trophies, it was also his last as captain. He retired as a professional the following summer, aged 32.*

In 1995, Surrey epitomised all that was wrong with English cricket. They had plenty of talent but were habitual underachievers whose glory days were receding into the distance: after winning the Championship seven seasons in a row in the 1950s, they had won it only once more, and that was back in 1971. The team was poorly run and visibly divided – literally so, with a separate dressing-room for capped players. In July 1995, Surrey hit rock bottom, tumbling to 18th place in the table.

It was a custom at The Oval not to appoint an official vice-captain, even though the then captain, Alec Stewart, was an automatic choice for England. That July, the task of standing in for Stewart was handed to a 23-year-old all-rounder, Adam Hollioake. Stewart was the ultimate Surrey insider, son of Micky, who had led the team to the 1971 Championship and later became manager. Hollioake, raised in Australia until he was 12, was much more of an outsider, as was the new coach, the former Australian seamer David Gilbert.

Hollioake's approach was refreshingly positive and results improved almost instantly: Surrey won three first-class games and hauled themselves to 12th in the Championship and ninth in the Sunday League (divisions, in those days, existed only in dressing-rooms). But there was still deep disquiet. A special general meeting was called by disaffected members in October: the incoming chairman, Mike Soper, was "staggered" by the depth of feeling. In December, the chief executive, Glyn Woodman, resigned, to be replaced by Paul Sheldon. "Surrey," said *Wisden* in 1996, "are nothing if not consistent in their inability to win something."

Stewart remained in place but Hollioake, now officially vice-captain, played a larger role. In 1996, he led the team to four Championship victories as Surrey climbed to third, and they confounded *Wisden* and other observers by winning the Sunday League. In 1997, Hollioake was appointed captain and Surrey won the Benson and Hedges Cup. In 1999, finally, they won the Championship. Unlike 1971, this was not an isolated triumph: they retained the title in 2000, won the B&H again in

2001, and the Championship for the third time in four years in 2002. They had become the most successful team in the country.

If Hollioake changed one thing, it was to defenestrate the tired thinking prevailing in most county dressing-rooms. "It was the blame culture," he reflects. "Captains and managers pointing the finger for not winning. People covering their tracks. We would not be like that. We'd do everything to win but there'd be no aimless stuff. No five-hour fielding practice for the sake of it. If we were fielding well, we wouldn't bother. We asked ourselves what we needed to do to win and suggestions could come from anyone. No one questioned another's desire to win. Democracy's hard to get in county cricket. It comes through trust. If we have to sit around in pink underwear for half an hour beforehand, we will."

The collective realisation of what was required brought with it a need for collective maturity. Martin Bicknell, Alistair Brown, Mark Butcher and Graham Thorpe were all aged 24 to 28 when Hollioake's reign began; they have grown wiser together. Hollioake was helped by his outsider's perspective, by two key confidants – his father, John, and Alec Stewart, who could have been old-laggish but went along with the new broom. Both had experience of Australian grade cricket and espoused its virtues. "I grew up with the Australian view," Adam says. "The main thing was to win, not how. I have carried that with me."...

While his captaincy work finally bore fruit in four-day cricket in 1999 and 2000 with Surrey's first Championship titles since the year of his birth, his batting average fell and bowling average rose for three successive seasons from 1998.

Liberation arrived last year by the most painful means imaginable. The death of Ben, in a car crash on the way home from a family reunion in Perth, forced Adam to reappraise his life. He stayed in Australia for the birth of his first child, Bennaya, and did not rejoin Surrey until two months into the English season, keeping in touch with the team's fortunes by phone and the internet. After some discussion, it was decided he should resume as captain – in another sign of a well-run club, both Mark Butcher and Ian Ward had led capably in his absence – and he immediately showed the old sureness of touch. But more practical skills felt different. When he picked up a bat for the first time in weeks, it felt like an axe.

He was soon wielding it like one as his batting assumed greater assurance than ever. In his Championship comeback against Somerset he struck 87 off 83 balls and he followed up with two brisk fifties against Warwickshire. Then, in the space of a few days, he hit 117 in 59 balls in a one-day quarter-final at Hove and a counter-attacking Championship century – his first for three years – at Canterbury. "That wasn't me," he observed. "I can't bat that well."

With the title in the bag, he rounded off the season with a maiden double-hundred against Leicestershire. The death of the placid Ben had taught his more aggressive brother to relax. "It made me get a perspective back on life as a whole," he said. "My job was important and I had pride in it but I realised that happiness was more important. I enjoyed hitting the ball into the crowd but to hit sixes you need to take risks. I had no fear of failure."

The year ended with Hollioake, now 31, called back to Australia as cover for England's one-day squad. He made it on to the field only once, in a warm-up game against a Bradman XI at Bowral, but took his chance with a hard-hit 53 off 38 balls. Although he could not push his way past Ronnie Irani into the World Cup squad, his name was bandied about as soon as Nasser Hussain handed in the one-day captaincy. The Hollioake story is not yet run.

Chapter 18

Surrey in the Modern Age

A fter eight trophies in eight years between 1996 and 2003, Surrey once again fell into a period of instability and underachievement. This was in stark contrast to the development of The Oval, which continued to build its reputation as one of the greatest grounds in the world. The OCS Stand was added in 2005, a new frontage to the pavilion followed in 2013 and the new Peter May Stand was opened in 2016. Surrey managed only one trophy in all that time.

After Hollioake stepped down, Jonathan Batty and Mark Butcher both tried their hand at captaincy with limited success. The one reliable element was the form of Mark Ramprakash, who time and again proved himself to be the great county batsman of his generation.

Former Sussex captain Chris Adams was appointed coach after Surrey suffered Championship relegation in 2008, and within a year he caused a shock by signing 22-year-old Rory Hamilton-Brown from his old county as the club's captain. Hamilton-Brown built the team in his own image: hard-hitting and aggressive. It was spectacular when it came off, but inconsistency remained the team's defining trait.

In 2012, ten years after Ben Hollioake's death, Surrey were again hit by tragedy. Tom Maynard, the 23-year-old Welsh batsman and close friend of Hamilton-Brown, died after an accident on a railway line in *south London one early morning in June. Surrey went into shock. Within a year both Adams and Hamilton-Brown had left the club.*

South Africa's Graeme Smith was appointed captain at the end of the 2012 season but injury forced him to retire in 2014 after just eight first-class appearances for Surrey. Alec Stewart returned as director of cricket in the same year, along with new coach Graham Ford, and feisty off-spinner Gareth Batty replaced Smith as captain. Batty led the county to promotion from the second division of the Championship in 2015, his first season in charge, and although they were defeated in successive Lord's finals, a new generation of Surrey-born players promises a bright future.

In recent years, the club's growing commercial strength has also attracted some of the game's biggest names to The Oval, including Hashim Amla, Ricky Ponting, the aforementioned Smith, and Kumar Sangakkara.

SURREY V GLOUCESTERSHIRE
2007

May 3, 4, 5, 2006. Surrey won by an innings and 297 runs.

The main bright spot for Surrey fans in the immediate post-Hollioake years was the unrelenting form of Mark Ramprakash, who would reach his 100th first-class century in 2008. On this occasion, it was Gloucestershire who were chastened by his blade.

The century-maker who took centre stage on the third day was 109-year-old Henry Allingham, the last known survivor of the Battle of Jutland, an Oval guest more than 100 years after his last visit, when he watched W. G. Grace in action. Surrey treated him to a statistical banquet: Ramprakash hit his 11th double-century (his sixth since moving from Middlesex in 2001) and became the first man to share in four century partnerships in the same Surrey innings. He motored to a career-best 292 – in 556 minutes and 425 balls, with 32 fours and seven sixes – with some imperious strokeplay, one front-foot pull for six leaving Kirby, the bowler, shaking his head, rather than his fist, in astonishment. Benning celebrated his 23rd birthday with his maiden

Championship hundred, including four fours off successive bouncers from Kirby. Surrey's highest total against Gloucestershire eclipsed Weston's first Championship century for almost two years. Mohammad Akram's best figures for Surrey then sealed a three-day victory, their biggest over Gloucestershire, but their first since 1995.

Gloucestershire 207 (W. P. C. Weston 102) and 135 (Mohammad Akram 6-34); Surrey 639-8 dec
(S. A. Newman 81, M. R. Ramprakash 292, J. G. E. Benning 112; M. C. J. Ball 6-134).

Surrey v Northamptonshire 2007
August 2, 3, 4, 5, 2006. Surrey won by seven wickets.

Ramprakash went one better later that summer, hitting Surrey's first triple-century for 80 years.

Once again Ramprakash stole the show, compiling an unbeaten triple-century – his first, and the first for Surrey since Jack Hobbs made 316 not out against Middlesex at Lord's in 1926. Dropped twice on 105, Ramprakash put on 353 with Butcher, a record stand for Surrey against Northamptonshire. He faced 445 balls in 530 minutes, and hit 44 fours and a six: it was his fourth score of 150-plus in five innings, and his second against Northamptonshire in three weeks. Newman had earlier made his only Championship hundred of the season. Northamptonshire conceded 600 for the second match running and, although Afzaal did reach his fourth hundred of the season, Surrey needed only 65 off 16 overs. They made a meal of it, losing three wickets – including the prolific Ramprakash – before limping home with 12 balls to spare. Surrey fielded three frontline spinners for the first time since 1972 (Intikhab Alam, Pat Pocock and Chris Waller), but one of them was almost enough: Kumble took eight wickets in the second innings against his former county.

Northamptonshire 347 (C. J. L. Rogers 59, B. M. Shafayat 91, B. J. Phillips 65) and 386
(C. J. L. Rogers 75, U. Afzaal 142, M. J. Nicholson 53*; A. Kumble 8-100); Surrey 669-5 dec
(S. A. Newman 143, M. R. Ramprakash 301*, M. A. Butcher 147) and 65-3.

SURREY IN 2009

David Llewellyn, 2010

Desperate times call for desperate measures. And the signing of the inexperienced Rory Hamilton-Brown, aged 22, as Surrey's captain on a three-year contract worth somewhere in the region of £400,000–450,000 certainly smacks of desperation. It is Surrey's professional cricket manager Chris Adams's first major signing, and *prima facie* a major gamble. Hamilton-Brown's primary brief is to take Surrey back to the first division of the Championship; failure to do so would almost certainly cost Adams his performance-related £90,000-a-year job.

Hamilton-Brown, the 40th captain in Surrey's history, is the least experienced in over 60 years, with just eight first-class matches to his name. Neither Swainson Akroyd (1869) nor Nigel Bennett (1946) had played any first-class cricket when they were appointed, while William Collyer (1867) with six matches and John Gregory (1871) with seven (three of them for Middlesex) edge Hamilton-Brown into fifth. None set the world alight with their cricket.

Adams, though, has faith. Hamilton-Brown, who will be the youngest captain in the 2010 Championship, caught his eye in early 2008, after he had been released by Surrey to join Adams at Sussex. So when Adams describes him as a "super-talented cricketer" possessed of "charisma, intelligence and the ability to get people to follow [him]," he speaks from first-hand knowledge.

SURREY V SUSSEX, CLYDESDALE BANK 40 SEMI-FINAL

2012

September 4, 2011. Surrey won by 71 runs.

Victory in the 40-over competition of 2011 was the sole piece of silverware in Rory Hamilton-Brown's reign as captain, which came to a swift end after the death of close friend and team-mate Tom Maynard the following year. One of Maynard's finest moments in a Surrey shirt came in the semi-final against Sussex.

Andy Flower turned down Surrey's request to release Jade Dernbach from the England squad for this match, but they won easily enough without him: brutal batting and unrelenting spin was a cocktail too powerful for Sussex. Rain reduced the match to 24 overs, though Surrey's score might have been defendable in 40, such was the impact of their spinners – bowling all but four overs – and their effervescence in the field. Surrey travelled at almost ten an over for the first 20: Maynard's 60 from 33 balls included four sixes which turned leg-side fielders into hopeless spectators. Sussex's fielding was exposed by four dropped catches and, wherever Yardy attempted to hide Panesar, the home batsmen found him. Hamilton-Brown had often opened the bowling himself in the group stage. This time he turned to Spriegel and was rewarded with two crucial blows, the second when the bowler stretched mightily to catch a top-edge from Goodwin, and tripped over the non-striker's stumps in the process. Sussex's hopes rested on Joyce and Nash, the most profitable of partners this season. They added 59 in six overs, but once separated, Batty and Schofield descended to secure Surrey's first Lord's final since 2001, when they beat Gloucestershire in the Benson and Hedges Cup.

Surrey 228-7 (24 overs) (T. L. Maynard 60; C. J. Liddle 4-38); **Sussex 157** (22 overs) (C. D. Nash 55; C. P. Schofield 4-22).

TOM MAYNARD – OBITUARY   2013

The 2013 Almanack *quoted from the emotional speeches made at Tom Maynard's funeral by Hugh Morris (a former team-mate of his father Matthew) and Glamorgan captain Mark Wallace.*

Maynard, Thomas Lloyd, died after being electrocuted on a railway line on June 18, 2012, aged 23. During the weekend before his death, Tom Maynard was a cheerful presence on television screens, as a guest on Sky's knockabout Saturday show *Cricket AM* and as part of *Finishing School*, a documentary about the England Performance Programme's winter training. There had been a chance to glimpse him in the flesh, too, in Surrey's Sunday afternoon Twenty20 match against Kent at Beckenham. Then, shortly after breakfast time on Monday, came the news that his body had been found on the tracks near Wimbledon Park tube station in south London. Not since the death in 2002 of Ben Hollioake – also of Surrey, also youthful, good-looking and precocious – had English cricket been so numbed by tragedy.

Five weeks earlier, against Worcestershire at New Road, Maynard's talent had been thrillingly laid bare. With Surrey following on, he made a career-best 143, moving to three figures with a six. The watching Kevin Pietersen called Andy Flower that evening to offer an enthusiastic endorsement. Not that this surprised Graham Thorpe, his EPP batting coach: "Tom scored runs when his team needed them, which is crucial for a player who has potential to get to the top."

The innings also underlined a new cricketing maturity acquired in his second season at The Oval. "He had moved to another level," said Dean Conway, the former Glamorgan and England physio who had known him all his life. "Before joining Surrey he had the talent but not the stats." At his funeral, at Llandaff Cathedral in Cardiff, Hugh Morris – the former Glamorgan opening batsman, now managing director of England cricket— said Maynard had first toddled into the dressing-room at Sophia Gardens with his father Matthew at the age of two. Thereafter, he was seldom out of it. Conway remembered: "He became like one of the team. We called him 'Bruiser'. Even then, he had massive arms and legs."…

Matthew Maynard's abundant talent was never successfully transferred to the international stage, but many believed his son had the temperament and ability to prosper there. Morris called him "a player who was surely destined for the highest reaches of the game, and whose authority and elegance at the crease reminded so many of his father".

Another speaker at Llandaff Cathedral was the Glamorgan captain Mark Wallace. "I will always remember him as the lad who could make me laugh more than anyone else I have ever met," he said. "I just wish he had never made me cry."

SURREY v NOTTINGHAMSHIRE 2014

July 8, 9, 10, 11, 2013. Match drawn.

With new captain Graeme Smith engaged with South Africa, Surrey needed an overseas player as cover in 2013. Director of cricket Alec Stewart dug deep into his contacts book and produced the name of Ricky Ponting. It was to be Ponting's farewell to first-class cricket, and he signed off with a characteristically pugnacious innings which saved the game against Nottinghamshire.

Ponting, widely feted as Australia's best batsman since Don Bradman, closed his first-class career on the ground where Bradman famously played his final Test, in 1948. The crowd was rather smaller, but – while The Don signed off with a duck – Ponting graced the occasion with his 82nd hundred, including some signature swivel-pulls and on-drives. He ensured that Surrey batted out the final day for a draw, and passed 24,000 runs in the process. In their first innings, they had thrown away the advantage of winning the toss, with only Burns and Davies making headway against a disciplined attack. Nottinghamshire then ran up a big lead. Mullaney had not reached three figures in the Championship since his second match, in May 2010, but warmed to his new role of opener with an adhesive 282-minute innings; Patel added a mature century, his third of the summer. The pitch, which had been used for a Twenty20 game the previous week, was expected to turn – Surrey fielded three spinners – but ended up providing more help for Dernbach and Tremlett. Neither side were willing to risk defeat, so Surrey batted out the match: Harinath knuckled down, but Ponting's seven-hour tour-de-force put everyone else in the shade.

Surrey 198 (R. J. Burns 57, S. M. Davies 65*) **and 395-8 dec** (A. Harinath 69, R. T. Ponting 169*); **Nottinghamshire 410** (S. J. Mullaney 104, S. R. Patel 110).

Surrey v Yorkshire   2014

September 24, 25, 26, 27, 2013. Match drawn.

After a disappointing summer, Surrey spirits were raised in the final match at The Oval of 2013 when young opener Dominic Sibley hit a double-century in his fourth first-class innings. Future England batsman Gary Ballance showed his international pedigree with a hundred in both innings for Yorkshire.

Surrey were cheered up by a record-breaking innings from Dominic Sibley, who in only his third first-class match was the youngest to score a double-century in the Championship. Earlier on the same day he had become Surrey's most youthful centurion. In all, he batted for a minute shy of ten hours for 242, faced 536 balls and hit 24 fours and two sixes. Just 18, and given special leave of absence by Whitgift School, Sibley – faced by six men in catching positions in front of the bat – inched nervily to three figures after starting the third day on 81. But he widened his range of shots, off front foot and back, and continued to concentrate fiercely. He put on 236 with Amla, who made his first hundred for Surrey, and was finally yorked by Sidebottom... Sibley's performance was overshadowed by a notable double from Ballance, who was named in England's squad for the Ashes tour the day before the match. He made 148 in the first innings and, after Yorkshire slipped to 84 for four in the second – still 116 adrift – another fine century to save the game, using his feet well as the spinners aimed into the footmarks, but frequently rocking back to force through square.

Yorkshire 434 (P. A. Jaques 88, G. S. Ballance 148; Z. S. Ansari 4-70) **and 265-6** (K. S. Williamson 60, G. S. Ballance 108*); **Surrey 634-5 dec** (R. J. Burns 82, D. P. Sibley 242, H. M. Amla 151, V. S. Solanki 51).

SURREY V LEICESTERSHIRE   2016

May 10, 11, 12, 13, 2015. Surrey won by seven wickets.

A subplot of Surrey cricket in these years was the soap opera of Kevin Pietersen's on-off England career. After joining Surrey on loan in 2010 and then permanently in 2011, Pietersen made big scores during his rare appearances for the club as a retort to his critics. This was never truer than in May 2015, when he came within a hair's breadth of breaking one of the club's most sacred records in a (futile) bid to win back his England place. It turned out to be his penultimate game in first-class cricket – barring a comeback of course.

Pietersen's monumental 355 not out – two short of Bobby Abel's 116-year-old county record – was the centrepiece of Surrey's victory, although Davies's scintillating 57-ball hundred was equally important as they sprinted home at ten an over on the final evening. Pietersen batted for seven and a half hours, faced 396 balls, and hit 36 fours and 15 sixes in his highest first-class score; next best was Sangakkara's 36. It was an easy-paced pitch, with a short boundary on one side, and he was dropped five times – but it was still a superb effort. Pietersen's characteristic crunching drives, whips and flicks were all in evidence, as well as the fist-clenched celebrations of landmarks on the ground where, ten years earlier, his 158 had secured the Ashes. For at least half his innings, he was battling to keep his side afloat, after Lewis Hill's century in his second Championship game had taken Leicestershire close to 300. Pietersen ended the second day unbeaten on 326 and – on the eve of Andrew Strauss's unveiling as England's new director of cricket – declared: "They say that timing is everything." His optimism lasted a couple of hours, until Strauss and ECB Chief Executive Tom Harrison told him during a meeting at a London hotel that there was no chance of an international return before the end of the summer. After penning an angry column in the *Daily Telegraph*, in which he said he felt "deeply misled" by the ECB, Pietersen carried on the next morning, taking the tenth-wicket stand to 139, of which last man Dunn made five; Tremlett also helped add 101 for the ninth. In that short time, Pietersen also picked up a calf injury, which meant he had to cancel his imminent spell with the Sunrisers Hyderabad at the IPL. Facing a deficit of 265, Leicestershire applied themselves well. Both Eckersley and O'Brien survived for around three hours and, with Tremlett tweaking a hamstring, the last three wickets used up 40 overs in adding 93. When Ansari, claiming a career-best six for 152, finished the resistance shortly after tea, Surrey had only 24 overs to score 216. But Roy tonked 67 from 39 balls, and the dazzling Davies made sure Pietersen didn't have to bat again.

Leicestershire 292 (L. J. Hill 126, B. A. Raine 57; M. P. Dunn 4-72) **and 480** (A. J. Robson 55, E. J. H. Eckersley 118, N. J. O'Brien 78; Z. S. Ansari 6-152); **Surrey 557** (K. P. Pietersen 355*; B. A. Raine 4-124) **and 218-3** (J. J. Roy 67, S. M. Davies 115*).

SURREY V DERBYSHIRE   2016

September 1, 2, 3, 4, 2015. Surrey won by an innings and 98 runs.

In his first full season as official captain, Gareth Batty bowled himself into club history during the win over Derbyshire which took Surrey back to the top flight of the County Championship.

The victory which confirmed Surrey's promotion – and took them top, ahead of Lancashire – was secured in spectacular fashion: skipper Batty had Palladino scooped up by Foakes (keeping wicket in place of the injured Wilson), before bowling Footitt and Cotton to complete a hat-trick. Batty and his team-mates – and a small but appreciative crowd – could barely take in the sudden achievement of their goal. They had the final day to bowl out Derbyshire, only for Madsen and Durston to settle in. But Batty, who finished with his best figures of the season, broke through shortly after lunch, and the floodgates opened. "My only other hat-trick came for Yorkshire Under-11 against Lancashire back in the late 1980s," he said. "I think Freddie Flintoff may have been one of my victims." On another rain-hit first day, during which five catches were dropped, Derbyshire had failed to take advantage of first use of a slow pitch which turned increasingly, if never violently. When Surrey batted, everyone reached double figures. Burns again looked good, but it was Ansari's five-hour hundred which hurt a tiring attack the most, as the last five wickets piled on 388. Durston achieved career-best figures, while Burke made his highest score.

Derbyshire 313 (C. F. Hughes 96; T. K. Curran 5-71, Z. S. Ansari 4-61) **and 149**
(W. L. Madsen 76*, W. J. Durston 57; G. J. Batty 6-51); **Surrey 560** (R. J. Burns 92,
Z. S. Ansari 106, G. C. Wilson 72, J. E. Burke 79; W. J. Durston 6-113).

Note: reports of some other Surrey matches at The Oval between 2007 and 2015 appear in chapters 11 and 12.

Chapter 19

Views from the Gasholders

We have seen how *The Oval has been the theatre for some of the most significant and dramatic events in cricket history, from the birth of the Ashes, through the Golden Age and the greats of the interwar era, to the Asian and Caribbean triumphs of more recent times. We have seen, too, how the ground played host to three great Surrey eras, including the team of the 1950s which dominated county cricket like no other. And we have seen how it played a central role in the advent of the shorter formats which have transformed the sport.*

But there are many more Oval delights to be found in Wisden, *even if they do not correspond to the broad themes charted by this book. Some of these are collected in this chapter. They are by design an eclectic bunch sweeping across the decades, ranging from Andy Sandham's recollections of his Oval debut in 1911 to an obituary of an aeronautical genius who was infatuated with the ground (and the art of leg-spin). The aim is to shed light on some of the characters associated with The Oval over the years, as well as the changing face of the ground itself.*

Included are several matches which produced some statistical quirks (Surrey supporters may wish to breeze through the game against Nottinghamshire in 1880). England's defeat by New Zealand in 1999, when the home team were booed by their own fans, provides a fascinating contrast to the unconfined joy of 2005 with which this book began.

C. W. ALCOCK – OBITUARY   1908

In 1908 Wisden *published the following obituary of Charles Alcock, Surrey's forward-thinking secretary without whom The Oval would almost certainly be a shell of its magnificent self.*

Mr Charles William Alcock, J. P., who was born at Sunderland on December 2, 1842, died at Brighton on February 26, 1907. He was educated at Harrow, but, not enjoying very good health, did not obtain a place in the eleven. In later years, however, he played occasionally for the Gentlemen of Essex, the Butterflies, Harrow Wanderers, and Incogniti, and once had the curious experience of captaining France against Germany in a match at Hamburg. *Scores and Biographies* describes him as a steady bat, a fair change fast bowler, and an excellent long stop or long field. On February 6, 1872, on the strong recommendation of Mr V. E. Walker, he was appointed secretary to the Surrey County C. C., a position he held until the time of his death. Of his work for Surrey cricket it would be difficult to speak too highly, for he was at all times both willing and anxious to do all in his power to further its welfare. He was a most voluminous writer on the game, and in 1882 founded *Cricket*, of which he was editor from the first until the day of his death. For 29 years he edited *James Lillywhite's Cricketers' Annual*, and was the chief contributor to *Surrey Cricket: Its History and Associations*, published in 1902. For many years he arranged the fixture list of teams visiting England, and it was due principally to him that the first meeting between England and Australia in this country – at The Oval in 1880 – took place. Mr Alcock's connection with Association Football was so prominent that it is not too much to say that he more than anyone else made the game. He captained England against Scotland in 1875, and it was under his leadership that the Wanderers won the Football Association Cup in 1872 and in four subsequent years. He was Hon. Secretary of the Football Association from 1867 until 1890, secretary from 1891 until 1896, and a vice-president from the last-mentioned year until his death.

Surrey v Nottinghamshire 1881

July 26, 27, 28, 1880. Nottinghamshire won by an innings and 65 runs.

In 1880 Nottinghamshire dismissed Surrey for 16, the lowest score in a first-class match at the ground.

Surrey's ill fortune in having the most popular matches in their programme for 1880 spoiled by bad weather still stuck to them. Rain prevented the game being commenced until nearly one o'clock, and caused several interruptions in the play, beside rendering the ground slippery and the ball difficult to handle. The end of the first day's play saw Notts still in, with four wickets to fall and a total of 208, which was augmented to 266 on the fine and sunny Tuesday ere the rest were disposed of. Wind and sun, following on the rain of the previous day, had caused the wickets to be in a very bad state, when Surrey began that memorable innings in which a good county eleven were dismissed for the extraordinarily small total of 16. Taking into consideration the calibre of the Surrey team it is probable that the bowling success of Morley and Shaw in this match stands unsurpassed in the history of the game. Morley was almost unplayable, as his wonderful analysis will tell. Surrey's second innings shewed a vast improvement in the batting, Jupp, Mr Lucas, Mr Wyld and Read especially playing some fine cricket, and it was due to their exertions that the game was prolonged over the second day. About half-an-hour's play on the Wednesday resulted in the addition of 20 runs to the overnight total, Pooley increasing his contribution to 29, the highest score made for Surrey, and an excellent innings. The end was the defeat of Surrey by an innings and 65 runs, a result achieved through the fine batting of Daft and others of the Notts Eleven, and the before-mentioned astonishingly successful bowling of Morley and Shaw.

Surrey

*A. P. Lucas c Flowers b Morley	2	–	†E. W. Pooley c Oscroft b Morley		3
J. Shuter c Shrewsbury b Morley	0	–	E. Blamires c Selby b Morley		0
H. Jupp c Sherwin b Shaw	1	–	T. Trodd not out		0
W. G. Wyld lbw b Shaw	0	–			
J. M. Read c Barnes b Morley	9	–	Lb I		1
R. Humphrey c Flowers b Morley	0	–			
G. L. Lyons c Shaw b Morley	0	–	1/2 2/3 3/3 4/12 5/12	(39.2 overs)	16
J. Potter b Shaw	0	–	6/12 7/12 8/15 9/15 10/16		

Shaw 20–16–6–3; Morley 19.2–12–9–7.

Umpires: R. P. Carpenter and J. Rowbotham.

A LIFETIME WITH SURREY

Andy Sandham, 1972

After 60 years as a player, coach and scorer for Surrey, Andy Sandham was asked by Wisden *to pen some reflections for the 1972 edition. This short extract recalls his first-class debut at The Oval in 1911.*

There was at that time a public house with a flat roof over on the gas-works side of The Oval, with six or seven tiered seats for customers who could see cricket for nothing. As the pubs were then open all day long and the beer was both cheaper and stronger, the customers by the afternoon got a bit under the influence and frequently gave us the bird. I got it on my first appearance and I thought it rather hard, for I naturally wanted to do well and took only two hours for my 53. All this, too, from people who were not in the ground!

SURREY v NORTHAMPTONSHIRE

1959

June 4, 5, 6, 1958. Match drawn.

Only twice has an opposition batsman hit a triple-century against Surrey at The Oval. The first occasion was when ex-Surrey player Raman Subba Row scored exactly 300 in 1958 (see chapter 15 for Neil Fairbrother's 366 in 1990).

A long struggle for the first-innings lead was a story of records but little entertainment. The match had lasted 15 and three-quarter hours when

Northamptonshire, who occupied nine hours of the time, went ahead. Stewart, with his first century of the season, and Constable batted particularly well for Surrey and at the close of the first day the score was 324 for four. McIntyre, captain in the absence of May, who, like Loader, Lock and Laker, was playing for England, chose to bat on for three-quarters of an hour next day on an excellent pitch, presumably in the hope of forcing a follow-on. With Northamptonshire 18 for three and then 95 for five, such an eventuality seemed likely, but Surrey had to wait another six and three-quarter hours and 376 runs before breaking the sixth-wicket stand. That partnership, between the former Surrey player Subba Row, leading his side at The Oval for the first time, and Lightfoot, created a record for any Northamptonshire wicket. Subba Row's 300 was the highest individual score for the county, as well as equal to the previous highest made against Surrey, and Lightfoot reached his maiden century, which took six hours 23 minutes and contained 14 fours. In all, Subba Row batted for nine hours 26 minutes and hit 42 fours.

Surrey 378-5 dec (T. H. Clark 71, M. J. Stewart 118, B. Constable 73, K. F. Barrington 62*; A. Lightfoot 4-96); Northamptonshire 529-9 (R. Subba Row 300, A. Lightfoot 119).

GEORGE EDWARDS – OBITUARY   2004

Aeronautical genius George Edwards was the Surrey president in 1979 and had a love of The Oval throughout his life. Edwards's obituary in 2004 included a delightful line about his influence on the Dambusters raids in the Second World War.

Edwards, Sir George Robert OM, CBE, FRS, DL, who died on March 2, 2003, aged 94, was one of the foremost aeronautical designers and administrators of the 20th century and chairman of the British Aircraft Corporation from 1963 to 1975. He was at the heart of almost every development in British aviation for 40 years, from biplanes to Concorde. He was also a skilful leg-break bowler, playing alongside the Bedser twins in club cricket, and married his two interests by insisting on the importance of backspin in the design of Barnes Wallis's bouncing bombs used in the Dambusters raids of 1943. He was president of Surrey in 1979 and also an accomplished painter whose "Cricket at Guildford" was offered by *Wisden Cricket Monthly* in 1989 to support Surrey's appeal to save The Oval.

SURREY V AUSTRALIANS   1900

May 15, 16, 17, 1899. Australia won by an innings and 71 runs.

The best bowling figures at The Oval belong to the Australian Bill Howell, whose medium-paced spin took 10 for 18 against Surrey in 1899.

The Australians played their first match at The Oval and lost no time in reasserting themselves. Though they had the bad luck to lose the toss on a soft wicket, they outplayed Surrey completely, winning the game by an innings and 71 runs. Howell, who had not played either at Crystal Palace or Leyton, made a sensational first appearance in England, taking all ten wickets in Surrey's first innings and having a record for the whole game of 15 wickets for 57 runs. Well as he often bowled later in the tour, he never did anything to approach this extraordinary performance. Apart from Hayes's vigorously hit 43 in the second innings, the Surrey Eleven had nothing on which to congratulate themselves. With Lockwood prevented from playing by a bad leg, their bowling was very weak and the batting gave no suggestion of the great things afterwards done by the team on the same ground. The Australian batting on the other hand was very consistent, Kelly, who hit ten fours, doing particularly well.

Surrey 114 (W. P. Howell 10-28) and 64 (H. Trumble 5-34, W. P. Howell 5-29);
Australians 249 (J. J. Kelly 50*).

KING GEORGE VI – OBITUARY   1953

The Oval has always been owned by the Duchy of Cornwall and enjoyed royal patronage, including that of King George VI.

H. M. KING GEORGE VI died at Sandringham on February 6, 1952. He was Patron of the Marylebone, Surrey and Lancashire clubs. When [he was known as] Prince Albert, he performed the hat-trick on the private ground on the slopes below Windsor Castle, where the sons and grandsons of Edward VII used to play regularly. A left-handed batsman and bowler, the King bowled King Edward VII, King George V and the present Duke of Windsor in three consecutive balls, thus proving himself the best royal cricketer since Frederick, Prince of Wales [1707-1751], took a keen interest in the game. The ball is now mounted in the mess-room of the Royal Naval College, Dartmouth.

SURREY V MIDDLESEX   1889

July 19, 20, 21, 1888. Surrey won by three wickets.

In 1888 Middlesex's George Burton became one of seven bowlers to have taken all ten wickets in an innings at The Oval.

A singularly even match, which was brought to a definite issue on the third day after a draw had seemed almost inevitable. Surrey won by three wickets, but the 52 runs required in the last innings cost considerable trouble to get on a very treacherous pitch. In the early stages of the game the ground had not dried sufficiently after drenching rains caused batting to be really difficult. Burton accomplished the great feat – very rare in a first-class match – of taking all the ten wickets in an innings, and Lohmann's fine bowling on the Saturday went far to make Surrey's victory possible.

Middlesex 161 (S. W. Scott 60; J. Beaumont 4-31) **and 53** (G. A. Lohmann 7-32);
Surrey 163 (K. J. Key 51; G. Burton 10-59) **and 52-7.**

BETTY SURRIDGE – OBITUARY   2014

Betty Surridge, wife of the great Surrey captain Stuart, was the first woman to be president of a county cricket club and was a fixture at The Oval for many decades.

Surridge, Betty Patricia, died on February 26, 2013, aged 91. Betty Surridge succeeded Sir Paul Getty as Surrey's president in 1997, becoming the first (and so far only) woman to hold the position at any county club. She was the widow of Stuart Surridge, who captained Surrey to five successive County Championship titles in the 1950s, and was president himself in 1981. "What I am good at is meeting people," she said. "I know a lot of cricketing people and I shall help entertain." She was also a founder member of the Lady Taverners section. Micky Stewart, who succeeded her as president, said: "Betty was a wonderful lady and was so popular during Stuart's reign as captain – with all the players and throughout the wider club. She will be remembered for her commitment to and love of Surrey CCC, and her amazing personality."

NOTES BY THE EDITOR   Graeme Wright, 1989

This brief extract from the editor's Notes in 1989 explains how a vote of the Surrey membership would be crucial to the survival of the ground in the early 1990s – and also how the ground paved the way for the modern phenomenon of commercial naming rights on stadia.

Towards the end of last season, the Surrey members voted to allow their famous ground to be renamed the Foster's Oval as part of a sponsorship agreement with the brewers, Courage. For some time Surrey had been struggling to achieve the target of their "Save The Oval" appeal, and this sponsorship allowed them to commence work on their £5.8 million development planned for the ground.

Without major renovations, it was said, The Oval's place as a Test-match venue would be in jeopardy. Stands which were condemned by the fire authority are now being rebuilt, and the development plans include a cricket school and facilities which will benefit the local community. The ground will be known as the Foster's Oval for a period of 15 years.

AN ALTERNATIVE FIVE   David Hopps, 1995

A feature in the 1995 Wisden *drew attention to five "unsung heroes who make first-class cricket possible". One of the five was the then Oval groundsman Steve Howes, who remains at the club 22 years later.*

For the past 13 years [Steve Howes] has been particularly responsible for the smooth running of the scoreboard at The Oval, the most efficient in the country. Only in cricket, and perhaps only in England, could a scoreboard encourage such affection. But cricket is a statistical game, its conclusion revealed over a considerable period of time. When major records are broken – Lancashire's 863 against Surrey in 1990, the highest Championship total this century; or Devon Malcolm's nine wickets for 57 runs against South Africa last year – The Oval scoreboard unfailingly poses for another round of photographs.

For most of the 1980s, Steve worked the box alongside his brother, Andrew, and they drew pride from their reputation for speed and accuracy. The advent of a second, electronic scoreboard on the ground a few years ago provided another incentive to maintain the highest standards. Recognition can easily depart and Steve admits that he used to feel a flutter of nerves before the start of a Test. "One year a number on the hundreds fell horizontal and no one could see it," he said. "I watched the Test highlights that evening and nearly had a heart attack."

The Oval box is now more than 40 years old and is struggling to disguise its age. Figures have been known to drop from the windows without warning – thankfully, there have been no recorded incidents of spectators being injured by Last Man's score – and are temporarily repaired with a hastily applied nail or screw. The box is spartan: a couple of chairs, a stool (Steve's preference), and a portable radio, tuned whenever possible to *Test Match Special*. There is not even a kettle in the box; they tried it once, but remembering to bring along a pint of fresh milk proved too challenging.

Steve took time out in 1990 to gain a degree in leisure management at Thames Valley University. But he returned in 1994, and the retirement in the autumn of Harry Brind caused him to move up a rung to No. 4 on the groundstaff. The only drawback with his promotion is that it might end his scoreboard duties, traditionally the novice's role.

Approaching his mid-thirties, Steve wonders about a proper job. But The Oval exerts a powerful pull: the renewal of old acquaintances, the charting of a player's career from its infancy, the discovery of the same old boys in the same old seats year upon year. "And you have to be mad on cricket to watch as much as I do," he said.

HUNDRED YEARS OF SURREY CRICKET H. D. G. Leveson-Gower, 1946

Surrey celebrated their 100th anniversary in 1946, a year late because of the war. Henry 'Shrimp' Leveson-Gower, a former England and Surrey captain and a hugely influential figure on the wider game, marked the occasion by recalling the birth of cricket at The Oval.

To those who started the Surrey County Cricket Club and to those who obtained The Oval for cricket a very great debt of gratitude is due. It would be as difficult to imagine county cricket without The Oval, Test matches without The Oval, as it would be to imagine The Oval without the gasworks...

Let us now imagine that we are entering The Oval in the year 1845. In the spring of that year an interesting ceremony was performed: the first sod of turf was laid on the present ground; 10,000 turves came from Tooting Common. Only a year before the same ground was nothing more or less than a market garden. In the early months of this year the members of the famous Montpelier Club had to vacate their ground adjoining the Bee Hive Tavern, Walworth, required for building purposes. It was due to the personal influence of their treasurer, Mr W. Baker, a fine all-round cricketer, that a lease of 31 years was secured from the Otter family, who held the ground on a 99-year lease, granted to them by the Duchy of Cornwall in 1835.

The autumn of 1844 may be said to have marked the foundation of the Surrey County Cricket Club, and the first game connected with the Surrey Club took place on August 21, 22, 1845 – Gentlemen of Surrey against Players of Surrey. Following this match a dinner was held at The Horns, Kennington…

The formal inauguration was deferred till later in the year, when another dinner at the same historic inn was held. The president on that occasion was the Hon. F. Ponsonby, afterwards Earl of Bessborough, and to him more than anyone we owe the continuance of cricket upon The Oval. The Surrey County Cricket Club was born, ever after increasingly to flourish, except for a few early vicissitudes. The question has been asked (and is worth answering): was The Oval ever in danger of being built upon? Yes, about the year 1851; this was prevented by the Prince Consort when acting for Edward, Prince of Wales, and Duke of Cornwall, afterwards King Edward VII.

In the late Sir Jeremiah Colman's beautifully illustrated book, *The Noble Game of Cricket*, there is a reproduction of a picture of The Oval painted two years after the inauguration of the Surrey Club. A label attached to the back of the canvas bears the following inscription, "Kennington Oval with the market garden dwelling turned into a Club House; date about 1847, before any pavilion stand was erected." Another reproduction from an oil painting shows the first members' pavilion erected in 1855. From a market garden to what was destined to become one of the finest cricket grounds in the country may truly be described as a wonderful transformation, and it is difficult to realise that here was the spot devoted to the cultivation of the cabbage and the cauliflower…

The Oval, with its reputation for famous wickets, can boast of famous groundsmen. There were in the past George Street, John Newton, and J. Over, all experts; while to the present generation the names of Sam Apted and Bosser Martin are associated with the splendid condition of the ground…

Many personalities apart from the players on the field cannot be dissociated from The Oval, and one figure I would not like to forget – the Surrey Poet, A. Craig. Without any official connection with the Surrey Club, he earned the name of Surrey Poet because he was most often found at The Oval. For many years his figure stood out as familiar to the spectators as that of the greatest cricketer. On the wettest days he would put the crowd in good humour. Captain of the spectators he loved to call himself, and the spectators, he said, were his constituents.

His skill in repartee was always pointed, and it was an unhappy moment for anyone who chaffed him. "Oh, take these things away!" snapped a spectator once at The Oval. "I beg your pardon, sir," replied Craig, with the greatest politeness; "these are not for you, these are only for people who can read." But he was happiest when conciliatory; and he checked a heated argument about the correctness of the title Gentlemen v Players with these words, "All the Players are Gentlemen and all the Gentlemen Players"...

GEOFFREY HOWARD – OBITUARY   2003

Geoffrey Howard was one of the most beloved cricketing administrators of the 20th century. As secretary of Surrey, he was at the helm of The Oval between 1965 and 1975, and later served as club president.

Howard, Geoffrey Cecil, died in Minchinhampton on November 8, 2002, aged 93, his place in cricket history secure as an enlightened administrator and popular tour manager. Geoffrey Howard was secretary of Lancashire and Surrey and had charge of three MCC tours of Australia and the Indian subcontinent...

He inherited... respect for people and his deep love of cricket from his grandfather, Sir Ebenezer Howard, a founder of the Garden City Movement. It was Ebenezer who first took him to The Oval, where the ten-year-old Geoffrey touched the hem of Jack Hobbs's blazer...

His outstanding operational and man-management skills were recognised in the RAF, which swiftly promoted him from auxiliary airman to acting squadron leader; the Essex secretary, Brian Castor, also noted them when Howard, restless after returning to civvy street, applied for his job in 1946. Castor was off to Surrey, and when Howard missed out at Essex he invited him to go to The Oval as assistant secretary. Two years later Howard went north to Old Trafford to be Lancashire secretary until 1964, whereupon he returned to The Oval as secretary from 1965 to 1975. These were years of reconstruction – of grounds, finances and the very game itself – and he was at the heart of the changes, pushing for reform and sitting on various MCC committees.

Sometimes his vision for cricket must have struck the game's establishment as downright revolutionary. Doubting the need for two major grounds in London, he thought the time would come when Surrey should move from The Oval into the county of Surrey, while Middlesex could play as London. Sporting a yellow shirt at one Surrey committee meeting, he said, "Why don't we wear these for our Sunday matches?" – and in time, albeit not until 1992, the counties came round to his way of thinking. In retirement he served the Minor Counties for eight years as honorary treasurer, and in 1989 Surrey honoured him with their presidency...

ENGLAND v NEW ZEALAND, FOURTH TEST   Hugh Chevallier, 2000

August 19, 20, 21, 22, 1999. New Zealand won by 83 runs.

New Zealand played their ninth and most recent Test at The Oval in 1999, a match which produced their only win at the ground. In the absence of any official Test rankings, Wisden *had devised their own system – and now it placed England at the bottom of the table.*

Ten minutes after lunch on the fourth day, Roger Twose, an English emigrant, held a steepling catch at mid-on that gave victory in the match – and the series – to a young and self-confident New Zealand side. The ignominy of a home defeat by the team previously considered the weakest in Test cricket unleashed a hail of criticism on the England players and – after the departure during the summer of the coach and two selectors – what remained of the management. This was no ordinary failure. As almost everyone noticed, the defeat meant that for the first time since the Wisden World Championship was launched in 1996, England were at the bottom of the heap.

In truth, England's performance was not wholly inept. Hussain's captaincy was inventive, the bowling thoughtful and the fielding near-faultless. The batting, though was execrable. Atherton held the second innings together for a while but, the moment he was out, the familiar, gaping deficiencies were cruelly exposed. The end, as it usually is with England, was swift, painful and rather embarrassing...

Heavy rain meant that the pitch had sweated for two days beneath the covers, prompting Hussain to bowl first... [Fleming and Nash] rebuilt the innings from the ruins of 104 for seven but, by the close... New Zealand were a precarious 170 for eight. Next morning, it all went wrong for England. Vettori got runs first from the edge of the bat, then from the middle. He scored 51 in 48 balls, put on 78 for the ninth wicket with Fleming at almost five an over and wrested the initiative...

Early on the third morning England were bowled out for 153, a deficit of 83... But just when the press were yet again preparing to fill their laptops with vitriol, the bowlers produced something special. England's previous six Test wins had come off the back of a first-innings deficit and, with New Zealand hurtling towards disaster at 39 for six – an overall lead of 122 – a seventh was on the cards... Then Cairns changed everything with an innings of uncompromising, Bothamesque belligerence. Playing off the front foot to minimise the effect of lateral movement, he hit 80 from 94 balls...

England were left needing 246, the highest score of the match... Once Atherton was fourth out for a positive 64... the batting descended into farce, the remaining six wickets adding 19 runs. Over their two innings, England's last three wickets fell for a total of two runs; New Zealand's 92. Chairman of selectors David Graveney belatedly promised that England would never again pick what amounted to three No. 11s – Mullally, Tufnell and Giddins – in the same Test... The crowd jeered as Hussain collected the loser's cheque.

New Zealand 236 (S. P. Fleming 66*, D. L. Vettori 51) and 162 (C. L. Cairns 80);
England 153 (C. L. Cairns 5-31) and 162 (M. A. Atherton 64; D. J. Nash 4-39).

SIR PAUL GETTY – OBITUARY   2004

Sir Paul Getty, who bought Wisden *in 1993 and was chairman of the company for ten years until his death, was Surrey president in 1996. He loved The Oval so much that the 'cricketing utopia' he built at his Wormsley home in Buckinghamshire was based on the ground's dimensions and shape.*

Getty, Sir John Paul KBE, who died on April 17, 2003, aged 70, described himself in *Who's Who* as simply a "philanthropist". Paul Getty inherited a fortune from the family oil business but, unlike his tycoon father, had little interest in adding to it. Instead, he settled in Britain and gave away huge chunks of his money to a vast array of beneficiaries, most of them institutions representing what he saw as the country's threatened heritage, including cathedrals, art galleries, the British Film Institute's archive and the Conservative Party. Cricket was close to the top of the list...

After an unhappy American childhood... he worked for the Italian subsidiary of Getty Oil before... marrying a Dutch beauty, Talitha, who died of a heroin overdose in Italy in 1971. He moved to London and lived as a recluse in Chelsea, subject to depression and his own drug dependence, a period that included the terrible kidnap of his eldest son Paul. During this period Mick Jagger, a friend since the 1960s, visited him, insisted on switching the TV over to the cricket and explained what was going on. Getty got the bug. Gubby Allen, *éminence grise* of MCC and at one time a fellow patient at the London Clinic, described by Getty as being "like a father", encouraged him into the cricketing community. Men like Brian Johnston and Denis Compton became friends, and he took delight in the game's history, traditions and etiquette, which were at one with the concept of Englishness that he embraced.

So he sprinkled cricket with some of the stardust that his wealth made possible. He gave an estimated £1.6 million to build the Mound Stand at Lord's, but this was the tip of an iceberg of donations: to every county, to countless clubs, to individuals fallen on hard times and to organisations like the Arundel Cricket Foundation, which received £750,000 from him to help disadvantaged youngsters play cricket. Even his pleasures were inclusive ones.

At Wormsley, his estate nestling in the Chilterns, he created his own private cricketing Eden project: a square like a billiard table with a thatched pavilion. Getty built his field of dreams, and they really did come: the Queen Mother and the Prime Minister, John Major, attended Wormsley's inaugural match in 1992; touring teams made it a regular stopover; and cricketers ranging from the great to the gormless delighted in playing there or simply sharing the idyll...

His ownership of *Wisden*, sealed in 1993, brought together the two great passions: cricket and books. In 1994 Getty sealed his own personal happiness by marrying Victoria, who had nursed him through the bad years, and four years later tied the knot with the country he had come to love, becoming a British citizen, which allowed him to use the knighthood that had been bestowed on him for his charitable services 12 years earlier. His presidency of Surrey, in 1996, was another honour he cherished. Those who knew him valued him as a generous spirit, a quality that has nothing to do with money. And cricket repaid him a little by giving him a sense of his own self-worth as a man, not just as a benefactor.

Acknowledgments

A great many people have helped hugely in the writing and compilation of this book and I owe them all a debt of gratitude. Specifically, I would like to thank:

Christopher Lane for his extraordinary knowledge of the *Wisden* archive and support with editing, proofing, additions and everything in between. To be totally honest, this book deserves his name on the front just as much as mine.

Alec and Micky Stewart for agreeing to pen the forewords for this book and doing such a spectacular job.

Rachel for her understanding of my need for a project and the constant flow of love and support.

Dad, who deserves to be thanked in print for a second time for taking me to my first Test match in 1988 – and also for taking me to The Oval for the first time in 1995 (see chapter 13).

Mum for her faith, pride and constant open door.

Charlotte Atyeo, Holly Jarrald and everyone else at Bloomsbury for placing their faith in me to write a good book and their help in getting it out there.

Richard Gould at Surrey CCC for incorporating this book so whole-heartedly in the celebrations around The Oval's 100th Test in 2017.

The many generations of staff at Surrey CCC who have built and maintained the club's formidable collections of the *Wisden Cricketers' Almanack*.

Jon Filby and all the volunteers at the Sussex Cricket Museum for also allowing me access to their superb collection of *Wisden*s.

Fats, Skinny and Gusto for their support and companionship during long hours at a laptop.

All Cricket Scorers and Statisticians for their dedication to the game, meticulous approach and huge efforts to ensure their work is easily accessible online.

All the *Wisden* reporters over the years for allowing us to enjoy such a complete record of our game with their words, passion and diligence.

Philip Bailey for the provision of all the match scores in the book.

James Watson for designing a beautiful cover.

Benj Moorehead, an excellent copy editor and fine all-round cricket man.

Charles Barr for his world-class proof reading expertise.

Index